CHINESE
CIVIL SOCIETY
and
SPONTANEOUS
ORDER

www.royalcollins.com

CHINESE CIVIL SOCIETY

and

SPONTANEOUS ORDER

Native Tradition and Overseas Development

Denggao Long and Wei Yi

Books Beyond Boundaries

ROYAL COLLINS

Chinese Civil Society and Spontaneous Order: Native Tradition and Overseas Development

Denggao Long and Wei Yi

First published in 2023 by Royal Collins Publishing Group Inc.
Groupe Publication Royal Collins Inc.
BKM Royalcollins Publishers Private Limited

Headquarters: 550-555 boul. René-Lévesque O Montréal (Québec) H2Z1B1 Canada
India office: 805 Hemkunt House, 8th Floor, Rajendra Place, New Delhi 110008

We are grateful for the support from the yonyou Foundation "The Great Wall of Commerce" Project.
We also appreciate the collaboration and support of the Institute for State-Owned Enterprises, Tsinghua
University.

ISBN: 978-1-4878-1111-2

To find out more about our publications, please visit www.royalcollins.com.

Table of Contents

PART ONE: NATIVE TRADITION

PART TWO: OVERSEAS DEVELOPMENT

PART THREE: BLEND AND CONTRAST

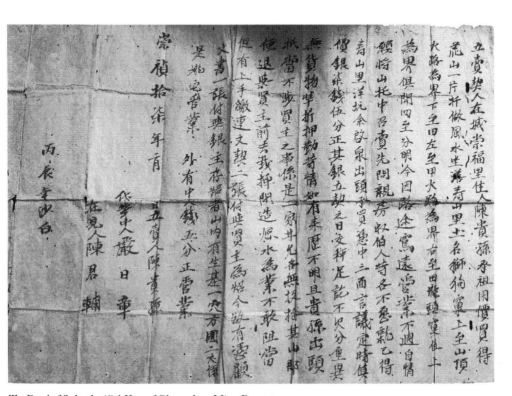

The Deed of Sale, the 17th Year of Chongzhen, Ming Dynasty.

Li-Guangming collections of folk documents, Center for Chinese Economic History, Tsinghua University.

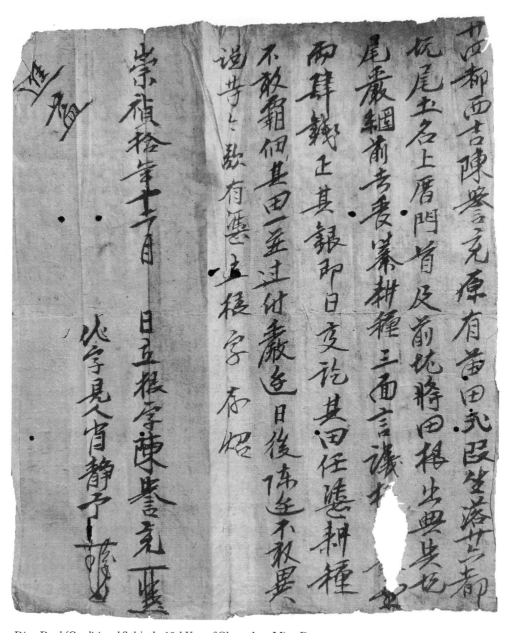

廿都西吉陳譽克原有黃田九段坐落廿二都

坑尾土名上厝門首及前坑將田根出典與其邑

尾嚴輯前去農業耕種三面言議時值

而肆轢正其銀即日交訖其田任憑耕種

不敢霸佃其田一至过付嚴逐日後係任不敢異

詞芽之欵有憑立檀字為照

崇禎拾年十一月　日立根字陳譽克一紙

此字見人肖靜子

Dian Deed (Conditional Sale), the 10th Year of Chongzhen, Ming Dynasty.

Li-Guangming collections of folk documents, Center for Chinese Economic History, Tsinghua University.

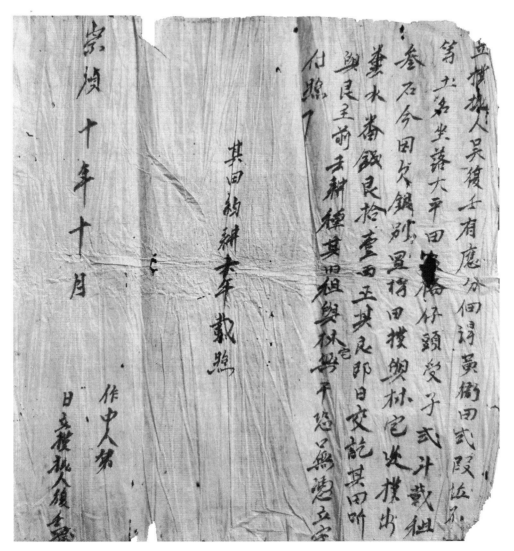

立賣批人吳復壬有應分佃得黃衛田貳叚壹坵

等土名尖落大平田塢坵存頭受子貳斗貳秬

參石今因欠鎁別置將田樸與林包坟樸出

葉水蕃鎁艮拾壹兩五其艮郎日交訖其田所

與艮主前去耕種其租與林無干恐口無憑立字

付照

崇禎十年十月

其田租耕本年�收[押]

作中人第[押]

日立賣批人復壬[押]

The Tenancy Contract, the 10th Year of Chongzhen, Ming Dynasty.

Li-Guangming collections of folk documents, Center for Chinese Economic History, Tsinghua University.

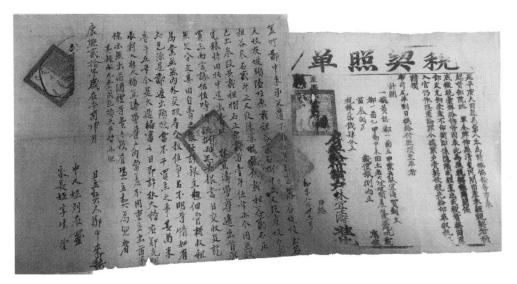

"Deed Tax Certificate," the 20th Year of Kangxi, Qing Dynasty.

Li-Guangming special collections of folk documents, Center for Chinese Economic History, Tsinghua University.

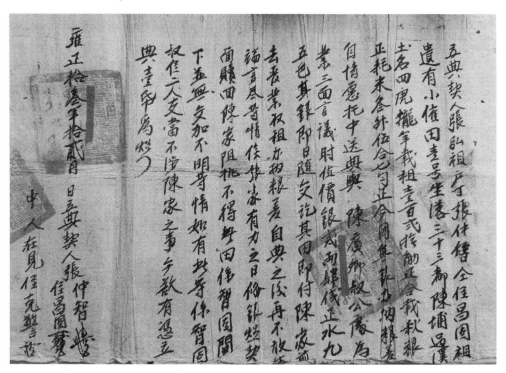

Dian Deed (Conditional Sale), the 13th Year of Yongzheng, Qing Dynasty.

Li-Guangming special collections of folk documents, Center for Chinese Economic History, Tsinghua University.

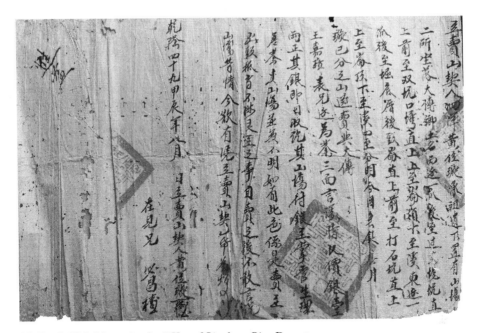

The Deed of Sale Mountain, the 49 Year of Qianlong, Qing Dynasty.

Li–Guangming special collections of folk documents, Center for Chinese Economic History, Tsinghua Univeristy.

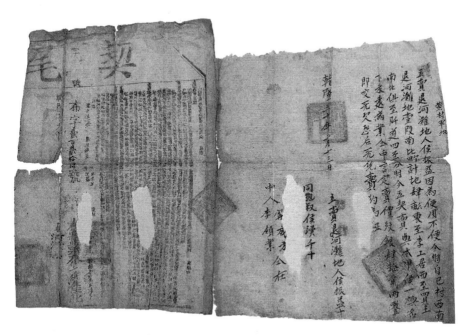

The Deed of Sale Beach, Hejin County.

Deed Tail: "No. Cloth 224," the 30th Year of Qianlong, Qing Dynasty.

Zhang–Wenda collections of folk documents, Center for Chinese Economic History, Tsinghua University.

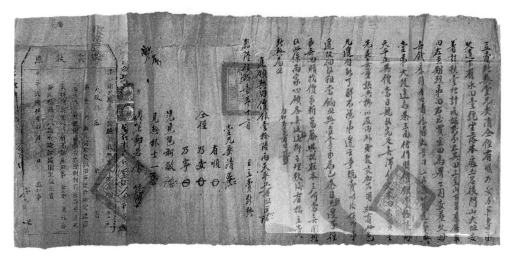

The Deed of Sale, the 51st Year of Qianlong, Qing Dynasty.

"Examination Licence," the 5th Year of the Republic of China.

Li-Guangming collections of folk documents, Center for Chinese Economic History, Tsinghua University.

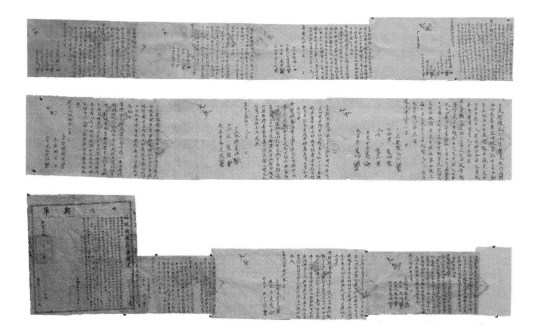

11 related Deeds, including Dian Deed, the 17th Year of Jiaqing, Qing Dynasty; nine additional Deeds during Jianqing, Daoguang, Xianfeng, and Tongzhi, Qing Dynasty and one official verification, the 2nd Year of the Republic of China.

Li-Guangming collections of folk documents, Center for Chinese Economic History, Tsinghua University.

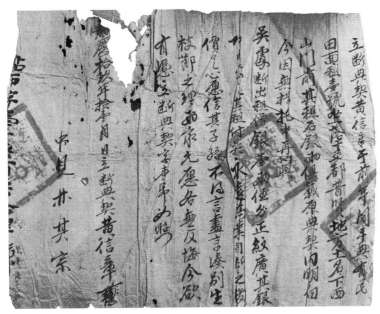

The Deed of End Dian Transaction, the 19th Year of Jiaqing, Qing Dynasty.

Li-Guangming collections of folk documents, Center for Chinese Economic History, Tsinghua University.

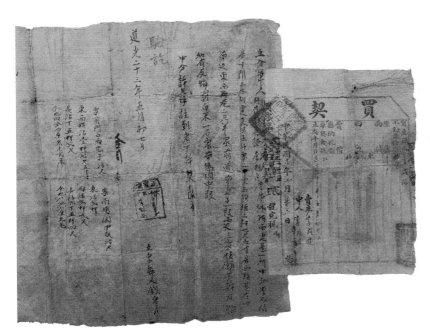

Deed of Dividing Up Family Property and Live Apart, the 23rd Year of Daoguang, Qing Dynasty. "Purchase Deed" Verification of ownership, the 3rd Year of the Republic of China.

Li-Guangming collections of folk documents, Center for Chinese Economic History, Tsinghua Univeristy.

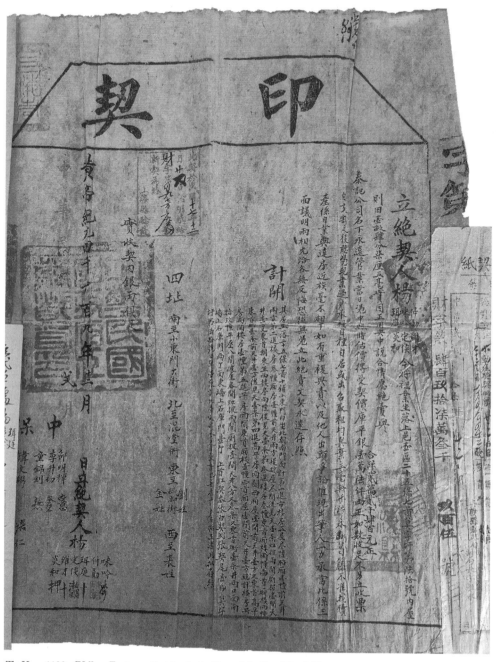

The Year 4609 of Yellow Emperor, that is, the 1st Year of the Republic of China, 1912.

Li-Guangming collections of folk documents, Center for Chinese Economic History, Tsinghua University.

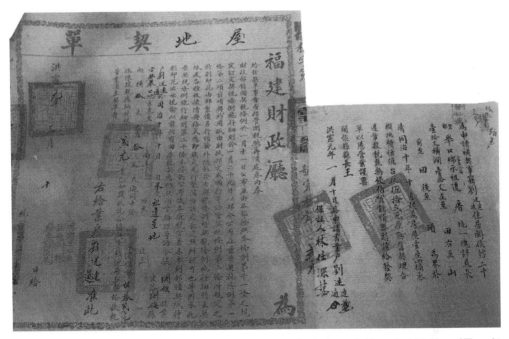

Deed of Repairing, Minhou County, the 1st Year of Hongxian, for the houses built at the 10th Year of Tongzhi, Qing Dynasty.

Li-Guangming collections of folk documents, Center for Chinese Economic History, Tsinghua University.

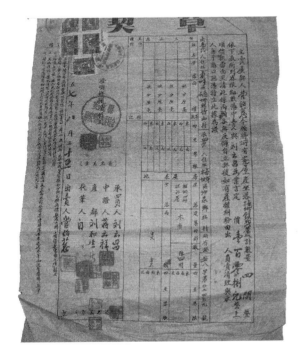

The Deed of Sale House, Anhua County, 1957.

Provided by Xiang Xinzhuang, Anhua County, Hunan Province.

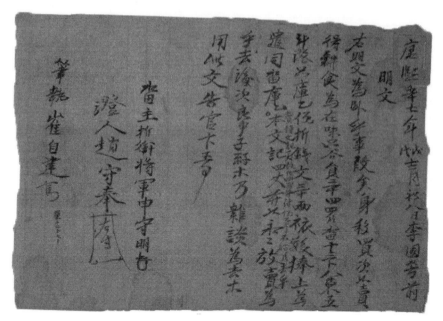

The Deed of Land in Korea, the 57th Year of Kangxi, Qing Dynasty.

Provided by Korean Professor Myung Cha.

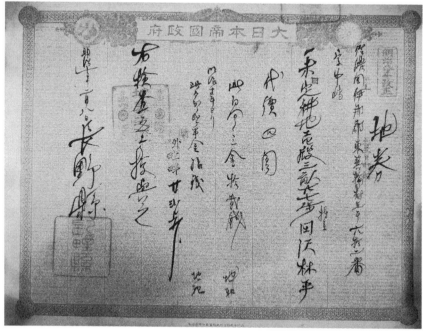

The Deed of Land, Meiji Period, Japan.

Li-Guangming collections of folk documents, Center for Chinese Economic History, Tsinghua University.

PART ONE

Native Tradition

*The Outline on the Institution of Land Transaction in Traditional China**

On the basis of the author's research findings in the last twenty years, this chapter comprehensively examines the land tenure system and its transmutation and function in the context of traditional Chinese socio-economic perspectives. It seeks to construct an interpretation framework with an internal logical system. In China's history, land tenures (or land rights) existed independently and were traded in the market at different levels and over different periods, thus forming multi-layered land rights such as ownership, possession, and usage rights. Correspondingly, land rights transactions have taken various forms, each with its characteristics and connectedness, thereby structuring a hierarchical and inherently logical system of land rights trading. By examining a large sample of primary documents, especially highly accurate land transaction deeds and *xingke tiben* (刑科题本, Routine-Memorials of the Board of Law), this chapter attempts to reconstruct traditional Chinese land property rights and its transaction system centering on *dian* 典 (conditional sale) and to dig deeper into the heritage of China's land system and its evolution over the last millennium. On this basis, the author explores the connection and interaction between the land rights market and the household farms, reflects on the old theories of "share tenancy" and "the equalization of land rights" based on historical evidence and theoretical logic, so as

---

* Long Denggao and Chi Xiang, "The Outline on the Institution of Land Transaction in Traditional China. European and Chinese Histories of Economic Thought Theories and Images of Good Governance," *Routledge Studies in the History of Economics* (2021). Chi Xiang, Assistant Professor at the Institute of Modern History, Chinese Academy of Social Sciences (CASS), and UCLA graduate of 2019.

to reveal the fundamental characteristics of the traditional Chinese economy, which sharply contrasted the economic path of Western Europe, and its modern transformation dilemma.

As the primary source of production in an agricultural society, land and its related institutions underlie the process of resource allocation and economic operation. It is the primary and most fundamental issue when one wants to understand the transformation of China from a traditional society to a modern one. It is the key to the current agricultural reform and is of special theoretical value for world economic history.

While previous understanding and assessments of this fundamental issue have been anything but uniform, during the last two decades dealing with the problematique has been especially fruitful and new breakthroughs have been made.[1]

By examining primary sources, especially land transaction deeds and the land disputes in the "Routine-Memorials of the Board of Law" (*xingke tiben* 刑科題本), this chapter reconstructs China's traditional land property rights and its transaction system. It offers an in-depth analysis of the institutional legacies of China's land system, as well as its transformation. On this basis, the author tries to provide a comprehensive analysis and explanation of the resource allocation and economic operation of the land tenure system based on economic principles and tools and offer a systematic framework of understanding and explanation of the historical transmutation of traditional economy revolving around land rights (or land tenures), including its impact on modern China's economic reform.

1 The Theoretical Construction of Forms of Land Tenure

Private (family and private) property rights, corporate property rights, and state property rights in land co-existed in traditional China. Among them, private property forms were much more mature. They demonstrated an innovation of Chinese origin based on

---

1. Until the recent decade, Zhao Gang, Fng Xing, and other middle-aged scholars, such as Qin Hui, Gao Wangling, Luan Chengxian, Cao Shuji, Li Deying, and others have made new explorations. See Zhao Gang, "The Land Tenancy System of Ming and Qing Dynasties From Another Perspective," *Agricultural History of China*, no. 2 (2000); Zhao Gang, "The Choice of Agricultural Land Management Mode in History," *Researches in Chinese Economic History*, no. 2 (2000); Fang Xing, "The Land Market of China's Feudal Society," *Researches in Chinese Economic History*, no. 2 (2001); Gao Wangling, "A New Perspective on the Tenancy Relationship," *Researches in Chinese Economic History*, no. 3 (2005); Gao Wangling, *New Theory of the Tenancy Relationship—Landlords, Peasants, and Land Rents* (Shanghai: Shanghai Bookstore Publishing House, 2005); Cao Shuji, "The Nature of Surface Land Rights in Southern Jiangsu Province," *The Journal of Tsinghua University*, no. 4 (2007); Cao Shuji, "Two Kinds of Permanent Tenancy and Rent Reduction in Zhejiang Province," *Journal of Historical Research*, no. 2 (2007); Cao Shuji and Li Feiqi, "Land Mortgage in Mountainous Regions of Southern Zhejiang during the Mid- and Late Qing: A Study Based on 'Land Mortgage Contracts' from Shicang Village, Songyang County," *Journal of Historical Research*, no. 3 (2008); Cao Shuji and Liu Shigu, *Traditional Land Property Rights Structure and Its Transformation* (Shanghai: Sahnghai Jiaotong University Press, 2014); Li Deying, *National Decree and Civil Customs: A New Probe into the Tenancy System of Chengdu Plain during the Republic of China* (Beijing: China Social Sciences Press, 2006).

the conceptual definitions and the systematically theoretical constructions of China's traditional land property rights.

First, land rights can exist independently and be traded in the market at different levels and at different times, thus forming forms of property rights such as ownership, possession, and usage rights, as well as their corresponding forms of transaction, which constitute the land rights transaction system.

Second, all these different levels of realization of various forms of property rights can be acquired through investment and trade. This results in rules that are universally accepted by society, licensed by the government, and regulated by the legal system, and thus have the force of law.

Third, documents of property rights and transactions expressed through contracts have a long history in civil practices and have been recognized and regulated by successive governments through laws.

Fourth, the property rights of legal persons (corporate property rights) were derived and developed from private property rights.

There has been a long-term sentiment whose influence continues today that, historically, China lacked an idea of property rights and had failed to develop a spirit of contract. In fact, however, a simple idea of property rights and a related system existed in traditional society and were deeply rooted in the people's hearts. Both private and corporate land was titled and traded by deed, and different levels of land rights could be acquired through investment capital (in addition to inheritance, etc.). Non-landowners also could obtain corresponding disposition of land rights by investing and controlling land yields and land appreciation and sharing land rights with the landowners. One instance is the so-called surface right of land (*tianmianquan* 田面权). It co-existed with the sub-soil right (*tiandiquan* 田底权) as a property right and differed from the regular tenancy right (*dianquan* 佃权). Similarly, the *dian* 典 (conditional sale) right resembled that of the right to the surface, and both were distinctive forms of land tenure.

Corporate property rights are the derivative extension of private property rights, reflecting the degree of development of the private property rights system. For example, clans, temples, academies of classical learning and private schools, non-profit organizations, organizations of charity, and various associations (*hui* 会) and societies (*she* 社) in the industrial, commercial, financial, cultural, sports, and entertainment industries could form a property unit, a transaction unit, and a taxing unit, with features such as integrity, indivisibility, and exclusivity, have developed an efficient management model based on the independence of property.[2] They were recorded as "properties of legal entity" (*gongchan* 公

---

2. Long Denggao, Wang Zhenghua, and Yi Wei, "The Governance Structure of Traditional Civil Organizations and Legal Person Property Rights System: A Study Based on Public Construction and Management in the Qing Dynasty," *Economic Research*, no. 10 (2018): 175–191.

产), as opposed to "governmental properties" (*guanchan* 官产) owned by the government and "private properties" (*sichan* 私产) owned by private individual and family.

State land has existed for generations and was usually not tradable. Only when privatized could it be traded; at that time, however, its character had been changed to private or corporate property, which did not happen in every dynasty. However, there was a general tendency that the share of state land was gradually diminishing.

2 A Systematic Discussion of the Land Transaction System

2.1 The *Dian* 典 Right and Its Transaction

As the form of land property rights and transactions with the "most traditional Chinese characteristics," there was a strong concentration of studying *dian* (conditional sale), but many controversies have remained.

Some regarded *dian* as the transaction of usage rights, while others argued that there is no difference between *dian* and the practice of "live sales" or "living sales" (*huomai* 活卖).[3]

Based on the analysis of original deeds and employing economic theories, the author finds that *dian* refers to a transaction regarding the management of land with all its profit and interest in an agreed period and not to the "balancing of rent and interest" (*zuxi xiangdi* 租息相抵) as claimed by some scholars.[4] A "conditional sale" (*dian*) is a property right in the form of a possessory right and can assume the function of a security interest. In other words, the *dian* practice is a transaction between the right to occupy land and interest on capital. It is different from both the sale and purchase of ownership and that of a tenancy as a transaction of the usage right, thus clarifying previous misunderstandings. The *dian*

---

3. Dai Jianguo and others argued that *dian* is a transaction of usage rights. See Dai Jianguo, "The Dian Transactions of Civil Lands and the System of 'One Piece of Land with Two Owners' in the Song Dynasty," *Historical Research*, no. 6 (2011): 99–117. Quite a few scholars, on the other hand, argued that *dian* is not-finalized sale (*huomai*), which means that *dian* is a transaction of ownership. For example, Ye Xiaoxin argues that *dian* "can also be called as *huomai*." See Ye Xiaoxin, *History of Chinese Legal System* (Beijing: Peking University Press, 1999), 249. Chen Zhiying clarified the meaning of *dian* and the difference between *dian* and sale, especially finalized sale (*juemai*), but still customarily thought of *dian* as "a not-finalized sale (huomai)." See Chen Zhiying, *A Study of Property Rights Relations in the Song Dynasty* (Beijing: China Social Sciences Press, 2006), 140–147. Li Li argued that Qing people saw *dian* as a sale. However, the deeds that his article used were all deeds of sales. See Li Li, "The Expression and Significance of Qing Dynasty Civil Land Deeds to the Dian," *Jinling Law Review*, no. 1 (2006): 111–118.

4. Some scholar, such as Wu Xianghong, misunderstood the core rule of *dian* practices. The author characterizes their misunderstandings as "balancing of rent and interest," because they have ignored the differences between different categories of *dian*. See Wu Xianghong, "Chapter 7," in *Customs and Laws of Dian* (Beijing: Law Press · China, 2009).

seller (*chudianren* 出典人) actually realizes the future interest in the land to obtain a loan, while the *dian* buyer (*chengdianren* 承典人) receives the possession for the agreed term, and could choose between either operating income (self-farming), investment income (leasing), or realizing future income (*dian* transfer), depending on his own preferences and needs. Moreover, the *dian* buyer could rent out the *dian* land, even to the landowner and *dian* seller himself. It reflects a pattern of shared land rights constructed by landlords, *dian* owners, and tenant farmers relying on market transactions and sheds light on the characteristics and orientation of the traditional land rights market.[5]

2.2 An Analysis of Various Land Transaction Forms

In different time periods, different levels of land rights could be transacted, forming a diversified regime of land transactions such as sales, conditional sales (*dian*), rent deposits (*yazu* 押租), tenancies, mortgages (*di* 抵), and loans through lands as collaterals (*taijie* 胎借). The system became mature during the Ming and Qing dynasties. Depending on the order of usage right, possession, and ownership, the greater the rights to the land, the higher the returns, and the higher the transaction price.

The multi-layered land rights and diversified forms of land rights transactions were quite complicated in reality. Ambiguities, disputes, and misunderstandings related to them in the past were mainly due to the lack of a theoretical explanatory framework. The author here therefore offers an analytical framework regarding the different levels of land rights and the development of regulations across time, distinguishing between the roles of the different land rights transactions and paying attention to differences and interconnections.

Dian (conditional sales) originated from sales. In the Tang and Song Dynasties (618–1279), the term *dianmai* (典卖) was used, and both transaction rules and tax payment procedures were not clearly separated. The main distinction between a "conditional sale" 典 (*dian*) and a "sale" (*mai* 卖) was made by the contractual form and by the fact that although even for a "conditional sale," the tax duty was transferred to the new owner, the administration continued to consider the original owner as possessing the "field bone" (*tiangu* 田骨). In the Qing Dynasty, the two were further clearly separated, while the "sale" (*mai*) of ownership was broken down into a "living sale" (i.e., a not-finalized sale) (*huomai* 活卖) and "finalized sale" (*juemai* 绝卖). The nature of a "not-finalized sale" was

---

5. Long Denggao, Lin Zhan, and Peng Bo, *Social Sciences in China*, no. 5 (2013): 125–141. The article was awarded the 18th Sun Yefang Prize in Economic Sciences (2018).

a proprietary transaction, with the ability to redeem, but only as a right of a proprietary transaction. In contrast, the redeeming of the *dian* was the end of the deal. The nature of a "living sale" is an ownership transaction. In a "living sale," the title to the land is able to be redeemed, but only as a right of first refusal. In a *dian* transaction, on the other hand, the redeeming of land ownership signifies the closing link of the transaction.

The tenancy is a transaction of the usage right. A regular tenancy is a post-rental payment, while a rent deposit (*yazu* 押租) is a partial pre-payment. There is a progressive relationship between tenancy and *dian* (典). When a rent deposit is maximized, it from the point of view of the landowner gets close to *dian*, as shown in Figure 1, but a rent deposit cannot create a security interest. Only a security right cannot be created. If we view the rent deposit as an investment in and purchase the right to use the land, then the surface right to the land, which is a further extension of the right, acquires rights similar to those of the *dian*, which is also a property right of possession. If the rent deposit is considered as an investment and purchase of land usage rights, then in the case of a rent deposit, the tenant can acquire the right to field surface in a similar capacity as the *dian* right. At this point, the surface right of land is also a right of possession with property attributes.

Both *dian* and mortgages can form security interests. However, land mortgages are usually short-term loans with a high risk of title transfer, whereas *dian* transactions effectively buffer the eventual transfer of land ownership. Therefore, the *dian* practice was popular and recognized by the government. This is one of the reasons for the long prevalence of *dian* in the market of land rights. As institutions of *dian* and *huomai* have effectively reduced the transfer of land ownerships and acted as hedge factors against the concentration of land ownership rights, they helped peasants to weather the storm and restore and re-establish independent farming. Practices such as "add-on" (*zhaojia* 找价) and "joyous-gift silver" (*xiliyin* 喜礼银)[6] could also be seen, to some extent, as a relief for landless peasants. Thus, the customary practices and legal provisions of *dian* have protected the vulnerable while preserving peasants' ownership rights and therefore contributed to the socio-economic stability of traditional Chinese society.

The above differentiation and analyses have revealed the interconnection and logical relations among various land rights transaction forms.[7] The land rights transaction system thus meets the different preferences and demands of factor market actors and reduces the

---

6. When a current landowner sold his land, the original landowner asked for and usually received "joyous-gift silver" from the buyer. This custom was widespread, and there were more than 20 cases recorded in *Memorials on Criminal Matters 2*.

7. Long Denggao and Wen Fangfang, "Identifying Traditional Forms of Land Rights Transactions: A Case Study of *Dian*," *Zhejiang Academic Journal*, no. 3 (2018): 172–182.

systemic risks of land rights transactions, especially ownership transfer.[8] The development of a land rights market is conducive to strengthening individual farmers' ability to operate independently and contributes to the stability and development of the traditional economy and society.

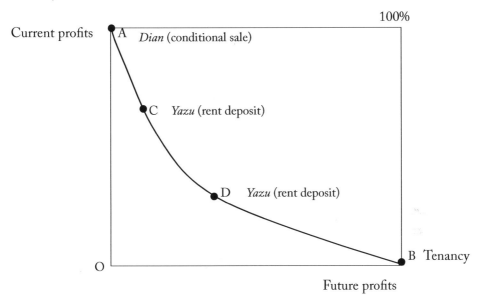

Figure 1 The Relations between *Dian*, *Yazu* (Rent Deposit), and Tenancy from the Point of View of the Land Owner

2.3 The Transmutation Process of Land Rights System

Since the Warring States period and the Qin and Han dynasties (471 BCE–220 CE), the forms of land rights transactions have gradually increased. The forms of land property rights have become more varied, including the *dian* rights in the Tang and Song dynasties, the permanent tenancy system in the Song and Yuan dynasties, and the emergence of

---

8. Some scholars today question the efficiency or rationality of pawn transactions, which is actually a misinterpretation. For details, see Long Denggao and Wen Fangfang, "On the Redemption Mechanism of Traditional Chinese Dian Transactions: A Study Based on the Shanxi Deeds in the Tsinghua Collection," *Economic Science*, no. 5 (2014): 172–182. In the traditional period, the opposite was true: the "conditional sale" (*dian*) was regarded as the "correct *dian*" and the mortgage was subject to moral attack. In fact, each transaction method has its own preferences and should not be viewed in isolation, but should be embedded in the trading system, so that it is understood that the coexistence of trading methods with different preferences can reduce systemic risk.

surface rights, rent deposit, and not-finalized sales in the Ming and Qing dynasties. The transformation of land rights from the Song to the Qing Dynasty and their differentiation reflect how the land-right transaction rules developed from spontaneous generation to gradual improvement and standardization. Social perceptions and government management also changed in this process.

The Song Dynasty was at the beginning of the development of the *dian* right. It was relatively easy to apply, and for this reason, it was easy to grasp the original nature of *dian*. In the Qing Dynasty, the development of the *dian* right led to complex and diverse forms and manifestations, and the rights derived from it gradually became explicit. They were no longer forbidden, as during the Song Dynasty. Nevertheless, they also contributed to obscuring and distorting the original nature of *dian*.

First, regarding the origin of *dian*, in the Song Dynasty, the fundamental norm was "selling the land off the property" (*diantian liye* 典田离业). The control of the land and the transfer of all operation income during the agreed period was the original and core of the *dian* right.

Second, the derived rights and the manifestation of diversity of *dian* are highlighted by the different ways to transact land in *dian* sales. Misconceptions about *dian* in the Song and Qing dynasties are also related to these different transaction procedures. For example, the practice of the *dian* buyer renting out land to the original landowner was not recognized in the Song Dynasty, while in the Qing Dynasty, this form was widely popular.

Third, the different policies and regulations of the Song and Qing dynasties regarding *dian* transactions were also compatible with the rules mentioned above. In the Song Dynasty, the transaction of *dian* fields required the transfer of the tax obligation of land tax and corvée and payment of a transaction tax. The form of the deed was correspondingly contractual, i.e., the deed consisted two parts, which would be put together at the date of redemption, a practice referred to as (*heqi tongyue* 合契同约). In the Qing Dynasty, the management of *dian* fields was simplified, and the tax was exempted for a long time, so there was no need to go through the procedure of transfer of farm tax. The contractual deeds of *dian* land also changed into a single deed form, which adapted to the increase of subsequent transactions or related transaction forms in the Qing Dynasty. On the original deeds and agreements, people could record and practice *dian* transfer, *dian* add-on, and other additions.

These phenomena and differences cannot be understood in isolation but are interrelated and corroborate each other with an internal logic and thus constitute an explanatory framework. The differences in the stages and characteristics of the development of the *dian* rights reflect the transformation of the rules of land rights transactions, thus enabling us to understand more fully the pattern of land property rights and transactions in traditional China.[9]

3   Land Rights Markets, Family Farms, and Characteristics of the Traditional Economy

3.1   The Connection and Influence of Land Tenure Market and Individual Family Farm

The markets for land rights and individual family farms were interrelated and constituted two of the most fundamental features of China's traditional economy and its unique development path. The two promoted and reinforced each other, improved economic efficiency and land output, contributed to the stable development of the traditional economy, and inhibited its transformation and change into modern economic forms. This helps to explain the difference in the evolution of the Chinese and Western economic forms and is one of the most important reasons that China's traditional economy was unable to move towards an Industrial Revolution spontaneously and powerfully.

Self-employed, semi-employed, and tenant farmers established individual family farms by virtue of their ownership, possession, and usage rights. They produced and reproduced with the help of a combination of market factors and resources. A multi-layered land rights transaction system enabled peasant households to make choices according to market prices and risk appetites, cater to their own needs, and help to achieve regulation between current and future profits, thereby facilitating the combination of land circulation and productive factors and improving economic efficiency.[10] The redemption mechanism, which included the use of *dian*, *huomai*, and *yazu*, effectively preserved the willingness of peasant households to secure and resume their land ownerships and made less complex but potentially usurious property transfers such as finalized sales or mortgages more unlikely.

The land rights market that supported individual family farms was characteristic of low threshold, separability, and easy replication. Farmers could support their families even when encountering natural and man-made disasters, and members of an increasing population coming from existing families and villages were able to establish their independent farms.

---

9. Long Denggao, Wen Fangfang, and Qiu Yongzhi, "The Nature and Rights of Dian Land—A Comparative Study of the Song and Qing Dynasties," *Historical Research*, no. 5 (2016): 54–70.

10. Long Denggao, "Land Rights Transactions and Production Factor Mix, 1650–1950," *Economic Research*, no. 2 (2009): 146–156; Long Denggao, *Land Rights Markets and Resource Allocation* (Fuzhou: Fujian People's Publishing House, 2012).

It was in this way that a system in which equal inheritance among sons was practiced (*zhuzi junfenzhi* 诸子均分制) instead of primogeniture, so that families, land, and individual farms were continually divided and regenerated. Since the Chinese used to have a system of equal inheritance among sons, rather than a system of primogeniture, people's family members, land, and individual farms were constantly divided and regenerated.

However, the self-regeneration and dynamism of individual family farms also inhibited the growth of large-scale and capitalist operations. As a result, it was difficult for new factors to emerge while the original essence of the Chinese agricultural economy was continuously reinforced. The changes in pre-modern Western Europe came mainly from new forces outside the manorial system. Because of the weak capacity of individual farmers to operate independently, farmers depended on the estate. At the same time, the estate was integral and inseparable, related to its property rights attributes and combined farming operations. As a result, the additional population of the estate or other descendants under the primogeniture system found it challenging to establish their independent agricultural operations to exist and develop outside the estate, promote the growth of new factors, and thus qualitative change.

3.2 Reconstructing Share Tenancy: A Reflection on the "Optimal Owner-Peasant"

Tenancy and land-rights transactions enabled the owners of factors with different endowments to cooperate effectively, increased the mobility and efficiency of the factors of production, brought about changes in different classes and changes in management, and thus reflected the social mobility of the time.

With regard to tenant peasants, previous studies have generally considered them to be the landowners' labour, similar in nature to hired labour, and remunerated on a par with hired labour, a stereotype that has led to a misconception of economic interpretation and historical understanding.[11] In fact, tenant peasants during the Ming and Qing dynasties already independently managed business, combined various factors and resources of production of their own, their landlords', markets', and families' through various channels and ways of personification and marketization to create wealth, and therefore formed diversified forms of farms. In fact, during the Ming and Qing dynasties, tenant farmers already managed businesses independently. Through the channels of personification and

---

11. Jing Su and Luo Lun, "Landlord and Labor in Late imperial China: Case Studies from Shandong," translated by Endymion Wilkinson (Cambridge, Mass.: Harvard University, Council of East Asian Studies, 1978).

marketization, they combined different factors of production from the family, the landlord, and the market to create wealth and form diversified forms of farming.

Moreover, they dominated the residual claims, reaping in uncertainty the rewards and risky returns that only an entrepreneur can earn, and the future benefits of his investment in the land and farm can be realized through trade. In all these cases, the hired farmers had no connection to them. Just as today's entrepreneurs do not own capital, land, labor, or technology but rather integrate these factors of production and resources through the market to build enterprises that create wealth. The economic efficiency and land output are driven by the transfer, selection, and allocation of factors of production under the system of land rights transactions, and the tenancy is an important source of dynamism for tenant farming and the smallholder economy.[12]

The dominant traditional myth that peasant farming is fair and efficient, while under the tenancy, the tenant farmer is exploited by the landlord and is less efficient, has been challenged both historically and theoretically. In a free market situation, the structure of land rights depends on the transaction costs and the level of the total surplus of the system. Drawing on the theory of optimal ownership structure to analyze the total institutional surplus of owner-farmers, tenant farmers, and hired laborers, the author argues that the optimal scale of land management, level of technology, land endowment, market conditions, and so on, will affect the choice of tenure structure, and owner-farmers are not necessarily optimal. By examining the impacts of the degree of marketization of agricultural products, transportation costs, the scale of land management, and the degree of dispersion of land rights on tenancy rates using statistical methods, and by comparing the scale of production and profits of modern owner-farmers with those of tenant farmers, it was found that the tenant economy exhibited advantages in many respects. The explanation lies in the fact that tenancy separates the asset function of land from the factor function of production, makes the area of land management independent of the area of land ownership, and also achieves the meritocracy of the cultivator.[13]

3.3 Corporate Property Rights, Civil Organization, and Grass-Roots Order

Suppose the right to private ownership of land is the cornerstone of the independent operation of peasants. In that case, the right to corporate ownership is the basis for the

---

12. Long Denggao and Peng Bo, "A Comparative Study of the Nature and Profitability of Tenants in Modern Times," *Economic Research Journal*, no. 1 (2010): 138–147.

13. Zhao Liang and Long Denggao, "Land Tenancy and Economic Efficiency," *China Economic Studies*, no. 2 (2012): 3–15.

independent development of civil society organizations, which together constitute the organic system of the private and public spheres of traditional society.

Non-governmental and non-profit micro-objects, represented by various civil society organizations, are prevalent in grass-roots society and the public sphere. They have independent property, especially estates and endowments (*huijin* 会金), with future value-added income for long-term operation. Such separate property is a corporate property right, exclusive, integral, and indivisible, and is guaranteed by the government and the law. Corporate property rights existed not only in "bridge societies" (*qiaohui* 桥会) and "voluntary ferry" (*yidu* 义渡) but also in water conservancy societies (*zhahui* 闸会), industrial and commercial societies, guilds, and secret societies, and more generally in families, temples, schools, and charitable and relief institutions. They are the cornerstone of the independent and sustainable development of civil society organizations, where they become the cornerstone of the independence and sustainability of any such social organization.

The micro subjects of corporate property rights have formed an effective organizational system and governance structure. They operated openly and transparently, were accountable to society and stakeholders, had clear regulations and institutional safeguards, and were able to embark on the path of sustainable development. Their effective incentive and discipline mechanisms were not only directly related to their economic interests but were also compatible with the prevailing religious, ethical, and moral values. The directors of social organizations were willing and committed; their employees worked hard. Meanwhile, strict regulations and public supervision prevented them from being able to take advantage of the situation and from being passive, thus effectively overcoming rent-seeking and corruption.

In short, independent property rights of corporate entities, clear statutes and rules, effective governance structures, open and transparent operations, incentives for social and economic interests, and supervision and restraint by the public all constitute the institutional arrangements of traditional Chinese civil organizations. The government manages grass-roots society indirectly through social organizations and social elites, which become the dominant force in the public sphere and provide public goods, services, and services to the grass-roots.[14] The grass-roots private and public spheres, provided by independent and autonomous micro-entities, allow the governmental authorities to achieve and maintain unity at a low cost.

---

14. Chen Yueyuan and Long Denggao, "The Property Attributes of Qing Academies and Their Market-Oriented Operation," *Zhejiang Academic Journal*, no. 3 (2020): 205–216; Long Denggao, Wang Zhenghua, and Yi Wei, "The Governance Structure of Traditional Civil Organizations and Legal Person Property Rights System: A Study Based on Public Construction and Management in the Qing Dynasty," *Economic Research*, no. 10 (2018): 175–191.

4 The Transformation of Modern Land Rights System and the Cognitive Misunderstanding

In modern times, the system and order of China's land rights have been undermined by power and violence. This deterioration led to the socio-economic upheaval and decline in the late Qing Dynasty and the early Republican era. People often blame it on the private property system itself, and, in particular, they infer that free trade in land rights leads to land appropriation and concentration. However, the cutting edge of economic historians' scholarship in the last two decades has shown that this traditional view has been significantly exaggerated.

4.1 An Examination and Analysis of Land Holdings

The amount of land held by wealthy landowners and peasants is an important indicator of the distribution of land rights in modern times after 1949 and a fundamental judgment of the land tenure system and modern economy. Yet, there has been a lack of convincing basic data. A detailed nationwide census has been conducted on land reform. Although accurate national data were not published, they laid the foundation for statistical work. Based on the land reform census data from 1949 to 1952, the author has examined that the proportion of land held by the top 10 percent of the rural wealthy on the eve of Land Reform was around 30 percent (±5 percent) in the southern provinces, while it was much lower than that in the north. This figure should be lower if the occupancy status of land rights, such as surface rights, permanent tenancy rights, and public land, was taken into account.[15] In other words, the rural rich held about 30 percent of land ownership, but their land rights and benefits were shared with the rest of the population.

Land concentration phenomena and trends are exaggerated. Another important reason lies in the perception that this is an inevitable consequence of free trade. The lack of convincing academic analysis has led to the neglect of the negative feedback mechanisms that inhibit and hedge against land ownership concentration.

The hedging factors for the concentration of land rights, or the factors and mechanisms for the fragmentation of land rights, have profound reasons other than the well-known system of equal inheritance rule among various sons. First, the more diverse the forms of transactions, the more likely they are to reduce systemic risk, such as redemption

---

15. Long Denggao and He Guoqing, "An Examination and Interpretation of the Distribution of Land Rights on the Eve of Land Reform," *Southeast Academic Research*, no. 4 (2018): 150–161.

mechanisms to protect the rights of vulnerable groups and also to delay the transfer of land rights, providing the possibility for farmers to weather the storm, recover and rebuild their farms and operate independently. Second, land tenure is not just about ownership but also possession. The fact the vast number of middle-and-lower-class farmers have the right to the surface of the land and the right to sell the land in a conditional sale, which is also a property right. Third, the land of corporate property rights, such as family-owned lands (*zutian* 族田), temple fields, school fields, various association fields, and community fields, has, to some extent, reduced the unevenness of private land occupation. For example, the proportion of public land (*gongtian* 公田) in Guangdong and Fujian could reach about 30%. These institutional arrangements have enabled individual farmers to gain ongoing competitiveness and vitality and have, to some extent, inhibited land concentration and mergers.

4.2 Equalization of Land Rights: A Reflection of History and Reality

Sun Yat-sen's political slogan, "equalization of land rights" (*pingjun diquan* 平均地权), has been the dominant ideological trend in China and was put into practice nationwide in the mid-to-late twentieth century. The Land Reform Movement of 1949–1952 was a compulsory change to equalize land ownership. In contrast, the Collectivization Movement since the late 1950s and the 1981 Family Contract Responsibility system were about equal distribution of land usage rights.

The initial equalization, whether of ownership or use rights, was quickly disrupted by factors such as female marriage, changes in household composition, population mobility, farming capacity, and so on. Therefore, the dynamic combination of land and labor was difficult to maintain when combined with other variables. In the twenty-first century, the shift in national policy towards encouraging land transfers meant a shift from government allocation of agricultural land to an enhanced role for the market.[16]

From an academic point of view, it is extremely rare to find economic "experiments" and research materials on how the tenure status changed after the initial state of tenure equalization, which is of irreplaceable value. Although there are many results on equal land rights and each land system reform, there are limited systematic studies on a coherent basis. In reality, each change has had a profound impact on the economy and politics of Chinese society. It not only provides inspiration and lessons for the current land system reform so

---

16. Long Denggao, "From the Equalization of Land Rights to Encouragement of Circulation," *Hebei Academic Journal*, no. 3 (2018): 142–147.

as to grasp the orientation and basic ideas of the reform but also summarizes the historical connotation of Chinese characteristics from the changes and provides historical support for grasping the changes and characteristics of Chinese society and economy as a whole.

In fact, the one-sidedness of the mainstream thinking of the 20th century, such as the theory of optimal self-farming, the theory of unfairness and inefficiency of tenancy, and the theory of equal land rights, is due to the lack of market mentality. They were all static thinking based on the premise of land immobility and other production factors. Still, they became mainstream thinking under the strong stimulus of China's economic backwardness and the quest for a strong state under foreign imperialism in the modern era.

4.3 Dilemmas and Perceptions of the Transition from Traditional to Modern Economies

Owning land properties and trading them to create wealth can be said to be a simple nature that the people in traditional China have unleashed. But in modern times, it has been lost in importance due to the chaos of backwardness and aggressions by foreign powers, both economically and forcefully. People sentimentally attribute poverty and backwardness to the concentration of land rights due to private ownership of land, which led to bankruptcy, exile, and poverty of peasants, and the disorder of the economy due to factors and commodity markets. People believed that only through government control and allocation of resources could we break out of the chaos and achieve a rich country and a strong military. This became the dominant ideology of the 20th century. However, the main external cause of the economic decline of modern China was the incessant wars, while the fundamental internal cause was the failure of the transition from a traditional economy to a modern economy (or the industrialization of the agricultural economy).

Many scholars have hypothesized that if China had been able to originate the Industrial Revolution, as Britain did, it would have been able to avoid being left behind and beaten. Similarly, many scholars have discussed why France, Spain, India, and the Muslim world did not have an industrial revolution. As a matter of fact, all other regions, except Britain, industrialized by learning and imitating the "British model." The absence of a spontaneous industrial revolution does not indicate the stagnation and lack of dynamism of the traditional Chinese economy, nor does it entirely negate the traditional Chinese system and culture.

Comparing the form of property rights and business operation between China and Western Europe in the pre-modern period, we find that the characteristics of traditional China—individual farming based on private property rights of land and market transactions, with low threshold, divisibility, replicability, and easy recovery, has created a substantial middle class of peasants in the agricultural era and achieved relative economic and social stability. This stability and the self-reinforcement of essential attributes, on the other hand, inhibited the growth of change and heterogeneous factors. This explains the essential characteristics of the traditional Chinese economy and its differences from the path of economic development in Western Europe.

Through systematic investigation of the traditional land property rights system over the past millennium, this chapter re-examines the land rights system and the traditional economy and reflects on some deeply influential existing theories in order to form a new understanding. Meanwhile, the all-round excavation of this irreplaceable institutional heritage, as well as the in-depth investigation of land property rights and the diversified forms of transactions, result in new academic discoveries and theoretical innovations and contribute to forming a systematic understanding and explanatory framework.

The interpretation of the relevant issues is not based on the deduction of some theories or models but on new insights based on the restoration of historical facts. The unique heritage of the traditional land tenure system has reference value for the current market-oriented reform of the agricultural land system. The recent construction of the market economy has specific traditional institutional and cultural foundations. However, these institutional legacies have not been properly explored for a long time; on the contrary, they have been neglected and distorted for a long time.[17] This chapter presents these valuable legacies clearly in front of the world so we can better understand the market economy system with "Chinese characteristics," which also shows its theoretical value.

References

Cao, Shuji, and Li Feiqi. "Land Mortgage in Mountainous Regions of Southern Zhejiang during the Mid- and Late Qing: A Study Based on 'Land Mortgage Contracts' from Shicang Village, Songyang County." *Journal of Historical Research*, no. 3 (2008).

Cao, Shuji, and Liu Shigu. *Traditional Land Property Rights Structure and Its Transformation.* Shanghai: Shanghai Jiaotong Univerisity Press, 2014.

Long, Denggao. *Land Rights Markets and Resource Allocation.* Fuzhou: Fujian People's Publishing House, 2012.

Cao, Shuji. "The Nature of Surface Land Rights in Southern Jiangsu Province." *The Journal of Tsinghua University*, no. 4 (2007).

---

17. Li Bozhong, "Preface," in Long Denggao, *China's Traditional Land Tenure System and Its Changes* (Beijing: China Social Sciences Press, 2018).

———. "Two Kinds of Permanent Tenancy and Rent Reduction in Zhejiang Province." *Journal of Historical Research*, no. 2 (2007).

Chen, Yueyuan, and Long Denggao. "The Property Attributes of Qing Academies and Their Market-Oriented Operation." *Zhejiang Academic Journal*, no. 3 (2020): 205–216.

Chen, Zhiying. *A Study of Property Rights Relations in the Song Dynasty*. Beijing: China Social Sciences Press, 2006: 140–147.

Dai, Jianguo. "The Dian Transactions of Civil Lands and the System of 'One Piece of Land with Two Owners' in the Song Dynasty." *Historical Research*, no. 6 (2011): 99–117.

Fang, Xing. "The Land Market of China's Feudal Society." *Researches in Chinese Economic History*, no. 2 (2001).

Gao, Wangling. *New Theory of the Tenancy Relationship—Landlords, Peasants, and Land Rents*. Shanghai: Shanghai Bookstore Publishing House, 2005.

———. "A New Perspective on the Tenancy Relationship." *Researches in Chinese Economic History*, no. 3 (2005).

Jing, Su, and Luo Lun. "Landlord and Labor in Late imperial China: Case Studies from Shandong." Translated by Endymion Wilkinson (Cambridge, Mass.: Harvard University, Council of East Asian Studies, 1978).

Li, Bozhong. "Preface." In Long Denggao. *China's Traditional Land Tenure System and Its Changes*. Beijing: China Social Sciences Press, 2018.

Li, Deying. *National Decree and Civil Customs: A New Probe into the Tenancy System of Chengdu Plain during the Republic of China*. Beijing: China Social Sciences Press, 2006.

Li, Li. "The Expression and Significance of Qing Dynasty Civil Land Deeds to the Dian." *Jinling Law Review*, no. 1 (2006): 111–118.

Long, Denggao, and Chi Xiang. "The Outline on the Institution of Land Transaction in Traditional China. European and Chinese Histories of Economic Thought Theories and Images of Good Governance." *Routledge Studies in the History of Economics* (2021).

Long, Denggao, and He Guoqing. "An Examination and Interpretation of the Distribution of Land Rights on the Eve of Land Reform." *Southeast Academic Research*, no. 4 (2018): 150–161.

Long, Denggao, and Peng Bo. "A Comparative Study of the Nature and Profitability of Tenants in Modern Times." *Economic Research Journal*, no. 1 (2010): 138–147.

Long, Denggao, and Wen Fangfang. "Identifying Traditional Forms of Land Rights Transactions: A Case Study of *Dian*." *Zhejiang Academic Journal*, no. 3 (2018): 172–182.

Long, Denggao, and Wen Fangfang. "On the Redemption Mechanism of Traditional Chinese Dian Transactions: A Study Based on the Shanxi Deeds in the Tsinghua Collection." *Economic Science*, no. 5 (2014): 172–182.

Long, Denggao, Lin Zhan, and Peng Bo. *Social Sciences in China*, no. 5 (2013): 125–141.

Long, Denggao, Wang Zhenghua, and Yi Wei. "The Governance Structure of Traditional Civil Organizations and Legal Person Property Rights System: A Study Based on Public Construction and Management in the Qing Dynasty." *Economic Research*, no. 10 (2018): 175–191.

Long, Denggao, Wen Fangfang, and Qiu Yongzhi. "The Nature and Rights of Dian Land—A Comparative Study of the Song and Qing Dynasties." *Historical Research*, no. 5 (2016): 54–70.

Long, Denggao. "From the Equalization of Land Rights to Encouragement of Circulation." *Hebei Academic Journal*, no. 3 (2018): 142–147.

————. "Land Rights Transactions and Production Factor Mix, 1650–1950." *Economic Research*, no. 2 (2009): 146–156.

Wu, Xianghong. "Chapter 7." In *Customs and Laws of Dian*. Beijing: Law Press · China, 2009.

Ye, Xiaoxin. *History of Chinese Legal System*. Beijing: Peking University Press, 1999.

Zhao, Gang. "The Choice of Agricultural Land Management Mode in History." *Researches in Chinese Economic History*, no. 2 (2000).

————. "The Land Tenancy System of Ming and Qing Dynasties From Another Perspective." *Agricultural History of China*, no. 2 (2000).

Zhao, Liang, and Long Denggao. "Land Tenancy and Economic Efficiency." *China Economic Studies*, no. 2 (2012): 3–15.

CHAPTER 2

The Diversification of Land Transactions in the Qing Dynasty*

There were three kinds of financial transactions involving rights of land during the Qing Dynasty: debt financing through rights of land, the direct transferring of the rights of land, and the transaction of shares. This chapter attempts to clarify the confusion between several types of debt financing through rights of land. *Ya* 押 was a loan through land as a guaranty and repaying the interest and capital by the rent of land or harvest. *Dian* 典 was a loan through temporary transferring of usage rights and harvest in a certain period of time. *Dang* 当 referred to various types of loans involving the rights of land. *Di* 抵 meant using a certain portion of land right as repayment of debt. Similar to modern financial methods, these financial transactions in the Qing Dynasty allowed peasants to preserve their possessive rights over the land and also satisfied their financial needs. The direct transactions of rights of land and repayment of a debt by harvest included *juemai* 绝卖 (finalized sale of land), *huomai* 活卖 (not finalized sale of land), *dianquan dingtui* 佃权顶退 (sell or purchase tenancy), *zhaojia* 找价 (price add-on after transaction), and *huishu* 回赎 (redemption). The main purpose of these transactions was to protect the land proprietors as far as possible. Share transactions and co-tenancy of land also appeared in the Qing Dynasty. Such diverse financial transactions were substitutes for modern financing tools that allowed peasants to weather financial hardship and promoted the changing ownership

* Long Denggao, "The Diversification of Land Transactions in the Qing Dynasty," *Frontiers of History in China* 4, no. 2 (2009).

of land, which further encouraged the combination of different production elements and the reallocation of resources in the land market.

Emerging in the forms of the rights of top soil (Tianmianquan 田面权, right of secure land usage) and the rights of subsoil (Tiandiquan 田底权, right of land ownership), the dissolution of property rights of land and administrative rights of land accelerated the tradable revolution of land rights in the Qing Dynasty.[1] The diversified ways of transaction included the extremely confusing *dian, dang* (and *an* 按), *ya* (and *taijie* 胎借—mortgage by land as guaranty and repay it with the harvest), *di*, as well as the forms of redeemable sell, unredeemable pawning of land, repayment by tenancy, and price add-on, etc. Although well known, some of the transaction rules and the differences in their functions are not yet clarified; some of them are even misread. This chapter distinguishes and categorizes the miscellaneous original contracts of land transactions and the cases of complicated land disputes[2] in China, Japan, and the United States. These cases could be differentiated into three categories as debt financing through rights of land, direct transferring of land rights, transaction of shares (of ownership or tenancy of land), to examine thereof. The paper also inspects the differences among distinctive rules of each transaction form, analyzes their functions in the market of land rights and the economy of the peasantry, and accordingly investigates the development of the market of land rights and the dislocation of resources in the Qing Dynasty.

1   The Analyses of *Ya, Dian, Dang, Di*: Four Transaction Forms that Property Rights Are Unchanged

Ya, dian, dang were all under the pre-condition that property rights were not ultimately transferred, transaction methods that manipulate the right of land usage and its profits to gain funds. *Di* was slightly different, for it happened with the division of land rights. These forms of transaction were popular in traditional periods; however, differences among them could not be distinguished easily. Moreover, the modern financing tools such as mortgage and pawn, different in their methods and usages, further confused these transaction forms.

---

1. Long Denggao, "The Market of Land Rights and the Allocation of Resources," in *Keynotes and Variations: China from 7–20th Century*, ed. Huang Kuanzhong (Taibei: Zhengzhi daxue lishi xi, Zhongyang yanjiuyuan, etc., 2008).

2. *Legal Cases Records of Grand Secretariat in Emperor Qianlong's Reign, The land Rent Exploitation in the Qing Dynasty* (Beijing: Zhonghua Book Company, 1982). The cases from *Xingke tiben* (XKTB) presented in this paper are adopted from *Qingdai dizu boxue*. Due to the complicated plots of each case, this paper does not quote the original texts but only gives the sources of each case, such as "XKTB: No. 214." The number refers to the serial number of each case in the book.

1.1 *Ya, Taijie, Zhiya*: The Loan that Uses Land Rights as Guaranty and Land Profits as Repayment

Ya[3] means using land rights as guaranty and land profits to repay the capital and the interests of the loan. The loan by the rights of land ownership was repaid by land rent; the loan by the rights of land usage was repaid by the profits of land, but the right of land was not transferred. For example, XKTB: No. 214 recorded, in Liu'an, Anhui Province, Zhang Nan'e leased the right of land usage of 7 shi 石 of temple land with 20 liang 两 of silver. In the 30th year of Qianlong (1765), he used the security right of land usage of 4 shi 石 of land to mortgage 57 liang 两 of silver from Zhu Congheng, which he was to pay back with 16 shi 石 of crops from his rented land every year. Through the transaction form of *ya*, he got the cash by mortgaging his future profits, and repaid the rent annually.

Taijie, which means "li tai jie yin" 立胎借银 (setting up a contract for borrowing silver), was popular mainly in Taiwan and Fujian. It was a special way of referring to *ya*; making a contract to borrow money with the land as a guaranty repaying the capital and interests of the loan with crops of the land. Profit of the land belonged to the creditor, and if the loan was not repaid according to the contract, the right of land would be transferred. What follows was an example from Taiwan of China:

> Drawers of the "dui dian tai jie yin" 对佃胎借银 (mortgage the tenancy for silver) contract, Jiang Gan included, according to their relatives' relations, were supposed to receive their rights to land located at Haishan. The land's boundaries of the north, east, south, and west, along with its rights to water, were all recorded in the contract. Due to the lack of money, Gan and others were willing to mortgage this land. We first inquired after uncles and nephews among the relatives, and then resorted outward to borrow 100 silver yuan 银元 from Li Jingyi through a middleman. The silver was collected by Gan's relatives on that day and the three sides agreed on the contract. It was agreed that each silver yuan 银元 was to be repaid with extra interests of sixteen percent, which meant 16 silver yuan 银元 of interests in total. The interests, divided into first and latter halves, would be paid separately in the early season by the end of June and the late season by the end of October. As to the current tenant Xu Laoyong, his rent of the land should be paid to the creditor, and none of the amount should be owed. The loan period was two years, from the winter of the 20th year of Guangxu (1894) to the winter of the 22nd year of Guangxu (1896).

---

3. There is also another form of *ya* as rent deposit. By paying a certain amount of cash, the rights to cultivate or rent the land can be gained, and accordingly the money is paid as the deposit to future payment of renting the land. On a certain level, *ya* is also a way to manage currency. This is also the consensus of the common people at that time. This paper, however, will not discuss specifically on this topic.

After two years, the beginning date of repayment was set to before the Moon Festival in August; 10 silver yuan 银元 were to be returned first, and the rest of the silver could be waited until the tenth day before the winter solstice, when all silvers were prepared, to be used to redeem the contract. The deadline should not be overdue; if by the time no silver could be submitted to the creditor, the term of the contract should be carried out. Gan and others should not dare to cause trouble accordingly. Such was the agreement of benevolence and righteousness, and both sides were willing and unregretful. In fear of the unreliability of speech, they drew up the dui dian taijie yin contract and submitted a copy, two papers in total, for evidence's sake.

Today the loan of 100 yuan 元 of silver is collected, as recorded in the contract.

This business is specified so that afterwards if the land is leased by other tenants, the new tenant has to pay the interest to the creditor and provide fingerprints at site.

Another note: current tenant Xu Laoyong terminated the lease during October in the 22nd year of Guangxu (1896), by which time Jianggan, Jingyi, and Xu agreed to lease the land to Liu Qi. Gan hence clarified the issues with the silver and land contract with the new tenant Liu Qi, and dared not act against the contract.

Now that the tenant has changed, recognize the person who is to submit the interests, Liu Qi.

On behalf of him: Li Guangwu

Current tenant and interests' payer: Xu Laoyong

Witness: Li Chens (Li Jianggan's mother)

Debtor: Li Jianggan

November, the 20th year of Guangxu (1894)[4]

In this example of "dui dian tai jie yin," debt owner Li Jianggan used the land as the mortgage and repaid with the harvests of the land with a 16% interest. Moreover:

(1) It was agreed that the tenant (Xu Laoyong) would submit the rent directly to the creditor (Li Jingyi).

(2) Corresponded with the two harvests of the land, the interests would be divided into two payments per year, one by the end of June, and the other by the end of October.

(3) If the tenant was changed, the new tenant (Liu Qi) would bear the responsibility of the previous tenant.

Similar to *ya* was *zhiya* 质押. *Zhiya* usually referred to the action of a loan that used movable properties as guaranty. When lands, as immovable properties, appeared in the

---

4. Wang Shiqing, "Official and Private Collections of Ancient Records in Taiwan" (Taibei: Fu Sinian Library of Academia Sinica), FSN01-10-479.

form of paper contracts, they could also be referred to as *zhiya*. In the accountant book of the Wang Family in Yi County, Hui prefecture, Zhang Youyi found that there were two lands that distinctively appeared on the record in the 8th and 12th year of Tongzhi (1869, 1873). Both of these two records were noted with words of *zhiya*,[5] which meant that the lands were used as a guaranty of the loans from the Wang family.

1.2 *Dian*: To Relinquish the Land Usage for a Loan and to Repay the Interests by the Rent of the Land

Dian means the persons in possession of land rights relinquish the rights to control the land as well as the rights to take profit from the land temporarily for loans. After due time, these rights could be bought back by the original sum of the loan. Mortgagers usually had to "leave the property," namely, to transfer the rights to use the land to the creditor and to "submit the rents to the creditors' interests of the loan." Interests in other forms and amounts would not be collected.

In the first year of Tongzhi (1862), "a couple of contract drawers including Li Xiehe" mortgaged their 11 mu 亩 and 8 fen 分 of land:

> Due to emergency, after discussions with grandmother and mother, it is agreed that we are willing to mortgage the land for a loan of 300 liang 两 of silver, in a time frame of ten years, from Kuihai year (1863) to the end of Rensheng year (1872). The creditor will not collect additional interests, and neither will the debtor collect the rent of the land. . . . After the loan is contracted, rents will be submitted as payment. It is not until the date of due can the land be redeemed. If the land is redeemed prior to the due dates, 32 liang 两 of silver are required as compensation to the creditor. This land is indeed inherited from the ancestors and is certainly not the guaranty or interests of other loans. If the rights of the land are questionable, they should be clarified, and the rent should still be submitted to the creditor as payment of interests.[6]

The contracted period of loan lasted as long as ten years, for the debtor needed a larger amount of silver—300 liang 两, Consequently, except for using the land as a guaranty of the loan, the interests needed to be repaid with rents of ten years. Land rights, tenant

5. Zhang Youyi, *The Study of Land Relationships in Huizhou in the Ming and Qing Dynasties* (Beijing: China social sciences press, 1984), 280.

6. Xiao Guojian and Bu Yongjian, "The Document Volume of the Xiao Family in Huaping of Xiaolan in Xiangshan County of Guangdong Province," *South China Research Resource Station Newsletter*, Jan. 15, 2008, no. 50.

rights, land rents, as well as tenant rents were all objects that could be used as a guaranty of a *dian* loan. *Dianzu* 典租 was, on the other hand, the action of contracting the loan by mortgaging land rents or tenant rents. This was exemplified in the fourth part of this chapter, in the instance of "li dian zu qi" 立典租契 from Taiwan in the 17th year of Jiaqing (1812).

There were two other examples of the transfer of tenancy by "drawing up dian tickets." In the 23rd year of Qianlong (1758), in Ninghai County of Zhejiang, Bao Youxiang originally leased three shi 石 of land from Bao Youcang. In the 23rd year of Qianlong (1758), he mortgaged his tenancy for a loan of 3000 wen 文 from his kinsman Bao Guangyu. A dian ticket was drawn up accordingly. In the 25th year of Qianlong (1760), the ticket was "redeemed and the tenancy was returned to the debtor" by the original amount of the loan.[7] The transfer of tenancy, in many contracts, equaled the mortgage of tenant rights. In Danyang of Jiangsu, Zhang Chaoyang had 4 mu 亩 and 4 fen 分 of land. Jiang Chaozong rent the land with a deposit of 16 liang 两 of silver and 2 qian 钱, and he submitted 2000 wen 文 as rent every year. Due to the illness of Zhang's mother, he lacked money and intended to sell the land with more than 50 liang 两 of silver. The prospective buyer Wang Jichang, however, was only willing to pay 19 liang 两 of silver and 4 qian 钱. Unable to reach an agreement on the sell price, they instead negotiated a dian contract. Owing to the few amount of the rent, Wang drew back tenancy rights to farm the land himself.[8] Meanwhile, the original tenant Jiang Chaozong faced two alternatives: either he could demand the return of his deposit silver from the original landlord Zhang, which would result in the loss of tenancy rights, or that he could demand compensations from the creditor Wang. It was additionally noted by the time of contract making that because of the low price to *dian* the land (the annual rent of 2 000 wen 文), compensation should be made from time to time to compensate for the loss of the original tenant Zhang. The *dian* contract could become the transition to the final sale of land; if Wang (who got the mortgaged land) prolonged or increased his rights of the land, Zhang could demand subsidies.

If the time was overdue and the debtor was unable to redeem the land, he could request a postponement from the creditor, namely, *yandian* 延典, or he could mortgage the land again. The debtor could also increase the price of *dian* (the annual rent of the land) again and again. The creditor would have to increase his subsidization to the original tenant until the *dian* contract become sale of the land,[9] and hence the transfer of property rights. In

7. XKTB: No. 318.

8. XKTB: No. 229.

9. Zhang Fumei, "The Evolvement of the Laws on Pawning and Purchasing Land Properties and the Price Add-on Issue of Real Estate in Taiwan," in *The Land Problems in the History of Taiwan*, ed. Chen Qiukun, Xu Xueji (Taibei: Institute of Modern History, Academia Sinica, 1992).

the 11th year of Daoguang (1831), in Anlishe, Taiwan, a case of land mortgage contract for loans reflected the relationship of *dian* and loans among Wang Chengzong, Wang Jingshan, and the aboriginal woman of Anlishe:

> The *dian* contract of this land has not yet been fulfilled in its time frame of six years by the winter of 1837. Because of the aboriginal landlord's lack of money, she demands cash of 380 yuan 元 of silver from the creditors Wang Chenzong and Wang Jingshan. An amount of 115 yuan 元, as the deposit silver without interests as previously noted in the dian contract, is handed to the aboriginal landlord in person. After due negotiation, the tenancy of the land will be given to the farmer to be cultivated and harvested for 17 entire years. Rents that are supposed to be received year by year will be listed in numbers to be counterbalanced.
>
> It is also noted that the aboriginal landlord will prolong the *dian* contract for another ten and a half more years until the early season of Dingmao (1867).[10]
>
> After the first time the aboriginal landlady mortgaged the land to the Han person Wang, she needed cash when there were yet six years to the due of the mortgage, and signed the contract again:
>
> (1) Prolonging the contract for 17 years and getting the cash of 380 yuan 元.
>
> (2) Adding the amount of 115 yuan 元 as a cash deposit of the land based on the previous *dian*.
>
> (3) The above amount and interest would be repaid with the rents supposedly received year by year.
>
> (4) In the attached section of the contract, the aboriginal landlady prolonged the *dian* for another ten and a half years, rendering the entire period of pledge 33 and a half years.

Such a long time of mortgage was rare, meaning the loss of property rights to the land in a generation or two. It could be inferred that the aboriginal landlady was in desperate need of money, or it could also suggest her weak anticipation for future income, especially if she was a woman of old age. She was reasonably willing to exchange the tenancy for cash.

The transfer of mortgage was another common phenomenon, although such transactions did not result in final transfers of land rights. During the Japanese occupation, a "document of reason"[11] in Taibei County made a clear explanation:

---

10. "Anli wenshu," no. 411, recited from Chen Qiukun, *The Land Ownership of Taiwan Natives in the Qing Dynasty* (Taibei: Institute of Modern History, Academia Sinica, 1997).

11. Zhang Yanxian and Wu Xiaoyun, "The Collection of Ancient Books in Xinzhu Area" (Taibei: Academia Sinica. 1993), vol. 6.

Niupu Village, Zhubei yibu, Taibei County, numbered 46 in the 4th district

An garden of 4 fen 分 of land

Zeng Shi's father Zeng Wen bought a garden located in Niupu Village. At that time, Zeng Wen lacked cash and therefore mortgaged the garden to Cheng Jin and his sons Chen Fan and Chen Tianhe. The contract of *dian*, and other documents were submitted to be kept by Chen Jin, etc. Later, when Chen Jin and others intended to do other businesses, they transferred the mortgage of the garden to Zeng Lianfa, and the contract was turned in. Unexpectedly Zeng Lianfa lost all four pieces of last contracts, and the *dian* contract was the only thing left. By the 14th year of Guangxu (1889), this contract was submitted for tax, and after due examinations, the examination sheet was issued to the name of Zeng Lianfa. This land, in fact, belonged to Zeng Shi, who lacked the money to redeem the land. Now thanks to the examination of lands, this document is conducted with a due reason as a sheet of fact.

June 12, the 34th year of Muji (1901)

Yada Village, Zhubei yibao, Taibei County. Inheritor of the diseased father, Zeng Wen, the rightful owner of the land: Zeng Shi (fingerprints)

Keyaxi Village, the same bao in the same county. Inheritor of the diseased grandfather Zeng Lianfa, the creditor: Zeng Wang (fingerprints)

The same village, the same bao in the same county. Person of the pledged: Zeng Shuicheng (fingerprints)

The same village, the same bao in the same county. Person of the pledged: Zeng Jin (fingerprints)

The same village, the same bao in the same county. Person of the pledged: Zeng Jiu (fingerprints)

The same village, the same bao in the same county. Person of the pledged: Zeng Ren (fingerprints)

Committee member: Xu De (stamper)

Head of the village: Chen Yunru (stamper)

The minister of the Temporary Bureau of Taiwanese Land Investigation: Gotoo Shinbeii (seal)

This document disclosed the following contents, illustrating the consolidation of land rights in the concepts of the people and legislation of the time.

Firstly, *dian* was constantly transferred, and yet the rightful owner of the land remained unchanged: Zeng Wen—mortgaged the land to Chen Jin and his son—Chen Jin, transferred the mortgage to Zeng Lianfa. In this document, the original creditors, Chen Jin and his son, did not sign their names, and neither did they leave their fingerprints. This explains that the transfer of the mortgage did not affect the status of the landlord.

Secondly, although the rightful property owner was incapable of redeeming the land, the "document of reason" had to specify the name of the property owner and emphasized that "this is the property of Zeng Shi."

Thirdly, even if the original contract of mortgage and land certificate got lost, as long as the evidence (such as one of the *dian* contracts) could be verified, the property owner could be recognized.

Fourthly, despite the change in the government, property rights remained the same. Although occupied by Japan, conventional regulations of property rights continued to function, and usually new rulers recognized them. From the Ming to the Qing, transactions and transformations of land rights by all parties to the contract were not at the least affected.

Dian did not involve with the change of land ownership. The Qing Dynasty inherited from the Ming laws and did not demand taxes from such transactions of *dian*, though people who sold their lands had to submit taxes after transferring the property rights. "For contracts of mortgaging lands or houses, taxes can be waived. Taxes are required for all kinds of sales, whether redeemable or not."[12]

This practically encouraged debt financing by transfering non-property rights and consequently cheating behaviors of using repeating mortgage in replace of sales appeared. The multiple transactions of mortgages result in the gradual decline of loan money. For the first time, the debtor received a larger amount of loan. The loan money through such mortgage decreased significantly for the second time and even lower for the third time. If the item was mortgaged again or turned to sale for the third time, the transaction price on the surface would be significantly low, and so would the tax burden. To prevent such cheating, the government regulated that the mortgage period of land had to be recorded; comparatively, along with long periods of mortgage came high prices.

1.3 *Dang* (And "*An*"): Loan by Means of Land Rights (as Guarantees, Mortgages, Repayments, etc.)

The definition of dang (henceforth pawn) was more obscure, and its extended use more widely manipulated. Therefore, it can be associated with almost all other methods of debt financing, such as *diandang* 典当, *didang* 抵当, *yadang* 押当. Overall, *dang* referred to using land rights as intermediary tools to process all forms of loans.

---

12. Kun Gang and Li Hongzhang, eds, "Collected Statues of the Qing Dynasty Compiled in Emperor Guangxu's Reign," *Guangxu 25 nian (1899) shiyinben*. no. 755.

For one thing, the loans based on the guaranty of lands did not rely on the land for debt payment. If the debtor was unable to repay the debt within the time of the contract, the lands or rights recorded in the contract would belong to the creditor. A contract of *dang* in Anhui in the 27th year of Kangxi (1688) reads:

> Contract maker Zhu Guochang, now due to lack of money, is willing to pawn his inherited garden of Chakezhuying, located at Libianwu, to his lineage uncle for 1 liang 两 2 qian 钱 and 5 fen 分 of silver with an interest rate of 20%. If no interest is paid for one year, the property will be transferred without further protests.[13]

An, same as this form of *dang*, usually came in the cases of "an di jie yin" 按地揭银 (pawn the land for receiving silver).[14] Two contracts in Xiangshan County, Guangdong Province, reflected such forms of transaction. One was "jieyinqi" 揭银契 (the contract of receiving silver):

> Kong Changhan and Kong Qiyuan, as two partners, for the purpose of making a living, pawn two hill lands called Tangyong and Nuotang, 3 mu 亩 in total, along with the 3 mu 亩 of Kong Qiyuan's inherited land of Dongguatan and Lijiaotou for a loan of 29 liang 两 of silver. The contract is negotiated through middleman Kong Xianshen and drawn up in the house of Feng Boxian, Kong's cousin. It was agreed that the interest rate per liang 两 of silver is 18% which should be paid as scheduled. No delay of interest payment is allowed. If the payment is delayed, both parties should follow the judgment of Boxian without protest. Now for record's sake, this contract of jieyin is drawn up, and two copies of fingerprints are made and handed to Kong Xianshen and Feng Boxian.
>
> The actual pawned lands were Tangyong and Dongguatankou, 6 mu 亩 in total, evidenced by the contract with fingerprints.
>
> The actual silver received by the debtors was 29 liang 两 and 5 qian 钱 of silver.
>
> Middleman: Kong Xianshen
>
> Fellow debtor: Kong Chaoyuan
>
> June 15, the 8th year of Qianlong (1743), debtor: Kong Changhan[15]

---

13. Zhang Youyi, *The Study of Land Relationships in Huizhou in the Ming and Qing Dynasties* (Beijing: China social sciences press, 1984), 93.

14. "Anjin" in certain dialects means "Yajin." Also called "Anjie" nowadays, same as mortgage.

15. Xiao Guojian and Bu Yongjian, "The Document Volume of the Xiao Family in Huaping of Xiaolan in Xiangshan County of Guangdong Province," *South China Research Resource Station Newsletter*, Jan. 15, 2008, no. 50.

Obviously, this was a way of mortgage by pawning the land, and its repayment was not paid with rent or crops of the land. The 18% interest had to be "calculated according to schedule, and delay of payment is not allowed." "An di jie yin" sometimes could be contracted again and again. Now let us look at another contract of "an yin" 按银 (pawning for silver):

> The debtor Li Xianxing, for the medical needs, discussed with his wife and father and negotiated to mortgage the house of two units within the ninth mill and a piece of land for silver. Guaranteed by the middleman Xiao Qi's letter, they received 80 liang 两 of silver from Guisheng Hall. It is agreed that the interest rate for each liang 两 of silver was 12% one month. The period of this loan is six months. When the time is due, the capital silver and the interests should be paid together without any delay. If a delay in payment occurres, Guisheng Hall has the right to lease the house, transfer the mortgage contract, and deconstruct the house for materials.
>
> Drafted on December 24, the 29th year of Guangxu (1903)
>
> February 10, the 30th year of Guangxu (1904), "another 40 liang 两 of capital silver is borrowed for medical needs, and the interests will be calculated as previous."
>
> And on May 28, "because of the insufficient money for the funeral, another 49 liang 两 of capital silver is again loaned to the debtor, and the interests calculated as previous."[16]

Therefore, to provide medical resources for their family member, the Li family mortgaged houses and land again and again. The medical care proved ineffective at last (the first time the three of the Li family signed, and the third time, only the wife and the son signed). The Li family still needed to borrow silver for the funeral expense. Three times in total, in less than a half year, they borrowed 120 liang 两 of silver.

The second form of *an* used the land as the guaranty for loan and repaid the debts with rents of the lands. Such a mean of financing was equal to ya. In Wuxuan, Guangxi Province, the Tong people farmed "the same land, regardless of the change of land ownership, as if the tenancy is a generational business." The tenant Wei Fuhuan leased 4 sheng 升 of land, and afterwards due to his disease of dysentery, he temporarily pawned the land to Qin Fufu for 4 liang 两 of silver, and lived on the amount. As "the tenancy is temporarily pawned and redeemed by rent," he still cultivated the land himself.[17] Wei Fuhuan used his future tenant rent as mortgages to repay the interests and got 4 liang 两 of silvers in cash.

---

16. Ibid.
17. XKTB: No. 246.

In Rui'an, Zhejiang Province, the tenant Li Shisheng leased 3 mu 亩 of land from the Yin family. Li paid the deposit according to the custom and received the rights of the land from the landlord. In the second month of the 15th year of Qianlong (1750), Li "pawned (*yadang* 押当) the land to Zhong Yingyuan for 5 liang 两 and 2 qian 钱 of silver and agreed to redeem the land in the first month of the following year." When the date was due, Li had no silver to redeem the land. He then "relinquished (*ding* 顶 or sell) his tenancy of 2 mu 亩 to Zhu Bao and received 5 liang 两 of silver which he gave Zhong Yingyuan as debt repayment."[18]

Here the *yadang* involved the transaction of the tenancy rights of the 3-acre land, its property rights, cultivation, and benefits in the following year. The debtor received the cash in exchange for future benefits from the land; by the due date of the contract, the debtor returned the silver and redeemed the land. When disputes happened, Li Shisheng stressed the fundamental distinction between *yadang* and *ding* (relinquishment or selling of tenancy rights), "I temporarily mortgaged the land to Zhong Yingyuan for 5 liang 两 and 2 qian 钱 of silver, originally with the agreement that by the first month of the next year the silver will be returned and the land redeemed. I did not intend to relinquish the tenancy rights of the land to Zhong." *Ding* was the long-term relinquishment of property rights, and its price was higher: 5 liang 两 of silver for 2 mu 亩 of land; *dang* was the temporary relinquishment of land rights within limited time frames (in this example, one year), and therefore the price was comparatively lower: 5 liang 两 and 2 qian 钱 of silver for 3 mu 亩 of land.

The pawning object was sometimes simply part of the profit from the mortgaged land, as shown in the accountant book of the Hu family in Qimen.[19] For the land mortgaged in the 12th year of Tongzhi (1873), the Hu family only "took the 10 jin 斤 of the harvest" instead of the entire harvest of the land. In the 3rd year of Guangxu (1877), 7.5 yuan 元 were paid, and the pawned a certain portion of the land and submitted payment of 2 cheng 秤 (1 cheng 秤=100 jin 斤) and 10 jin 斤 of grain annually. Six years later, another 7.5 yuan 元 were paid, "with the interest of 2 cheng 秤 and 10 jin 斤 of grain from the land." Mortgaged with the land, the payment should be turned in with the profit of the harvest.

Besides, there were also *dang* cases in which the right of land was relinquished as well. *Dang* usually did not result in the relinquishment of land rights, but in certain cases, such things did happen. For example, in the Qimen Hus' accountant book, quoted by Zhang Youyi, it is recorded that: "In the 8th year of Xianfeng (1858), a land was pawned for 15 jin 斤 of harvests," "in the 11th year of Tongzhi (1872), a land was pawned for 20 jin 斤 of

---

18. XKTB: No. 309.

19. Zhang Youyi, *The Study of Land Relationships in Huizhou in the Ming and Qing Dynasties* (Beijing: China social sciences press, 1984), 402.

harvests," "in the 5th year of Guangxu (1879), a land was pawned for 15 jin 斤 of harvests," and "in the 20th year of Guangxu (1894), a land was pawned for 15 jin斤." In Gui County of Guangxi Province, in the 14th year of Qianlong (1749), Li Shebao rented Huang Durong's land and *dang* (relinquish) his tenancy to Zheng Laohuo to cultivate the land. Li received 8 liang 两 of silver. In the 16th year of Qianlong (1751), he intended to redeem the land to cultivate on his own.[20] But here, the *dang* of relinquishing the tenancy was actually accomplished by making a deposit. Here, the meaning of pawning the land was the same as pawning one's possessions in pawnshops. Movable properties, as guaranties, were taken to pawnshops under the charge of the pawnshop keepers; immovable properties, on the other hand, only needed contracts of both sides as covenants. "Zhuandang" 转当 (the transferring of the pawning) were allowed, and although there would be no final transfer of land rights, the "pawning debtor" could transfer the land to be cultivated by the third person.

In Bobai County of Guangxi Province, Liu Ya and his brothers, in the 8th year of Qianlong (1743):

> I received the relinquished a piece of shared land called Guanyinshan from Pang Yasan, Pang Shaonan, and Pang Shaorong with tax 2 dou 斗 and 5 sheng 升 and 3 he 合 of rice, total 4 shi 石 seeds, which worth 36,000 wen 文 and 15 liang 两 of silver. Later, because we were in need of cash, and the Pangs had no money to redeem the land in the last month in the 13th year of Qianlong (1748), through the middleman Zou Guangzu, we had drawn up a contract that relinquished the land right to Long Tiande for 51,000 wen 文. We also gave our contract with the Pangs to Long Tiande, who then had the right to cultivate the land.[21]

If the debt could not be cleared, the transformation from debt rights would become the transaction of land rights and, therefore, the occurrence of transfer of land rights.

1.4 *Di*: Division of Property Rights as Repayment of Debts

The use of property rights of the land or profit from the land to repay previous debts was usually referred to "di huan qian xiang" 抵还欠项 (to repay the owed items).

> In Guangze County of Fujian Province, Mao Shouzhao was unable to repay his debts owed to Wang Gonghuan. Mao Shouzhao drew up a contract, using the land as the

---

20. XKTB: No. 257.
21. XKTB: No. 036.

guaranty to *di* (repay) his debt to Wang by the rent of land submitted by the tenants. After Shaozhao died, his son spent the rent and did not give it to Wang. Gonghuan, therefore, found another tenant to cultivate the land. Disputes occurred, and the government ruled that "the land should be managed by Wang Gonghuan."[22]

Here *di* 抵 was to transfer the rent of land in the form of the harvest from the land to the creditors. Yet different from the general transfer of land rights, in such cases, the original landlord kept the right to use the land. Therefore, it is not accurate enough to say simply that *di* involved the transfer of land rights. Misunderstanding is consequently easily incurred. It should be put this way that what happened with *di* was the division of land rights. Such could be the route to form the right of a secure tenancy. When tenancy rights were mortgaged as property rights of land, the creditor got the "lizu" 利租 (profit from land as repayment of loan).

In Nanjing County of Fujian Province, Xu Bao rented Wang Jin's 4 dou 斗 of land to cultivate, yet he was unable to do more farming because of his illness. In contrast to him, Xu Zhen had four sons, and his family was rich with labor. As a consequence, he used 32 liang 两 of silver to take over 2 dou 斗 seeds of Xu Bao's tenanted land in the 16th year of Qianlong (1751), and he paid 2 shi 石 and 8 dou 斗 to the landlord Wang Jin annually. In the 22nd year of Qianlong (1757), Xu Bao owed Xu Zhen 17 liang 两 3 qian 钱 and 5 fen 分 of silver, and he could only repay such a debt by relinquishing the profit from the rest 2 dou 斗 of land to Xu Zhen. Xu Bao still cultivated the land, but he had to give Xu Zhen 3 shi 石 and 5 dou 斗 of grain harvest from his land as repayment of his debt owed to Xu Zhen.[23]

Xu Bao owned secure right of land usage, and he used it to repay his debts of 17 liang 两 3 qian 钱 5 fen 分 of silver, namely, using the future profits of rent income, 3 shi 石 and 5 dou 斗 of the harvest to repay his debt. Tenancy rights were transferred nominally, but the powers to control and to cultivate the land were still held by Xu Bao; the creditor (Xu Zhen), on the other hand, enjoyed the rights to a portion of the profit from the tenanted land. This was a kind of division of land rights, the creditor got the land rights in the form of profit, like the asset, and the original tenant held the rights to administrative and cultivate the land. Of course, these were all negotiated by both debtor and creditor, and it was possible to end up with a complete transfer of property rights. For example, here is a "contract of tenancy" in the 49th year of Kangxi (1710):

---

22. XKTB: No. 188.
23. XKTB: No. 327.

The drawer of this tenancy contract Wang Yuansun leased 2 qiu 丘 land called Fangkengkou, with a supposed rent of 11 zu 租 and 5 jin 斤 of harvest. Because of the delay of land rents for years, now through a middleman and Wang relinquished his tenancy right to the landlord Wang. When negotiated, the three agreed on the price of 4 liang 两 of silver, and the silver was used by Wang as repayment of his delayed rents to the landlord. The landlord would find another tenant for the land, and no objection is allowed.[24]

Because of the mortgage and repayment of debts owed, Wang Yuansun lost his right of land usage.

1.5 Distinctions and Analyses on All Transactions of Debt Financing

An: similar to pledge, was a loan by using the lands as guaranty.

Ya, taijie, zhiya: same as collateral, was loan by using the land as guaranty and profit from the land as repayment. Their distinctions from *an* were that they repaid the capital and the interests with profits from the land. Accordingly, when it came to the relationship with the land, *ya* was closer than an.

Dian: also pawn broking, whose relationship with the land was rather closer. The right to use lands changed within the agreed limit of time and the debtor of a *dian* contract had to relinquish the rights of the land and profit from the land to the creditor and used land rent as repayment of loan interests. But the precondition was that the debtor had to redeem the land at the end. Even if all profits from the land and land rights were eventually transferred to the creditor, the owner of the land remained the same legally.

Dang: equals to pledge or hock, was to gain loans by using land rights as mediums. It could simply use lands as guaranty (as in contracts of *an*), or use the land to mortgage the loan (similar to *ya*), and could also be pawned with the condition that the debtor relinquished his rights of land and profit of the land to the creditor. It could therefore be inferred that the use of dang was most popular and flexible. *Dang* could also be associated with other forms of transactions, such as *diandang, yadang, didang, zhidang*.

Di: compared with the above three forms of debt financing, it significantly differed with two fundamental disparities: one was "to repay previous debts" by land rights, whereas other forms were all to mortgage new loans; the second was the division of land rights that

---

24. History Department of Nanjin University keeps the original document. Recited from Fang Xing, Jing Junjian, and Wei Jinyu, eds., "A Comprehensive History of Chinese Economy, the Qing Dynasty," Beijing: *Economic Daily*, 2000.

accompanied "di." Of course, nominally, the debt had to be repaid by land rights, but the original landlord maintained his rights to use and control the land, although the rent of the land or rent in the form of harvest had to be paid to the creditor according to the agreement.

Distinctions of the above forms of transactions are rather subtle, yet surprisingly, most of the contracts from all places strictly distinguished between different forms of debt financing,[25] and only in very few areas or cases were these forms confusedly used.

In modern times, there are more and more combined usages of *dian, dang, di, ya, an, jie*, and so on, such as *diandang, didang*, and *diya*. This is also the reason to the difficulty in distinguishing the above forms of debt financing. From the linguistic perspective, it is probably because the customary usage of Chinese vocabularies prefers terms of double syllables; from the legal perspective, it is probably due to the slight difference in transaction regulations of laws in the Qing Dynasty and the modern era, rendering distinctions even more difficult.

Nevertheless, in traditional times, differences among them should be clear and generally consistent in all places of China. Similarly amazing is how these forms of debt financing have continued in their distinct methods and names and remained identical to the names of transaction in other fields. These proved the highly developed state of debt financing that used land rights as mediums. Such a state also further affected the development of financing methods at the time and for later times.

2   Transfer of Land Rights and Its Remaining Effects of Profits: Protections for Owners of the Land Rights

The above relationships of debtors and creditors, based on land and its profits, did not involve the transfer of land ownership. Transactions like *an, dian, dang, ya* did not come with the transfer of property rights, but they were easier to transform into the transacting relationship of land rights. The transfer of property rights occurred when pawning became selling and land became unredeemable.

Transacting forms and regulations of direct transfer of land rights, though not as complicated as the debt financing mentioned above, had their distinctive characteristics to reflect the financing function through the transfer of property rights and all aspects of benefit bargaining that surrounded the property rights.

---

25. The author could not clearly distinguish them at first, and considered such phenomenon as randomness due to regional differences or the lack of strictness with language or laws. After due examinations, the author found it was myself who was obscure, not the Qing people. Other scholars also had this kind of misunderstanding.

2.1 Transfer of Property Rights of Land: *Huomai, Juemai, Ding,* and *Tui* (Including *Bao*)

Huomai 活卖 (Redeemable sale, not-finalized sale) was a form of land transaction, and similar to *dian*, the contract regulated that the original landlord kept the rights to redeem the land and bargain the prices. This was the arrangement to associate with and protect the disadvantaged people who were forced to sell their land rights. Different from *dian*, in redeemable sales, property rights were transferred in the end.

When the final transfer that came after the not-finalized sale occurred, the actual action of trading had to take place. On buyer's part, buying out by increasing the price was called *jiajue* 加绝 (the finalization of the sale) or *duangu* 断骨 (breaking the bone). The seller called it *zhaojia* 找价 (price add-on after the transaction). If the continuant and the repetition of *dian* were the leftovers prior to the final transfer of property rights, *zhaojia* was the compensation after the transfer of property rights. The only distinction was, if any, that there was only one time for the buyer to call for the finalization of the sale, whereas the seller could bargain the prices twice, three times, or more. For example, in the 28th year of Qianlong (1763), the Ni brothers in Yuanhe, Jiangsu Province, "received the relinquished right of the 10 mu 亩 and 5 fen 分 of land from Chu Cangpei with 22 liang 两 of silver." In the 32nd year of Qianlong (1767), Ni used 8 liang 两 and 5 qian 钱 of silver to finalize the sale of land from Chu Cangpei.[26] In Shanghai County, Zhang Zhongshan sold 4 mu 亩 of land to Zhu Feng for 43 liang 两 of silver but kept the sale not-finalized. In the 25th year of Qianlong (1760), Zhang bargained with Zhu for an extra increase of 6 liang 两 of silver for the price add-on and 3 liang 两 of silver as a commission fee for the middleman who drew the contract of finalized sale.[27]

Some people consider that people in the Qing Dynasty regarded *dian* as sale,[28] which is a misunderstanding of the Qing concept. *Dian* and not-finalized sale appeared similar on the surface: *dian* required the temporary relinquishment of secure usage of land rights, and redemptions were allowed. *Dian* was allowed to prolong or contract additional items, while sales of land allowed price bargaining or price compensation. However, the distinction between *dian* and not-finalized sale was clear. In Qing concepts and laws, *dian* was a kind of debt financing through temporal relinquishment of land right in the contracted period, which could be as short as one or two years or as long as more than 10 years. Even when the contracted period was as long as 37 years, the property rights remained under the name of

---

26. XKTB: No. 293.

27. XKTB: No. 208.

28. Contracts of price finding listed in this article are all contracts of sale, yet the author Li Li termed them with *dian*. Li Li, "The Expression and Significance of *Dian* in the Folk Land Contracts during the Qing Dynasty," *Jinling Law Review*, no. 1 (2006).

the original landlord, as clearly verified in the case of the Taiwanese "document of reason" above. In fact, the Qing laws accurately regulated that taxes were not required for *dian*, though in selling actions, tax was mandatory. The owner of the property remained the same in cases of *dian*, and so were his rights and obligations, which included submitting tax to the government.

Secondly, there was a distinct difference between price bargaining and redemptions. The price bargaining after the transfer of land rights was processed. *Dian's* continual or addition was, on the other hand, processed prior to the transfer of property rights. The continual of *dian* was simply to prolong the time of *dian* in order to get more funds; after the continual of *dian*, property rights remain unchanged. *Dian's* "receipt of redemption" or "redemption" took place at the end of the contracted period, while there was no time frame for redemption in not-finalized sales of land. It depended entirely on whether the original seller had the financial capacity to redeem. To illustrate with concepts of modern civil laws, what the buyer got was the real right, and what the creditor of *dian* contract got was the usufructuary right. The creditor's right to control the object was limited to the control of usages and the right to profit from the object. Such distinction, like in modern times, was also clearly defined in the Qing Dynasty.

Juemai 绝卖 (finalized sale) was, on the other hand, the final relinquishment of the rightful possession of the land, and the original landlords could not redeem or bargain prices in such cases. However, cases in which the original owner pleads for the chance of price bargaining were not rare. During the Qianlong period, it was once regulated that price bargaining was allowed even in cases of finalized sales, with the purpose of protecting the rights of the disadvantaged in receiving profits of the land.

Ding 顶, *tui* 退: transactions of tenancy rights, named "tui" from the perspective of the original tenant, and "ding" from the perspective of the new tenant, were equal to "sell" and "purchase," respectively. Subsequent transactions of ding and tui were, on the other hand, called "zhuantui" and "zhuanding"; these transactions all involved trades of money. For example: In Yudu of Jiangxi Province, Xiao Zuoqiu had a land, yet because of the distance, he could not cultivate the land himself. In the 15th year of Qianlong (1750), Xie Xiuyong purchased the tenancy right of the land from Xiao with an agreed price of 135 liang 两 of silver. He paid 115 liang 两 of silver when the contract was being drawn, owing 20 liang 两 of silver. In the 17th year of Qianlong (1752), Xie sold the tenancy right (tui) of the land to Ma Boliang with an agreed price of 110 liang 两 of silver. Xie received 49 liang 两 of silver as the contract was being drawn. It was agreed that the rest of the payment should be made in the second month of the following year. When disputes occurred, the government ruled that "20 liang 两 of silver would be given to Xiao on that very day; the compensation was waived. When Xiao was capable, he should redeem the land with its original price of sale."[29]

The form of *bao* 包 (outsourcing) appeared in certain contracts and transactions, yet no explanations of this type of transaction had been made. *Bao* was neither trading of land rights and sale of tenancy right, nor tenant farming; it also had a fundamental distinction from employment. A case that involves *bao* farming and transfer of *bao*, in Jingjiang, Jiangsu Province, goes as follows: Yu Wenxuan, in the 13th year of Qianlong (1748), contracted the cultivation of Xu Shunzhang's 20 mu 亩 of land and received wage payment of 1 liang 两 8 qian 钱 and 5 fen 分 of silver. According to the local tradition, "it is agreed that the harvest of rice belongs to the landlord, and the harvest of wheat goes to the tenant." Wenxuan later transferred a part of his contracting land (6 mu 亩 and 5 fen 分) to Gui Yuan, and paid him with 6 qian 钱 of silver. Gui also divided half of the land to be cultivated by Yu Wenxuan's lineage nephew Yu Wusheng, paying him with 3 qian 钱 of silver. Both Shunzhang and Wenxuan were not notified of this arrangement.[30]

This piece of contracted land was additionally contracted twice. If any of the elements of this contracting chain was interrupted, disputes would easily arise. Later, Yu Wusheng failed to harvest the contracted half share of rice because he was away. Shunzhang urged Wenxuan, and Wenxuan urged Gui Yuan. Gui was busy doing work he contracted from another household and was not able to harvest the rice. The interrupted part of this contracting chain was not able to be restored and disputes occurred consequently.

We can see here the obvious distinctions between *bao* 包, *dian*, and *gu* 雇 (employment):

Dian—the tenant submitted a deposit, gained tenancy of land, and managed it independently. *Dian* could be transferred, bought or sold (*ding, tui*).

Bao—the landlord paid the capital in advance, and the recipient of the *bao* was administered independently. *Bao* could be transferred, but not bought or sold.

This had a lot in common with modern corporations' use of external contractors for exclusive production of products.

Gu—the landlord paid the salary and administrated the business. The employees could neither transfer the employment nor could they involve in its buying or selling. In other words, the landlord purchased the labor.

Both *dian* and *bao* belonged to entrustment, and hence a relationship of principal-agent was formed. *Gu* and *bao* both belonged to the investment of the landlord, but *bao* did not constitute a relationship between employer and employee.

29. XKTB: No. 310.
30. XKTB: No. 307.

2.2 Additional Profits: *Zhaojia, Jiajue* (Both Mean Price Bargaining), and *Huishu* 回贖 (Redemption)

After the not-finalized sale of the land took place, if the buyer bargained the sale price, the sale would become finalized. From the seller's point of view, it was termed *zhaojia* (*zhaoxi* 找洗 or *zhaotie* 找貼). After the sale of the land was finalized, due to reasons such as the increase of land value or life difficulties of the seller, the seller could request to increase the sale price. This custom was actually supported by the government and was specified in legislation. Price bargaining could be found usually in transactions of not-finalized sales, but it also existed in cases of finalized sales. Not only did it take place in transactions of the rights of land ownership, but also in those of secure usage.

In 1723, Xu Zhenxun from Jieyang bought Li's 6 mu 畝 of land. The land was originally leased and cultivated by Xu Yingjie. The owner of the tenancy remained the same (Xu Zhenxun). Because of flood and landslide, the land was overflown, and Yingjie quit farming, relinquished his tenancy and took back the original deposit of the tenancy 18 liang 兩 and 5 qian 錢 of silver, and went away to make a living. Zhenxun restored the land to a cultivable state with his own fund and labor. In 1741, Yingjie returned with the hope of getting the compensation of 10 liang 兩 of silver for his previous relinquishment of the tenancy.[31] Xu Yingjie was the original tenant of the right of land usage, and he hoped to get compensating money from the usage rights he gave away 19 years ago.

Pan Tansheng sold his land to the Han tenant Xu Lüeguan. Later, however, Pan raised a petition: "Today, due to the lack of food, the famine is severe. I entrust a middleman to pledge the current tenant Xu Lüeguan to provide me with some edible food as compensation for my previous sale of land. I asked for four dou 斗 of grain which should be submitted in two seasons annually, and an extra 5 yuan 元 for supporting my diet."[32]

This case of price bargaining was special, for the original landlord asked the original tenant—the new landlord—to give him not only 5 yuan 元 of cash but also 4 dou 斗 of grain annually. Such a request was almost a restoration of the previous relationship between the landlord and the tenant, although the petitioner spoke with a pleading tone. It is unknown as to what reason was involved in such a case of price bargaining after the sale of the land was finalized, probably having to do with the Han immigrants' disadvantage when dealing

---

31. XKTB: No. 249.

32. Xie Jichang, ed., *The Ancient Books of the Minority Group Kaidagelan* (Taibei: Department of Anthropology, National Taiwan University, 1999), 78.

with the aboriginal people. If they came as outsiders of their residing community, many landlords in China usually could not help but face strong power holders in the community.

Cases of repeating price bargaining were not rare. Often, the new bargaining price would be added to the original contract of sale. In an original contract of Yilan, Taiwan, I found Qiu Zhenkun's two contracts which involved three price bargainings: In 1862, "again bargaining the price": sold in the year before last year, "the sale price was bargained, and 10 yuan 元 plus the 9 yuan 元 owed to Kun previously were paid," which made 19 yuan 元 in total. In 1868, "to bargain the sale price for the third time": "Kun had pleaded for another price bargaining twice as proved by words on the contract. Ever propelled by others, he filed a lawsuit against the buyer of his land. Kun later repented for his action. His income was not sufficient to support his family; therefore, he implored the buyer Zhang Quanguan to give him another 10 yuan 元 of silver as compensation for the sale of his land."[33]

The repeating price bargaining illustrated the power of property rights and the effects brought by the land profit. Such power and effects were actually sympathized with and recognized by society. On the other hand, as reflected in the previous example, the seller was usually local people; if the buyer was an outsider to the local community, he could probably only yield to local people in certain aspects. Yilan's Qiu Zhenkun seemed to manipulate this to force the buyer to allow the third price bargaining. In addition, by demanding the seller to confess and apologize in the contract, the buyer sought to avoid trouble by losing money.

For the original land owner, price bargaining was, for the first thing, compensation for the market price of land; for the other, the last resort of weathering risk and hardship. Usually, it included the most imploring language under reluctant conditions. The pleading language of the two contracts from Yilan was rather common.[34] Such price bargaining was more like begging for the seller and merciful acts of the buyers. In 1834, "the seller finalized the sale of his land with a contract;" however, as she later appealed, "my husband is dead, my son is young, and my family is poor. Because of my poor life and lack of money, I can not pay for the funeral expense. I have no way but to entrust the original middleman to implore the buyer," for 20 yuan 元 of silver as compensation for sale price. "I will never initiate such price bargaining again. This is for emergency's sake."

A contract dated 1847 stated: "how dare I say I am here to bargain the sale price, however, life has been hard, and I cannot afford daily food . . . I plead to the buyer for 20,000 wen 文 of copper coin to save my need for food." Price bargaining also reflected an arrangement of convenient transactions. As Mio Kishimoto explains, "decreasing in advance the sale price

---

33. Qiu Shujin, ed., *Yilan Archives Series* (Yilan xianli wenhua zhongxin, 1994), 003, 004.
34. Ibid., 001, 002.

of land became virtually a custom of later payment for the finalized sale of the land."[35] This actually lowers the standards for land trading, and it can also be referred to as the blooming of installment in land trading.[36] In 1729, Lai Yongsai from Guishan County, Guangdong, had 6 dou 斗 seeds of land, which he sold to Peng Guozhen and his brothers for 39 liang 两 and 5 qian 钱 of silver. In 1732, he bargained the sale price for an extra 1300 wen 文, and drew up an additional contract in which he stated that he would never bargain for the price again. But in 1738, when Lai saw the rise in land value, he intended to further bargain the price.[37]

Therefore, price bargaining at least reflected the following meanings: first, the compensation for the change of market price of land was a kind of protection for the disadvantaged seller; second, it was the last resort of means and protections for the original land owner in time of hardship; third, it was a custom of lowering the sale standard so to make transactions convenient; last, it illustrated the strong recognition with property rights in society. The effects on land profits were always there. Such effects continued the sellers' time of receiving land profit and allowed a certain amount of compensation even after losing property rights of the land for a certain period of time.

The custom of redemption was also meant to protect the seller's legal status and his hope and legitimacy of restoring the sold land. The Qing laws had regulations on redemption accordingly.

2.3   Tendencies of Transaction Methods: Protecting the Interests of Land Right Owners

In the traditional agricultural society, where financial tools were scarce, and the ways to earn a living were exclusively singular, land rights presented the means of making a living and the hope of the land possessor. Consequently, land rights carried a diversified function. On the other hand, the owner and the government both made their utmost efforts to protect the peasants' possession of land rights.

The first level of effort was to fulfill the financing needs of the peasants through land profits or rights of usage. In agricultural times when financial tools were few, arrangements

35. Kishimoto Mio, "The Price-Adding Problem in the Qing Dynasty," *Tōyō shigaku (Oriental History)*, no. 4 (2003).

36. Wen Ming, "The Similarity between the Transaction Arrangement of the Land Ownership in the Qing Dynasty and Modern Financial Tools" (M. A. thesis, Tsinghua University, 2006).

37. XKTB: No. 260.

that relied on or used land rights as a medium, such as *ya, dian, dang, di,* were a kind of effective substitute.

The second level was the redeemable not-finalized sale of land and selling or purchasing of tenancy, leaving the possibility of renegotiation after the transfer of land rights was finalized so that the original landowner might have a chance to restore his ownership.

The third level was the finalized sale of land, symbolizing the ultimate loss of the ownership of land. It was often the last resort for desperate peasants. The fourth level: even after losing land rights, price bargaining could be attempted so that the original owner of land rights was not cut off from the land profits completely, and by bargaining subsidies, he was able to live through the difficult times.

During the Kangxi and Yongzheng periods of the early Qing Dynasty, some governor generals announced limitations in the system of bargaining sale price add-on, prohibiting the seller from bargaining the finalized sale price or redeeming the land.[38] This was mainly because the disputes caused by bargaining sale prices became a huge burden for local officials. However, subsequent legislations inclined to protect the original owner of land rights. In the 8th year of Yongzheng (1730), a government statute states:

> If the contract did not record words of finalized sale of the land, or there was a limited time frame for redemption noted in the contract, the seller of the land shall be allowed to redeem. If the seller was incapable of redemption, a middleman should negotiate a price bargain and then draw a new contract for the finalized sale of the land.[39]

In the 51st year of Qianlong (1786), the Shandong Provincial Administration Commissioner reported:

> And yet the property of these common people was the source of food and clothing for them. For the sudden need for money for emergency's sake, it was empathetic how they ended up losing their previous properties eternally.
>
> Therefore I think in order to promote Your Majesty's benevolence, we should follow the example of Henan Province and allow redemption, regardless of whether the sale of the land is finalized or not, so that the impoverished would not grow old without properties.[40]

---

38. Li Wenzhi, *The Decay of Feudal Land Relationship in the Ming and Qing Dynasties* (Beijing: China social sciences press, 1993), 510–511.

39. Kun Gang and Li Hongzhang, eds., "Collected Statues of the Qing Dynasty Compiled in Emperor Guangxu's Reign," *Guangxu 25 nian (1899) shiyinben,* no. 755.

40. The memorial in July of the 51st year of Emperor Qianlong (1786). The Provincial Commissioner of Shandong once announced the Emperor's oracle that officials and rich merchants were banned in cross-boundary purchase of property.

The policies of unconditional redemption carried out in Henan and Shandong were approved by the Qianlong Emperor. Of course, such policies also caused an increase of disputes, sometimes resulting in market disorder. It was not until the 60th year of Qianlong (1795) that it was clearly regulated that no redemption was allowed for any land sold more than 30 years ago or when the contract did not specify the term of the sale. Similar to this, *Daqing lüli* (The Qing codes) protects the rights of the *dian* debtor, stipulating that even the date for redemption passed, redemption was still allowed:

The time frame for redeeming the houses and gardens passed, and the original owner had prepared money to redeem the land. If the creditor was unwilling to return the land, he shall be flogged 40 times. The debtor should make up the payment of interest for the years after the contracted period ended and the land shall be redeemed with the original price of the loan.[41]

3   Transaction of Share and Partnership of Land Rights

3.1 Transactions of Partnership

Huodian 伙佃 and *gongdian* 共佃 both mean co-tenancy. "Co-tenancy," or partnership of tenancy, was a kind of incorporating management of land cultivation. When tenancy became a type of property rights, co-tenancy was formed. Co-tenancy and co-ownership were similar to modern cooperative businesses. The partners contracted agreements and funded and managed business, enjoyed the profit, and took risks together. They also shared unconditional responsibility for the business debts, and each partner had an obligation to repay the business debt as a whole.

In 1771, Lin Laoli borrowed 20,000 wen 文 from Ye Tianxin, and he submitted 6 shi 石 of the harvest to Ye every year. During the 12th month of the same year, they bought the tenancy of a land from Peng Shirong, each paying 33,100 wen 文. Ye Tianxin borrowed another 52,000 wen 文 in his name, and resulted in a fund of 118,200 wen 文 in total. "The land was given to Lin Laoli to cultivate, and it was agreed that except for paying rent to Peng, the rest of the rice would be harvested together and shared." However, Lin Laoli harvested by himself, and conflict then took place. Ye Tianxin considered that, Lin Laoli's investment, minus his previous debts owed to Ye (33,100–20,000=13,100 wen 文), was not even enough to counterbalance the money he owed. Therefore, Ye controlled the land alone,

---

41. Yao Yuxiang and Hu Yangshan, *A New Compilation of the Qing Codes*, vol. 2 (Taibei: Wenhai press, 1987), 979–980; Xue Yunsheng and Huang Jingjia, *Queries in Reading Legal Cases* (Taibei: Wenhai press, 1964).

and he later contracted the land to others in 1773.[42] In this case, the partnership of tenancy was actually the incorporation of capital (Ye), labor (Lin), and land (Peng).

In Dianbai, Guangdong Province, Lai Shixuan leased 24 shi 石 of land from Xiao Dasan. In 1754, he sold the secure tenancy of 10 shi 石 of the land to Deng Rong. In the next year, the two of them became partners and cultivated together. Deng Rong provided labor and ox, while Lai provided fertilizer and seed. The harvest would be divided equally between them. Because Lai was ill and could not tend to the farming and Deng Rong did not want to cultivate either, "hence the tenancy of the land was sold to Ling Zhuochao for 13,000 wen 文. Deng Rong received 5,000 wen 文 as a labor fee and had his ox back. I should be entitled to receive seeds and 8,000 wen 文 as the price of the cottage."[43] This was a very reasonable arrangement, because whereas the harvest was divided into two, Deng Rong had not yet paid his part of labor at this point. From co-tenancy to the sale of tenancy rights, the process was a transaction through partnership. From the term "total sale of tenancy," it could be illustrated that the property rights were transferred as a whole.

There were many cases of property transactions in types of co-ownership of property among the contracts of Huizhou. According to the accountant book of Sun Juyi's family in Yi County edited by Zhang Youyi, 48 in 89 land transactions were co-ownership. Such co-ownerships involved as few as 3 or 5 households and as many as 28 households. (Table 1) The share of rental income for each house was usually between 20 to 50 jin 斤of harvest. In the accountant book of the Hu lineage in Qimen, among the 34 land properties with recorded names of landlords, the number of landlords was up to 105. Among these, one land belonged to 11 owners. Among contracts of the forestland in the Miao area in Guizhou, organized by Tang Li and Luo Hongyang, co-ownership of the property was also very common.[44]

Table 1 Land Co-ownership as Recorded on the Account Book of Sun Juyi's Lineage in Huizhou

Number of households involved in the co-ownership	2	3	4	5	7	8	28	Unknown
Number of land property	16	13	10	5	1	1	1	1

42. XKTB: No. 289.

43. XKTB: No. 313.

44. Tang Li, Yang Yougeng, et al., "A Compilation of the Contract Documents Concerning Forestry of Miao Nationality in Guizhou Province" (Tokyo: Institute for the Study of Languages and Cultures of Asia and Africa, Tokyo University of Foreign Studies, 2001); Luo Hongyang, "The Study of the Miao Nationality Selling Contracts Concerning the Forests in Jinping, Southwest Guizhou, in the Qing Dynasty," *Ethno-National Studies*, no. 4 (2007).

3.2 Transactions of Share of Land Rights: Case Study of Wood Trading in Guizhou

The Miao mountainous area in Guizhou was an important area for forest plantation and trading of woods. The remaining documents of contracts reflected the transaction of share of property rights. A case in the first year of Daoguang (1821) was amazing:

> Drawers of this contract of trading fir trees, the Yanwan natives Fan Xianzong, Xianxiu, Weiyuan, Shaopei, and Shaozhai, for the lack of silver, were willing to give away a log of fir, located at Ranlou . . . the right of this log would be divided into two shares, Zaishou (the planters) took one while the landlord took the other; the landlord's share could be further divided into four shares: Wenjin took one, Shaobang took one, Wenxiang and Xianfeng shared one, Jinqiao took one; Jinqiao's one share was further divided into two shares: Shaozu took one, and the other one went to the 19 households.
>
> Today the share was sold by the 19 households to Jiang Yinghui. The parties agreed on a sale price of 10 liang 两 1 qian 钱 and 5 fen 分 of silver. After the transaction, the property would be under the administration of the buyer, and the sellers' brothers and irrelevant people should not utter any protest. In fear of the lack of evidence later, this contract of sale was to be kept for examination's sake forever.
>
> Note: The 19 households were listed in the following (including the contracts with the landlord): it is indeed the truth that the 19 households sold their share together (There was also share division within these households. Youcai and Decui each received half of one household's share).[45]

As the contract was charted in Figure 2, the relationships between all parties became clear, and the history of the transaction of shared rights of woods was recovered.

In Figure 2, "landlord" included 4 shares. Three shares belonged to three natural persons or families (Wenjin, Shaobang, Wenxiang, and Xianfeng), and one belonged to a legal entity (Jinqiao). "Landlord," "Jinqiao," and "19 households" were all legal entities, not natural persons, and formed on the basis of shareholding.

Share was the transferrable right of receiving profit and was purchased by the shareholders with a certain amount of funds. From the economic perspective, the share was part of the property right, which was the rightful possession of the property, excluding property rights of legal entities. The transfer of share rights would not change the completeness of property rights; neither would the trading of share rights. In the contract, as part of Jinqiao's share,

---

45. Luo Hongyang, "The Study of the Miao Nationality Selling Contracts Concerning the Forests in Jinping, Southwest Guizhou, in the Qing Dynasty," *Ethno-National Studies*, no. 4 (2007).

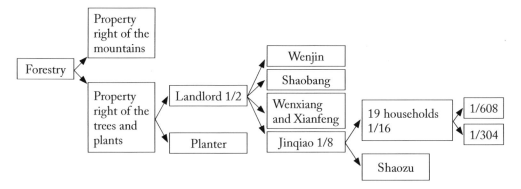

Figure 2 Transaction Contracts of Shared Rights to Woods and Trees in Guizhou

"19 households" could place their share on the market for sale, and the property right as a whole would not be affected. The responsibility and profit of share rights were both limited. Neither of them was the system of partnership. Since being not the property management through partnership, the partial share could be detached from the entire property right. Based on the trading price of 10 liang 两 1 qian 钱 5 fen 分 of silver, every household could receive a sale profit of approximately 0.5 liang 两 of silver, and 0.25 liang 两 for Youcai and Decui. If we use the share of these 19 households to estimate the whole value of the woods, the value would be 162.4 liang 两 of silver.

Some people regard the phenomenon that two landlords share the rightful possession of land as the beginning of the share system;[46] such assumption is wrong. The property rights of land ownership and land secure usage were two independent property rights that were completely different from each other. Although these two rights were attached to the land, they did not share rights of an identical property right. The concept of land with two landlords and that of share system were opposite logics. In the share system, the property right as a whole was composed of many transferable share rights. In cases of two landlords co-owning a land, the land right was divided into two independent property rights, namely, the right of land usage and the right of land ownership. When there appeared a mutually independent right of land usage and that of land ownership, the land was no longer *qingyetian* 清业田 (land whose right of usage and ownership belonged to one holder). In other words, the form of property rights of *qingyetian* no longer existed.

Transaction of woods was also a transaction of futures, which means that the prospective grown woods that were the objects of transactions. It was also called "purchasing in

---

46. Jiang Taixin, "The Initiation of Land Share Ownership System and the Division of Land Rights in the Ming and Qing Dynasties," *Researches in Chinese Economic History*, no. 3 (2002).

advance," a custom that came to existence as early as the Song Dynasty (960–1279). After the transaction took place, the buyer received future profits; if he was "the hand in charge of the planting," usually, he would even be in charge of the management of wood trading. Dated in the 10th year of Daoguang (1830), a contract of "buying out fir woods" stated: "after being sold, the care of the sold wood will be undertaken by the buyer. Later after the trees were grown, cut down, and transported downstream by the river, the land still belonged to the original landlord." In such a case, "rent" referred to profit from the land—forestry. This kind of rent was not submitted annually as the profit of harvest but was submitted every 10 or 18 years. Because of the lengthy period of awaiting profit, the cost of hired labor for caring for the forest was excessively high and hence often resulted in partnership. From thousands of contracts of mountain sale in Huizhou in the Ming Dynasty (1368–1644), Zhang Chunning finds that most forest farms were often co-owned by lineage members. A couple of contracts even showed that the buyers and sellers had relative relations or co-ownership.[47]

3.3 Fair Profit Divisions According to Share Holding Were not Share Trading

In the case of Haishan, Taiwan "Angu junfen" 按股均分 (equal profit division according to share holding) constantly appears in all kinds of contracts; Are they the transactions of share rights? In "Guwen qishu" 古文契书 (Contracts in ancient times), which were collected in Fu Sinian Library, I found two relevant contracts in Haishan, Taiwan, dated in the 59th year of Qianlong (1794). These two contracts described different ways of transactions on an identical land. One was constructed in November, "li heyue zi" 立合约字 (words of contract), followed by December's "li dumai tianwu qizi" 立杜卖田屋契字 (contract about land and house selling).[48] With detailed analysis, distinctions on systems of partnership and of rights of share could be discovered.

> Contract drawer Yuanhui and Zhaolin combined their investments, and bought the tenancy of a farm field from Peng Fuzai of Haishan, along with gardens, houses, ponds, and so on. The landlord has measured the land as 11 jia 甲 3 li 厘 and 3 hao 毫, and Dazu (rent to owner) submitted to the landlord is 80 shi 石 6 sheng 升 4 he 合. Xiaozu (rent to tenancy owner) submitted to tenancy holders and their deposits are divided into 8 shares according

---

47. Zhang Chunning, "The Study of Dissipated Selling Contracts in Huizhou in the Ming Dynasty" (M. A. thesis, Chenggong daxue (Tainan), 2003).

48. "Ancient Records of Contracts" (Taibei: Library of Institute of Modern History, Academia Sinica), FSN01-02-037.

to their investment. The rent: 5 share for Shiye, 1 share for Master Meng Wulang, and 2 for Hao and his brothers. The brothers were willing to sell their tenancy of 2 jia 甲 and 7 fen 分 of land; Yuanhui and Zhaolin have prepared silver of 1 300 yuan 元 and bought the tenancy as partners. Each of them shares half of the tenant's rent and the deposit. Now that they together signed a contract on two separate papers, each one kept a copy for records.

The contract disclosed forms of transactions and relevant parties in transactions of land rights:

(1) Owner of property: got rent to the owner of more than 80 shi 石 grain. In this contract, the property owner was neither mentioned nor he signed. Usually, the landlords were aboriginal people.

(2) Owner of tenancy: got rent to tenancy owner and provided the deposit. The distribution of profit was practiced with shareholding: eight shares in total, and Hao and his brothers had two shares.

(3) Two shares of the transaction: the buyers Yuanhui and Zhaolin bought the property together. Such partnership signified that they, as legal entities, had unlimited responsibilities among the owners of the tenancy. Their purchase price for tenancy was 3 000 yuan 元.

(4) The transaction of two shares was an independent action, so other shareholders did not have any function in the contract. It was not necessary for them to appear in the trading, nor did they need to sign. This explained that the transaction share did not influence the property right as a whole. Fair division, according to 8 shares, was the division of profit and did not involve the management of the property right as a whole. From the perspectives of profit distribution, this was extremely similar to the transaction of rights of share.

Yet the following contract of relevance required further examinations and corrections on the fourth point mentioned above. There was another contract set a month later by both sides of the transaction, providing more information on the parties involved:

Drawers of this contract of sale, lineage nephews Zhenhao and Zhenfeng, have a farm bought together with other uncles and nephews a few years ago. The land was located in the village of Pengfu, Haishan, along with houses, bamboo gardens, ponds, vegetable gardens, and so on. The owner of the property had measured the land to be 11 jia 甲 and 3 fen 分. The land also had convenient watering facilities with bamboo gardens and houses around it. Those facilities were all recorded in the contract. The entire property was separated into 8 shares. Hao and his brother had 2, and they held the tenancy of 2 jia 甲 7 fen 分 8 li 厘 3 hao 毫 of fertile land. Now due to the need for silver cash, Hao and his brother were willing to sell their share. They first inquired about lineage brothers, but they were unable to purchase the shares. They entrusted a middleman to carry the message to two lineage uncles,

Yuanhui and Zhaolin, who were willing to purchase the shares. The three parties agreed on the market price of the shares, 1,300 yuan 元, on that very day. The money and contracts were also exchanged.

The farms and houses were immediately given to Yuanhui and Zhaolin for cultivation and administration, rent submission, and so forth, as their own property in the future.

Four pieces of paper on the sale contract from Jiang Chaofu and Liu Xiushen, from whom the property was acquired, along with the paper of contract on the sale of the house by Liu Xiumei, were kept by Zhaolin for the record. A paper on the sale of land by Liu Xiumei, along with two papers of original cultivation contract, and a contract on land measurement, five papers in total, were kept by Yuanhui for the record.

Owner of property

Witness: lineage uncle Rongguang, son Guanfu

Middleman: lineage uncles Dingjin, Wei Tailiang, lineage uncles Panyang

Upon close examination of the size of land, prices, and times of transaction, and both sides of the transaction, it should be the transformation of the transaction on the same land—from the transaction of rights of share to the transaction of property rights. The first contract and signature only involved the distribution of profits, not the entire property rights and administration. In the second contract, however, land rights were clearly divided and given away. If the property rights attached to the sold shares had been clearly in the divided status, it could not be called as a system of share, for the property rights attached to the sold two shares could not represent the whole property rights held by other shareholders, though the profit of that land was divided among its holders. As for the transaction in the second contract, it was surely not a system of share, but of partnerships. Nevertheless, the partnership between Yuanhui and Zhaolin in the first contract was not affected by the second contract.

To this point, it is clear that: First, the sale contract in December was the division and transfer of tenancy rights, so the terms of the contract were much stricter and more detailed than the one in November. Second, the contract of November was only the equal distribution of profits according to shares, and its property rights of land distinctively belonged to each shareholder. The right of each shareholder did not represent the property as a whole. Although it was possible that the property was managed by all shareholders, such a management was not part of the shares of rights. Third, "sale contract" and "contract" rightly distinguished differences between the transaction of property rights, partnership administration, and profit distribution. Many of the equal distributions according to shares were only limited in the distribution concerning land profits. The property right of each shareholder was substantial and independent and did not represent the whole property right; hence, the equal distribution according to shares should not be considered as trading of shares.

4   Diversified Ways to Promote Transaction of Land Rights and Satisfy the Peasants' Need for Financing

The diversification of land rights transactions ways enabled peasants to manipulate any form of transactions, whether large or small, long or short term. The multi-layered market resulting from the division of property rights enabled the expensive unmovable properties to accommodate many independent owners of property rights and made the trading of land rights convenient. By lowering the standard for entering and exiting land rights markets, large population of petite peasants could participate in transactions. Hence, land rights became generally accepted and commonly used financial tools, satisfying peasants' need for financing and promoting the combination of productive elements. The following cases testify to such results.

- *Case 1 Wang Hanying and his son use land right markets to process all kinds of arrangements*[49]

In Zhuji County, Zhejiang, Wang Hanying had a rented land of 4 mu 亩. In the 9th year of Qianlong (1744), his father sold the tenancy to Jiang Yuqian, though the land was still cultivated by the Wangs, with a yearly rent of 10 shi 石 of grain. Being originally the landowner of qingyetian, the Wang family sold the property right of land for the need of cash, and in the meantime maintained the tenancy rights of cultivation for labor profits. In the 30th year of Qianlong (1765), the Wangs sold the tenancy rights to Su Bangxin, with a price of 6,400 wen 文—giving away tenancy rights in exchange for cash.

In the 34th year (1769), due to the rise of tenancy prices, the Wangs intended to redeem the sold tenancy right and resell it to repay the debt for the market price of the previously sold tenancy right increased to 10,000 wen 文. By redemption, the Wangs received profit resulting from the change in market price of the tenancy right. However, the buyer Zhou Shangwen only had cash of 3000 wen 文, so he mortgaged his tenancy right of other lands to Wang Hanying. In other words, Zhou used his own tenancy right to repay the 7,000 wen 文 which he owed to Wang Hanying. By flexibly using the method of "di," these peasants were able to overcome the drawbacks of transaction barriers and the lack of financial tools so the transaction of land rights could be completed. Although the

---

49. XKTB: No. 330.

Wangs could not get sufficient cash as they hoped, they accomplished the anticipation of future labor profits.

In the 35th year of Qianlong (1770), Zhou Shangwen's another 4 mu 亩 of land was contracted by Wang Hanying for cultivation and paid him 320 wen 文. Again, the form of "bao" appeared, and the Wangs received cash of 320 wen 文 as the payment of the labor contribution in the future. Wang Hanying and his son processed four land transactions in 29 years and flexibly used transaction methods involving rights and land profits like qingyetian, right of land usage, sale of tenancy right, purchase of tenancy, and contracting farming. This was similar to modern investment by using a combination of different investment objects. Of course, it appeared that land right markets provided multiple tools to be chosen from, though in reality, such tools were reluctant compromises forced by life. Yet, it was better to have choices. These tools of debt financing indeed enabled the Wangs to withstand the difficulties a couple of times and to prolong their own reproduction and life.

- *Case 2 Four times trading transactions processed by the family of Dayu Ganjin, to maintain their property rights*

In the documents of Dadu Village, Taiwan, I have discovered the Dayu Ganjin family's three contracts with 4 land transactions conducted within 32 years.[50] The first two were the contracts made by Dayu Ganjin for his father-in-law. The latter ones were about the transactions by him and his son, respectively. Let us look at the two contracts conducted within 10 years regarding the same piece of land by his father-in-law, Pu Lishe:

> In the 7th year of Jiaqing (1812), due to the lack of money, Pu Lishe rented the security tenancy of his land for 160 yuan 元. "A rent of 4 shi 石 and 8 dou 斗 of grain was submitted to the landlord after measuring a set of land and hills." "By the arrangement of a middleman, a Han Chinese, Chen Tingguan, agreed to purchase the eternal tenancy, be in charge of cultivation, and submit the rent without any increase or decrease annually. Pu's descendants should never attempt to redeem the tenancy and make trouble."
>
> In the contract dated in the 17th year of Jiaqing (1812): the aboriginal Pu Lishe of Beidadu village had a land inherited from his grandfather. The tenant Chen "paid rent of 40 shi 石 each year. Now due to the lack of silver, Pu was willing to mortgage 2 shi 石 from the rent for a loan. He had first inquired aboriginal relatives if they were interested, and yet they had no desire to take the deal." He, therefore, negotiated through a middleman with the uncle and nephew of the Chens, the original tenant, "and they were willing to take the

---

50. Liu Zemin, ed., "Ancient Records of Dadushe" (Taibei: Library of Taiwan Historica, 2000), 119, 135, 173.

deal. The three parties agreed on a price of 7 yuan 元 of silver. The money was submitted on the day with a record. Pu's 2 shi 石 of rent will be given to the creditor (Chen) as interest payment, and nobody should dare to stop him. This contract started in the year of Kuaiyou (1813) and would be terminated in the year of Yihai (1815). The debtor retains the right to redeem the original contract. If the silver is not ready when the date is due, the creditor will still have the contract as interest payment."

Dayu Ganjin's father-in-law Pu Lishe, in need of cash, sold the security right of land usage at first and got 160 yuan 元 of silver accordingly. He himself kept the right of land ownership. Ten years later, he needed cash again. This time he adopted the transaction form of mortgaging the rent to the original tenant Chen, using the 2 shi 石 of harvest for the subsequent two years as interest payment. Pu received a loan of 7 yuan 元 of silver. Because the creditor was the original tenant, Pu gave a rent discount of 2 shi 石 for the next 2 years to get the desperately needed cash.

In the 16th year of Daoguang (1837), Dayu Ganjin mortgaged his land for 100 yuan 元 of silver. Three years later, his son prolonged the period of this mortgage. At the end of the original contract, it was additionally noted, "In October of the 19th year of Daoguang (1840), Amei Ganjin implored the original creditor Li Hongguan for an additional mortgage of 2 yuan 元 of silver. The mortgage sum was 102 yuan 元 of silver in total. The land was to be cultivated by Li from the spring of the year of Gengzi (1840) to the winter of Renying (1842)."

The periods of these two mortgages were both two years. The first mortgage resulted in a loan of 100 yuan 元, yet for the second mortgage, it was only 2 yuan 元. Obviously, these mortgages were almost the sale of the land. However, unless there has not any other choice, the landlord always wanted to have the last opportunity of keeping the land right. The continual of the mortgage offered him this opportunity, which was equal to the price bargaining in cases of not-finalized sale.

However, while the price bargaining was the compensation after the loss of property rights, the continual mortgage was the final debt financing before the ultimate loss of property rights. These diverse trading ways provided all kinds of transaction choices.

• *Case 3 The resale, partnership, and mortgage of tenancy rights*

In a contract collected at Fu Sinian Library of Academia Sinica, 4 transactions were conducted in a period of 90 years (1729–1811). In a contract initiated in 1729, additional terms had been added in 1732, 1737, and 1811:

The ones who drew this resale contract are Qiu Ruozhuan and Qiu Ruodou. The landlord was Yang Huangda from Xishi village, Taloushekou. Previously, the Qiu brothers purchased the tenancy of 2 jia 甲 and 8 fen 分 of land, along with one and a half houses, half of the bull fence, some domestic belongings behind the house and half of the vegetable garden. Since the brothers cannot cultivate the land and are now in need of silver cash, they are willing to resell the tenancy to Yang Gui and Yang Shan through a middleman. The three parties agreed on a sale price of 620 liang 兩 of silver. The land was given to the buyers for cultivation, and the resellers should not protest. Any unpaid rent was the responsibility of the resellers. The resellers and the buyers were all willing to conduct this transaction. For fear of no evidence left, a contract is drawn.

The 7th year of Yongzheng (1729), reseller: Qiu Ruozhuan

Contract constructor Yang Shan and his lineage uncle Yang Gui bought a land of 2 jia 甲 and 8 fen 分. Now because they live separately, the land should be divided and the uncle received 1 jia 甲 and 4 fen 分, which was given to the lineage uncle for farming. If he does not intend to farm, the tenancy could be sold to others. No one should intervene or protest. The term is now added to the original contract as a record.

Witnesses: Qiu Yuzhang, Bu Rishang, Gu Guiyuan

Middleman: Chen Fuxing, Yang Youfa

Recorded of the oral statement: Qiu Yixian

In December of the 10th year of Yongzheng (1732), Yunzhang got a divided land of 1 jia 甲 and 4 fen 分 and gave it to Uncle Bao to cultivate, as recorded.

In December of the 2nd year of Qianlong (1737), it is recorded that Yunzhang redeemed the land from Uncle Bao, and gave it to Guisheng to manage and receive rent. Yunzhang shall never attempt to redeem or make trouble. Representative: Huang Xiuying.

In June of the 16th year of Jiaqing (1811), 1 jia 甲 and 2 fen 分 of the land are drawn and the tenancy of this land was mortgaged to Wang Fusheng, as recorded.[51]

In this contract, neither the landlord Yang Huangda, nor the original tenant Qiu Ruozhuan and Qiu Ruodou, is the protagonist, but the several generations of the Yang lineage, are the new tenant.

In 1729, the Qiu brothers transferred (tui, sell) the tenancy to Yang Sheng and Yang Gui, and the two of them bought the 2 jia 甲 8 fen 分 of land with 629 liang 兩 of silver. The contract also indicated that the Qiu brothers reserved the right to redeem the sold tenancy.

---

51. Wang Shiqing, "Official and Private Collections of Ancient Records in Taiwan" (Taibei: Fu Sinian Library of Academia Sinica), FSN01-10-479, FSN05-01-004.

In 1732, the uncle and nephew's business partnership encountered difficulties because they lived separately. Consequently, the land was divided, and Yunzhang gave 1 jia 甲 and 4 fen 分 of the land to Uncle Bao for farming. This arrangement should be a relinquishment of tenancy by Yunzhang to Uncle Bao. In 1737, Yunzhang redeemed the tenancy and transferred it to Guisheng for management. He should not attempt to redeem the tenancy later. This arrangement seemed to be the relinquishment of the right of land usage.

In 1811, *dian*: the tenancy of the main part of the land, 1 jia 甲 and 2 fen 分, were mortgaged to Wang Fusheng.

These confusing transactions of tenancy transfer, redemption, mortgage, partnership administration, and property division were not all clearly reflected in the details of the contracts. However, what was confirmed was that productive elements were in a state of flowing. Through rearrangements of all kinds of transactions, peasants' need for debt financing was satisfied, and the reallocation of resources approached its most effective result.

5   Conclusion

In an agricultural society where the harvest had strong seasonal qualities, the peasants' need for financing in life and production was an inevitable truth. However, due to the lack of financial tools, such a need could only be satisfied by using land rights and their profit for financing. The complicated diversified forms of transactions, either relying on land rights, using the land as a medium tool or directly processing the transfer of land rights, explained the strength of the function of transactions in lands. One was the transaction of debt rights in the land itself. One was the transaction of the property right of land. Occasionally, there were also trading of share and partnership. It can be observed that many modern finance methods already emerged in land rights transactions in the Qing Dynasty, reflecting the continuity of history. In other words, the continued usage of these financial tools and terms presented the strong power of these grassroots means of financing.

Concretely speaking, distinctions between all forms of debt financing are the following: *an*, loans with land as the guaranty; *ya*, mortgaged with land as the guaranty and land rent as the payment for interests; *dian*, to return the dept by temporary relinquish the usage right of land or land profit with an agreed time period; *dang*, all forms of loan by pawning the land; *di*, division of land rights, which was used to repay the debts.

The land right was the life of peasants, and they usually made the utmost attempts to keep land rights. In the Qing Dynasty, forms of transaction that involved the transfer of land rights and the compensation of profits included not-finalized sale, finalized sale, sell and purchase of tenancy rights, price bargaining, etc. Their purpose was to protect the owners of land rights. There also emerged transactions like partnership or share of rights and contracting, which was a kind of entrusted commission of management not including employment and tenancy. By examining original documents, this chapter discusses, clarifies, and investigates these forms of debt financing in order to construct more thorough knowledge about the diverse forms of transactions of land rights. These diversified forms of land rights transactions were substitutes for financing tools when such tools were scarce. By applying these substitutes, peasants were able to withstand hardship and continued the family economy and production. Meanwhile, the transfer of land is stimulated, rendering arrangements of production elements such as labor, land, and capital. The reallocation of resources also promoted the realization of a fluid market of land rights and furthered increased productive efficiency and economic profit. This is one of the ignored basic factors of economic development in the Qing Dynasty.

References

"Ancient Records of Contracts." Taibei: Library of Institute of Modern History, Academia Sinica, FSN01-02-037.

Chen, Qiukun. *The Land Ownership of Taiwan Natives in the Qing Dynasty* (Taibei: Institute of Modern History, Academia Sinica, 1997).

Fang, Xing, Jing Junjian, and Wei Jinyu, eds. "A Comprehensive History of Chinese Economy, the Qing Dynasty." Beijing: *Economic Daily*, 2000.

Jiang, Taixin. "The Initiation of Land Share Ownership System and the Division of Land Rights in the Ming and Qing Dynasties." *Researches in Chinese Economic History*, no. 3 (2002).

Kishimoto, Mio. "The Price-Adding Problem in the Qing Dynasty." *Tōyō shigaku (Oriental History)*, no. 4 (2003).

Kun, Gang, and Li Hongzhang, eds, "Collected Statues of the Qing Dynasty Compiled in Emperor Guangxu's Reign." *Guangxu 25 nian (1899) shiyinben.* no. 755.

Li, Li. "The Expression and Significance of Dian in the Folk Land Contracts during the Qing Dynasty." *Jinling Law Review*, no. 1 (2006).

Li, Wenzhi. *The Decay of Feudal Land Relationship in the Ming and Qing Dynasties.* Beijing: China Social Sciences Press, 1993: 510–511.

Liu, Zemin, ed. "Ancient Records of Dadushe." Taibei: Library of Taiwan Historica, 2000: 119, 135, 173.

Long, Denggao. "The Diversification of Land Transactions in the Qing Dynasty." *Frontiers of History in China* 4, no. 2 (2009).

———. "The Market of Land Rights and the Allocation of Resources." In *Keynotes and Variations: China from 7–20th Century*, edited by Huang Kuanzhong (Taibei: Zhengzhi daxue lishi xi, Zhongyang yanjiuyuan, etc., 2008).

Luo, Hongyang. "The Study of the Miao Nationality Selling Contracts Concerning the Forests in Jinping, Southwest Guizhou, in the Qing Dynasty." *Ethno-National Studies*, no. 4 (2007).

Luo, Hongyang. "The Study of the Miao Nationality Selling Contracts Concerning the Forests in Jinping, Southwest Guizhou, in the Qing Dynasty." *Ethno-National Studies*, no. 4 (2007).

Qiu, Shujin, ed. *Yilan Archives Series.* Yilan xianli wenhua zhongxin, 1994: 003, 004.

Tang, Li, and Yang Yougeng, et al. "A Compilation of the Contract Documents Concerning Forestry of Miao Nationality in Guizhou Province." Tokyo: Institute for the Study of Languages and Cultures of Asia and Africa, Tokyo University of Foreign Studies, 2001.

Wang, Shiqing. "Official and Private Collections of Ancient Records in Taiwan." Taibei: Fu Sinian Library of Academia Sinica, FSN01-10-479, FSN05-01-004.

Wen, Ming. "The Similarity between the Transaction Arrangement of the Land Ownership in the Qing Dynasty and Modern Financial Tools." M. A. thesis, Tsinghua University, 2006.

Xiao, Guojian, and Bu Yongjian. "The Document Volume of the Xiao Family in Huaping of Xiaolan in Xiangshan County of Guangdong Province." *South China Research Resource Station Newsletter*, Jan. 15, 2008, no. 50.

Xie, Jichang, ed. *The Ancient Books of the Minority Group Kaidagelan.* Taibei: Department of Anthropology, National Taiwan University, 1999: 78.

XKTB (Xingke tiben).

Xue, Yunsheng, and Huang Jingjia. *Queries in Reading Legal Cases.* Taibei: Wenhai press, 1964.

Yao, Yuxiang, and Hu Yangshan. *A New Compilation of the Qing Codes*, vol. 2. Taibei: Wenhai press, 1987: 979–980.

Zhang, Chunning. "The Study of Dissipated Selling Contracts in Huizhou in the Ming Dynasty." M. A. thesis, Chenggong daxue (Tainan), 2003.

Zhang, Fumei. "The Evolvement of the Laws on Pawning and Purchasing Land Properties and the Price Add-on Issue of Real Estate in Taiwan." In *The Land Problems in the History of Taiwan*, edited by Chen Qiukun, Xu Xueji. Taibei: Institute of Modern History, Academia Sinica, 1992.

Zhang, Yanxian, and Wu Xiaoyun. "The Collection of Ancient Books in Xinzhu Area." Taibei: Academia Sinica. 1993, vol. 6.

Zhang, Youyi. *The Study of Land Relationships in Huizhou in the Ming and Qing Dynasties.* Beijing: China social sciences press, 1984.

CHAPTER 3

Civil Society in Traditional China: Governance and Ownership System— Evidence from Construction and Management of Public Facilities in the Qing Dynasty*

This chapter focuses on the bridge council and free ferry services as the private organizers of public infrastructure construction in the Qing Dynasty, uncovers the legal entity ownership system and governance model with China's native origin, and reveals the attributes and characteristics of ownership by legal entities in China's traditional era. Bridge councils and free ferry services are non-profit and non-government public-interest institutions, whose members were elected by local communities. These councils were responsible for the fundraising, construction, and long-term maintenance and operation of public facilities and infrastructure at the grassroots level. They adopted open and transparent management procedures and could coordinate cross-jurisdictional affairs and mediate disputes. They possessed independent assets such as lands and fund reserves, and such exclusive legal-entity ownership received protection from the government and under the laws. Such a

* Long Denggao, Yi Wei, and Wang Zhenghua, "Civil Society in Traditional China: Governance and Ownership System—Evidence from Construction and Management of Public Facilities in the Qing Dynasty," *China Economist* 14, no. 5 (2019): 83–97. Wang Zhenghua, History Department, School of Humanities, Tsinghua University.

form of legal-entity ownership provided the institutional foundation for the development of clans, temples, charitable groups, academies of classical learning, and various associations and societies. These self-organizing groups demonstrate remarkable mobilization and organizational capabilities and institutional creativity of civil society in traditional China. They served as a link between the government and communities and played a unique and active role in maintaining social order at the grassroots level.

1 Introduction

There has been a deeply entrenched notion that in traditional China, the government played a dominant role in building public facilities and infrastructure. This idea is so widely accepted that the results of earlier academic studies, though convincing, cannot change this mainstream assumption.[1] Over recent years, many studies,[2] have demonstrated the importance and influence of private players in public infrastructure and public-interest undertakings in traditional China. According to historical records on ferry services and bridges across various places in the Qing Dynasty (1644–1912), the ratio of bridges and ferry ports constructed by the government, private groups, and unknown entities is 155:1,338:1,994 for bridges and 90:288:861 for ferry ports in Hubei,[3] 62:537:158 for ferry ports and 9:122:6 for bridges in the Southeast Guangxi.[4] As can be seen from these figures, most bridges and ferry ports were built by private groups in these two provinces, which were also the cases for other regions.

In the 19th century Anhui, roads and ferry ports were almost entirely built by local clan gentry (族绅) or town gentry (邑绅). According to historical records, there were 323 free ferry (义渡) ports in Sichuan, 228 bridges constructed on charitable lands in Longyan

1. Yang (2005) rejects the view represented by Karl August Wittfogel's (1989) Oriental Despotism. See Yang Liansheng, *Comments on Chinese History* (Beijing: New Star Press. 2005); Karl August Wittfogel, *Oriental Despotism: A Comparative Study of Total Power (Chinese translation edition)* (Beijing: China Social Sciences Press. 1989); Chung (1991) makes an earlier revelation that the local gentry were actually in charge of numerous local affairs in the 19th century China, including the construction of roads, bridges, river dams, and irrigation works. See Chang Chung-Li, *The Chinese Gentry, Studies on Their Role in Nineteenth-Century Chinese Society (Chinese translation edition)* (Shanghai: Shanghai Academy of Social Sciences Press. 1991).

2. Zhang Jun, "Study on the Construction and Management of Bridges and Ferry Ports in Hubei in the Qing Dynasty," *Theory Monthly*, no. 3 (2004); Lin Shiyun, "Study on Bridges and Ferry Ports in Southeast Guangxi in Qing Dynasty" (M. A. diss., Guangxi Normal University, 2013).

3. Zhang Jun, "Study on the Construction and Management of Bridges and Ferry Ports in Hubei in the Qing Dynasty," *Theory Monthly*, no. 3 (2004).

4. Lin Shiyun, "Study on Bridges and Ferry Ports in Southeast Guangxi in Qing Dynasty" (M. A. diss., Guangxi Normal University, 2013).

Prefecture of Fujian, and 47 free ferry ports in Dapu, Guangdong during the Jiaqing Emperor's reign (1760–1820). All the 70 ferry ports in Liling County of Hunan were free.[5]

These facts do not support the conventional wisdom that the government played a dominant role in building public infrastructure in traditional China. As mentioned earlier, new studies are yet to challenge such conventional wisdom despite the evidence. An important reason is that many of such studies are yet to consolidate fragmented findings into a systematic framework of interpretation, while supporting discussions and coherent logical system are still absent at some critical points.

Did private groups in ancient China possess such powerful organizational and mobilization capabilities? In most cases, the construction of bridges and ferry ports by private groups was not a profit-seeking investment behavior. How did private groups raise capital for and organize the construction of such large public-interest infrastructure projects that required long-term maintenance? What was the ownership and operational mode of such public goods? Answers to these questions are yet to be systematically unraveled.

Based on the latest studies on free ferry services and bridges and newly-discovered tablets and inscripts, including the *Inscript of Yongxi Bridge* (永锡桥志) in Hunan,[6] private contracts, and documents and other original materials housed at Tsinghua University, this chapter uncovers the ownership and governance model of public infrastructures built by private groups. Then, this chapter discusses the underlying systems for the existence of various self-organizing groups such as charity programs, temples, clans, and academies of classical learning. In traditional China, the Imperial Court followed a laisser-faire economic policy for private groups at the grassroots level, allowing their self-governance without assigning officials to below-county levels.[7] At the grassroots level, public facilities and

---

5. Almost all roads and ferry ports of the 19th century Anhui were built by local clan gentry or town gentry. According to historical records, there were 323 charity ferry ports in Sichuan, 228 bridges constructed on charity lands in Longyan Prefecture of Fujian, and 47 charity ferry ports in Dapu County of Guangdong during Emperor Jiaqing's reign. All the 70 ferry ports in Liling County of Hunan were all charity ferry ports. See Zhang Yan and Niu Guanjie, *Evolution in Dual Governance Pattern in the 19th Century China* (Beijing: Renmin University Press, 2002); Yang Wenhua, "Integration of Social Functions by Private Free Ferry Services in Sichuan in the Qing Dynasty," *Seeking Truth*, no. 7 (2016); Wang Rigen, "On the Development of Social Undertakings in Fujian in the Ming and Qing Dynasties." *Research in Chinese Economic History*, no. 3 (1993); Li Jian, "Ferry Ports in Hanjiang River Basin in the Qing Dynasty," *National Maritime Research*, no. 11 (2015); Xiao Ben, "Free Ferry Service in Huna, Perspective from Ferry Logs in the Qing Dynasty and the Nationalist Period," (Master's diss., Hunan Normal University, 2014); respectively.

6. (Qing Dynasty) He Huiqi (Styled Zhuchun), *Inscript of Yongxi Bridge*, the Eighth Year of Emperor Guangxu (1882), reprinted by Anhua County CPPCC, Anhua County Jinliang Printing Agency, 2015. The inscript was discovered by Zhao Yafei from Anhui County, and the content is consistent with the tablet inscriptions. We acknowledge Zhao's donation of the inscript and information.

7. Long Denggao, "Liberalist Traditions of China's Private Economy in History," *The Ideological Front*, no. 3 (2012).

affairs were taken care of by private groups in traditional China, which is unlike institutional arrangements for public goods in the traditional society of Western Europe. A comparative perspective helps unravel the government-private boundary for the provision of public goods, which is of general theoretical significance and historical value. Through systematic discussions on the governance structure and ownership heritage of private organizations, this chapter reveals China's traditional grassroots socio-economic landscape and creates a framework of interpretation to clear the myths and offer variable historical inspirations.

2   Governance Mode of Councils with China's Native Origin

A "wind and rain lounge bridge" (风雨廊桥) is a wooden structure that usually consists of a bridge with a tower and a pavilion that offers shelter against wind and rain. As a representative public infrastructure in traditional China, lounge bridges were widely seen in mountainous areas of southern China, including Hunan, Fujian, Zhejiang, Anhui, Jiangxi, Guangdong, Guangxi, Guizhou, and Sichuan provinces. Inside the bridge pavilion were benches for passers-by to rest, and tea was served free of charge. Compared with ordinary wooden bridges, a lounge bridge is more durable and shelters against the elements, but more complex and costlier to build. Free ferries were even more prevalent. Unlike official ferry ports, free ferry ports were non-profit and run by private groups. Such public facilities widely existed in traditional China and were adeptly run by local private organizations.

2.1 Composition of the Council

Before the construction of the Yongxi Bridge, a free ferry in Xishan capsized in flood in the second year of Emperor Guangxu's reign (1876), in which over ten persons drowned. The incident prompted local villagers to gather at the free ferry office to discuss the construction of a porch bridge. Villagers elected a head (首事) and formed a bridge council. They unanimously elected eight persons as directors (董事) or heads who were in charge of the council's affairs.[8] During the bridge construction, the eight persons were appointed "chief organizers" (主修) and supported by 22 assistants. Aside from the heads, there were accountants (司会) responsible for financial affairs. Initially built in the Southern

---

8. Board of directors was normally the authority of for-profit corporations, while council was the authority of non-profit corporations.

Song Dynasty (1127–1279), Pingnan Longjing Bridge bears the names of nine directors, nine deputies, and 17 associates, who represent three hierarchies.[9] The council adopted a collective responsibility system, under which key decisions were deliberated among its members. Any head who violated the rules of council charter would be dismissed and replaced by a new one. Despite the responsibilities, the head and/or director received no compensation, bonus, or income. Typically, a head would donate a large amount of money or materials for bridge construction to set an example for others. There was no strict rule on the number and tenure of the head, but over time, written or unwritten rules took hold. It was not uncommon to see leadership passed down from a father to his son.[10] Family inheritance was considered a reasonable practice.

It should be stressed that bridges and free ferry ports usually span across both sides of a river, which is often the boundary between administrative zones. Therefore, bridge or ferry councils were often cross-jurisdictional institutions involving different townships, counties, prefectures, or urban and rural areas, making it cumbersome to overcome administrative barriers and differences in local customs and coordinate responsibilities, obligations, and interests. Therefore, the composition of councils was often determined by two or more administrative regions in consultation with each other.[11]

2.2 Council Responsibilities and Management Mode

The first responsibility was the construction of bridges or ferry ports.

The Construction of a wind and rain lounge bridge was a massive project. It took six years and hefty human, material, and financial resources for Yongxi Bridge Council to complete the construction of the bridge from the second year of Emperor Guangxu's reign (1876) to the seventh year of his reign (1881). Without the power to issue mandatory orders or offer money and rewards to mobilize resources, the council still managed to call upon various stakeholders to complete the project, thanks to a public consensus on the importance of the bridge and the council's knack for management.

---

9. The bridge was destroyed in a fire during Emperor Qianlong's reign. In the 25th year of Emperor Jiaqing's reign (1820), the bridge was re-constructed with a stele Inscript of Longjing Bridge erected.

10. Yu Xiqiang, "Memories Evoked at the Ancient Ferry Port in Guazhou: Stories of My Grandfather at Shuzi and Zhenjiang Guazhou Free Ferry Council," *Zhenjiang Daily*, August 5, 2011.

11. (Qing) Liu Caibang, Zhang Yanke et al., *Archive of Changsha County during Emperor Tongzhi's Reign*, vol.5 of *Jinliang: Rules on Charity Ferry Crossings*, published in the tenth year of Emperor Tongzhi (1871). All the following information about charity ferry ports in Changsha are from this source without additional notations.

The first step was to create a bridge council in charge of bridge construction. The bridge council assigned tasks to different persons, including those responsible for accounting, fundraising, supervision of artisans, and procurement of materials, among others. Then, the bridge council retained stone workers, carpenters, and tilers for various bridge construction activities. Yongxi Bridge is a stone pier structure with wooden beams and a stone foundation. The bridge body features a mortise-and-tenon structure, which is an ancient Chinese carpenter technique. With handpicked workers and materials, the lounge bridge was built with remarkable craftsmanship and stringent management. The project cost 14,466,818 *wen* (copper coins), and labor costs made up 55.5%.

In many cases, a Master Carpenter (主墨) was appointed as the general contractor of a bridge project under a "bridge contract" signed with a bridge council. In provinces like Zhejiang and Fujian, 21 such bridge contracts were found, all of which were signed by council directors and heads with bridge craftsmen.[12] "Contract for Shuanglong Bridge in Pingnan County in the Third Year of Emperor Tongzhi Era" stipulated bridge specifications, construction compensation, and penalty clauses. Directors were responsible for supervision and inspection. In Pingnan County, there was a reputable craftsman family surnamed Zhang, whose bridge contracts spanned over 100 years from Emperor Jiaqing to Emperor Guangxu and the Republican Period. Heritage helped the succession and improvement of bridge construction as a lucrative profession for craftsmen.

The second responsibility of the councils was to raise money.

Private groups financed the construction of those wind and rain lounge bridges. Upon its establishment, the Yongxi Bridge Council created a donation record book, which was endorsed by the county government with an official seal. Donations came from townships in the vicinity of Yongxi Bridge and the neighboring county Xinhua. In addition to cash, donations also included land plots and materials. Seeking donations was a long and twisted process. The council spared no efforts to solicit donations and sent associates to persuade affluent households to donate. Yongxi Bridge received donations of 14,752,000 *wen* from 2,278 donors. Among them, 101 donors each donated more than 30,000 *wen*, accounting for 4.4% of all donors but as much as 43% of total donations. Thirty donors each donated more than 100,000 *wen* with a total amount of 3,404,000 *wen*, representing 23.07% of total donations. Wealthy households played a pivotal role in fundraising. Most donors donated a small amount of money, but the number of donors was significant, reflecting the council's influence and broad public participation.

---

12. Wu Jilei, "Historical Contracts for Wooden Lounge Bridge Construction," *Lantai World*, no. 13 (2015); Lin Lijin, "History and Culture of Lounge Bridges and Land Bridges in Northeast Fujian," *History of Heilongjiang*, no. 5 (2012).

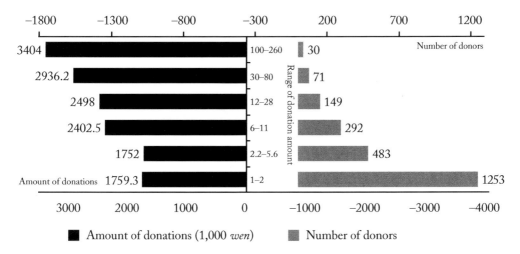

Figure 3 Composition of Donors and Amount of Donations for Yongxi Bridge

Note: Vertical axis denotes the range of donation amount (1,000 *wen*); left horizontal axis denotes the number of donations (1,000 *wen*); right horizontal axis denotes the number of donors.

The third responsibility was to supervise the maintenance and operation of public facilities.

Rules were essential for the long-term maintenance of bridges. Heads were responsible for coordinating the deliberation of relevant affairs, conducting regular inspections, and timely addressing problems. Moreover, heads were also responsible for organizing solemn sacrificial ceremonies for Yongxi Bridge. Daily management of free ferry ports was more complex. Any candidate applying to serve as a ferryman must sign a contract, pay a deposit, and have a guarantor due to security reasons.

The fourth responsibility was outreach and dispute settlement, including liaison with the government and stakeholders and settlement of disputes with the masses. Free ferry services were often at odds with the interests of private and government-run ferry services.[13] Heads must handle various external affairs, such as bridge damages, property disputes, and government-assigned tasks.

---

13. Xiao Ben, "Free Ferry Service in Huna, Perspective from Ferry Logs in the Qing Dynasty and the Nationalist Period" (M. A. diss., Hunan Normal University, 2014).

3 Ownership, Operation, and Management of Public Infrastructures by Legal Entities

Ownership of assets and proceeds from their future appreciation was the premise for bridge councils and free ferry services to operate sustainably. Take Yongxi Bridge, for instance, and its assets primarily included the lounge bridge, public housing, surrounding riverbanks, stone steps, land plots, and the bridge council's fund reserves.

3.1 Property Purchase and Land Management

Land management was the linchpin of bridge asset management. Bridge lands were either donated or purchased. Yongxi Bridge Council purchased the land plots with donated funds and collected revenue from bridge lands for future maintenance and management expenses.

First, the council followed strict procedures for purchasing bridge lands and completed ownership handover with formal contracts.

The "Bridge Lands" volume of the *Inscript of Yongxi Bridge* records the purchase contract and formalities of each land transaction. There were two types of land plots: first, land plots for bridge foundation, riverbanks, and stone steps on the bridge approach, as well as public houses on land; second, land plots for the earning of future revenues. In the land purchase process, Yongxi Bridge Council, as a legal entity, signed a land purchase contract with the seller to complete the ownership handover. The owner of Yongxi Bridge was a legal entity known as "Yongxi Bridge Pier" (永锡桥柱), which paid taxes as a taxpayer to the government. The "Pier" existed as an independent owner, transaction entity, and taxpayer. Moreover, donation agreements also served as valid documents for property handover.

Second, the bridge council was responsible for land management.

Criteria for selecting land plots for purchase included the convenience of land management and soil fertility. A tenant applying to lease a land plot from the council must seek endorsement from a reputable person in a township as his guarantor. The council formulated detailed rules on the management of tenants, forbidding them to sub-lease land to others. Payment of land rents was also subject to detailed rules. Usually, the council needed to swap in-kind land rents for currency. The council could not freely dispose of the land rents until it completed the tax payment. Generally, the government did not exempt taxes for public-interest undertakings such as Yongxi Bridge. When the famous philanthropist Wu Xun (武训) (1838–1896) set up free schools, the local gentry applied to the county government for a tax exemption for the school lands to make up for the shortfall of funds but only received a partial exemption.[14]

Third, the council was also responsible for managing public houses and delivering free public services.

The bridge council purchased lands to construct public houses, which were released to bridge keepers as their residences. Although tenants paid no rents, they were required to place a deposit as an "entrance fee" (进庄钱) and be endorsed by a reputable guarantor, who must assume joint and several liabilities for any misdeed of the tenant. Keepers of Yongxi Bridge were responsible for offering free tea to passers-by, the expenses of which were disbursed from revenues from bridge assets. A tenant could renew his leasehold upon expiry, provided his performance was satisfactory. If he committed an act in breach of rules within the five-year lease term, his guarantor must be held accountable. The public houses also served as a venue for the bridge council to deliberate bridge affairs. Public houses were properties owned by most bridge councils and free ferry services, which often provided docks or shelters for boats to keep them from the elements. They were also equipped with wharves and connecting roads. Bridge councils and free ferry services also had other properties. For instance, Taojiang (桃江) Free ferry Service was equipped with lifeboats at Hengkoutan shoal (横口滩).

3.2 Management of Council Funds

"Council funds" are the special funds of bridge councils for the maintenance and daily expenses of lounge bridges and necessary social activity expenses. Sources of council funds included donations, the balance of annual land rents, and investment income. Yongxi Bridge Council Fund initially had a balance of over 226,000 *wen* after bridge construction. The fund was managed by an accountant, who could seek to increase the value of the fund through market investment. The council fund offered loans to earn interest but attached great importance to risk control. In most cases, a financial institution was appointed to manage the lending business.

Expenses of bridge councils and free ferry services also included donations to the same types of institutions. Yongxi Bridge received donations from other free ferry services and could only donate to the free ferry services and bridge councils.

---

14. Long Denggao and Wang Miao, "Wu Xun Making Finance for the Setting up of Schools," Researches In Chinese Economic History, no. 3 (2018).

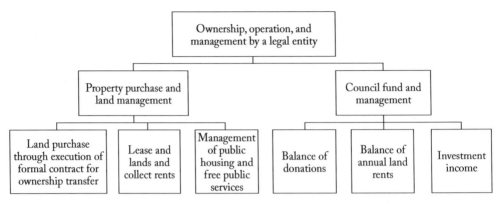

Figure 4 Ownership, Operation, and Management by a Legal Entity

3.3 Ownership by Legal Entities

In traditional China, the system of private land ownership was highly sophisticated.[15] However, no study has been carried out to uncover the system of legal entity ownership in China's history. Ownership by legal entities refers to the ownership by a specific group, institution, entity, organization, or enterprise. Other types of ownership include ownership by natural persons and public ownership, and the latter includes ownership by the state, government, or the public. Property rights were exercised by the public. When anyone was to exercise a right over a public resource, he or she could not exclude others from exercising the same right over such resource. Unlike public ownership, the ownership by legal entities at least features the following attributes:

(1) Ownership by legal entities was independent and exclusive. No individuals, groups, or institutions other than the owner—not even the government—could claim rights over properties owned by a legal entity.[16] The free ferry at Guazhou was opened to serve passers-by and adopted a rule that no merchants or government officials should order its service. It applied to Zhenjiang and Yangzhou government offices for the issuance of edicts that the free ferry service was not open to the government and military.[17]

(2) Ownership by legal entities was holistic and indivisible. After an asset was donated, the original owner ceased to be entitled to any rights of such asset. No director, manager, or even founder could claim or divide any rights over such an asset based on his contribution.

---

15. Long Denggao, *China's Traditional Land Ownership System and Transformation* (Beijing: China Social Sciences Press, 2018).

16. Xiao Ben, "Free Ferry Service in Huna, Perspective from Ferry Logs in the Qing Dynasty and the Nationalist Period" (M. A. diss., Hunan Normal University, 2014).

17. Gong Jun and Wei Zhiwen, "History of Guazhen Free Ferry Council," *Archives and Construction*, no. 5 (2016).

(3) Ownership by legal entities was protected by the government and the law. For instance, the Rules on the Protection of Yongxi Bridge were promulgated through a "county government announcement" with legal validity. The rules stipulate that no one is permitted to contaminate the bridge and public houses, engage in short-term for-profit activities or unapproved charity activities, or peddle or keep beggars. Offenders shall be subject to penalties.

4   Institutional Creativity and Influence of Private Groups

4.1   Public-Interest Legal Entities in Traditional China

Bridge councils and free ferry services, similar to today's public-interest legal entities, were a type of non-profit institution established lawfully to perform social administration functions for public interests. Without elaborating on the legal definition of such organizations,[18] this chapter focuses on the basic characteristics of bridge councils and free ferry services.

Public-interest: Such private groups built public facilities and infrastructures free of charge. Heads and organizers of such private groups did not seek compensation from running such public-interest programs, except for nominal allowances to those overburdened with various tasks.

Non-profit: Free ferry services and bridge councils collected no fees from users and did not seek profit. Incomes from their land plots or funds were used for their operations and could not be distributed. Namely, there were no shareholders and no dividend distribution. Contemporary charity and public-interest institutions also followed this rule.

Non-government: They were not government organizations or public institutions.[19] It should be noted that their internal documents still used the references of "public deliberation" and "common property 公产" following traditional customs. "Common property 公产" in

---

18. Yu Zucheng, "Japan's Public-Interest Legal Entity Recognition Systems and Inspirations," *Journal of Tsinghua University (Philosophy and Social Sciences)*, no. 6 (2017).

19. "Zhenjiang Private Guazhen Charity Ferry Council" and Taichung "Private Dongshi Free Ferry Council" have the legal status as private groups. Established during Emperor Daoguang Era, Taichung Dongshi Free Ferry Council (台中东势义渡会) was registered at Taiwan Governor's Office, and was renamed into "Dongshi Free Ferry Foundation" in 1925 corresponding to the Japanese system. After the free ferry was no longer in service, the Free Ferry Foundation applied to Taichung county government in 1953 for renaming into "Taichung County Private Dongshi Free Ferry Charity Society." In 1986, it was renamed into "Taichung County Private Dongshi Free Ferry Social Welfare Foundation." See "Dongshi Free Ferry Service: the Oldest Charitable Organization in Taiwan's History," *Philanthropy Times*, June 3, 2015, 16.

the traditional sense is similar to "collective ownership" in modern China but differs from the Western concept of "public property."[20]

Open and transparent management: Heads were elected democratically at the grassroots level, and donations, assets, and accounts were open to public supervision. There were detailed records of incomes and expenses of bridge lands and rents paid in grains to prevent rent-seeking.

4.2 Organizational Capabilities and Institutional Creativity of Private Groups

First, private groups created rules and systems akin to modern laws and regulations.

China's *Charity Law* enacted in 2016 is highly consistent with the charters and operational procedures of traditional bridge councils and free ferry services in traditional China. China's *Charity Law* stipulates the following requirements:

> *A charitable organization shall conduct its activities without seeking profits and shall use its incomes and operating balance for the charitable purposes stipulated in its charter; it shall not distribute properties and interests among its sponsors, donors, or group members; it shall stipulate in its charter that its remaining properties shall be transferred to other charitable organizations of the same or similar purposes.*

Similar clauses may also be found in the charters and rules of traditional bridge councils and free ferry services, which reflect the institutional creativity of traditional private groups. Similar rules were adopted not only by small bridge councils and free ferry services but worked well by large institutions.

Large-scale free ferry services even developed hierarchical organizations, such as Wuning Pontoon Bridge Council (武宁浮桥局) and Zhenjiang Free Ferry Council (镇江义渡局). In the sixth year of Emperor Tongzhi Era (1867), seven free ferry organizations, including Geyi Hall (葛翼堂) and Liji Society (利济会), jointly enacted the Regulations on the Public Deliberation of Pontoon Bridge Affairs and put the pontoon bridge council in charge of coordination and centralized management. The original free ferry

---

20. For members of an organization or institution, it was a "common property 公产." Relative to the government or external commons, it belonged to a specific group or institution. "common 公" and "private" property ownership is defined differently under Chinese and Western systems, and such difference will not be discussed in this paper. Although Harvard and Yale universities are "independent private institutions," they are not privately owned by individuals or families. In this regard, the concept of "private" is different from perceptions in the Chinese context.

councils remained independent under centralized management.[21] In other words, the head office and its subsidiaries were all legal entities. They went about their business independently, but the head office had the power to dispatch resources between various subsidiaries. With jurisdiction over both sides of the Yangtze River, Zhenjiang Free Ferry Council was the largest public-interest institution in traditional China. In the 10th year of Emperor Tongzhi Era (1871), a Zhejiang merchant named Wei Changshou (魏昌寿) and his followers established the Guazhen South and North Free Ferry Service with a head office and two branches operating with an annual budget of 6,000 strings of coins—a significant amount.

Fortunately, the free ferry service received abundant donations, and the ferry council had a knack for wealth management.[22] Rents from houses and lands became a steady source of income for financing the expenses of the free ferry service. In 1923, the local gentry in Zhenjiang City raised money to purchase a steel ship with a capacity of over 400 passengers. In 1936, the ferry service handled 500,000 passengers. In about 80 years, more than 10 million passengers had used the free ferry service.[23] Modern Sino-foreign dredging operations in Tianjin and Shanghai in the late Qing Dynasty also adopted the public-interest legal entity system, which could have been influenced by traditional practice.[24]

Second, private groups had powerful mobilization and organizational capabilities.

From simple wooden bridges to luxurious wind-and-rain lounge bridges, from mountainside tea pavilions to the bustling ferry ports at the Yangtze River, all these public facilities provided services to passers-by as public-interest legal entities. Stable properties, incomes, and good systems laid the foundation for the century-long development of free ferry services and bridge councils. The success of such public-interest facilities is a manifestation of the mobilization, organizational, and managerial capabilities of private groups in China's traditional society.

---

21. Hong Ziya and Wu Tao, "Bridge and Ferry Services: Control and Management of Transportation Routes during the Development of Wuning in Ming and Qing Dynasties," *Local Culture Research*, no. 4 (2015).

22. Zhu Ruihong, Pang Xun, and Zhang Zhengrong, "Jingkou Life-Saving Society and Zhenjiang Free Ferry Council," *Southeast Culture*, no.6. (2016); Gong Jun and Wei Zhiwen, "History of Guazhen Free Ferry Council," *Archives and Construction*, no. 5 (2005).

23. Yu Xiqiang, "Memories Evoked at the Ancient Ferry Port in Guazhou: Stories of My Grandfather at Shuzi and Zhenjiang Guazhou Free Ferry Council," *Zhenjiang Daily*, August 5, 2011.

24. Long Denggao, Gong Ning, and Meng Dewang, "The Institutional Innovation of Public Service: Public Interest Organizational Mode of Various Related Parties: Study based on Chinese and Foreign-Language Archives of Haiho Conservancy Commission," *Journal of Tsinghua University (Philosophy and Social Sciences)*, no. 6 (2017).

4.3 Actors in the Construction of Public Infrastructures

Construction of public infrastructures used to be considered a government responsibility. Ostrom[25] discussed the possibility of self-management of public resources outside the realms of government and the market from the game theory perspective. The institutional heritage of traditional China provides the experience of public-interest infrastructure construction. Some public facilities were built by the government using its tax revenues. Others were built with private investments following a market-based approach. Public facilities built by private non-profit groups relied on donations. These three modes of financing for public infrastructures are characterized by different fund sources, organizational forms, and profit distribution. Different actors in infrastructure construction raised funds and organized and distributed dividends in different ways.

In 18th century Britain and 19th century America, which roughly coincided with China's Qing Dynasty, infrastructure construction was carried out in ways very different from China's tradition. Most investments in roads, rivers, and ports in Britain came from local property owners, including gentry, factory owners, merchants, and professionals. With road toll revenues as collateral, turnpike trusts issued bonds and raised funds primarily through the issuance of shares and mortgage loans to construct canals.[26] The 19th century America was a small-government and low-tax state dominated by market-based resource allocation. Private companies extensively participated in constructing toll roads, bridges, and canals. Profit-seeking companies attracted Western capital through the stock market, enabling rapid development of infrastructure construction.[27]

In the 19th century, the central government of China's Qing Dynasty only had a budget of 1.5 million silver taels[28] to construct public facilities. Given the central government's paltry resources, private groups played a dominant role in constructing public facilities at the grassroots level—mostly through public-interest programs. However, public-interest legal entities could only accept donations in the vicinity of the local places. Their non-profit nature prevented them from business expansion with profit accumulation. Unlike Britain, bond financing from future earnings did not appear in the Qing Dynasty. These barriers

---

25. V. Ostrom and E. Ostrom, "Legal and Political Conditions of Water Resource Development," *Land Economics*, no. 1 (1972).

26. Shen Qi, "18th Century Transportation Revolution: A New Direction for the Research of Britain's Transportation History," *Guang Ming Daily*, June 18, 2018.

27. Han Qiming, *Construction in America* (Beijing: China Economic Press, 2004).

28. Jia Misen, "Report on Fiscal Incomes and Expenditures in the Chinese Empire," in *The Cambridge History of China Late Ch'ing, 1800–1911*, eds. John King Fairbank and Liu Guangjing (Beijing: China Social Sciences Press, 1993).

stunted infrastructure construction in the Qing Dynasty. In the Qing Dynasty, private for-profit ferry services were less common than free ferry services.[29] In China's traditional society, per capita tax payment was low, officials seldom intervened in local affairs below the county level, and the government normally encouraged private groups to develop public facilities.[30] In the planned economy era (1949–1978), however, the government was responsible for constructing almost all public facilities with revenues. Government-led infrastructure construction had limited business operation modes. In the mid-and late 20th century, China's infrastructure construction seriously fell short of demand.

5 Legal Entity Ownership and Diversified Private Organizations

5.1 Diversified Private Organizations and Grassroots Order

Private groups and institutions existed in traditional China's grassroots society and were responsible for organizing various affairs in the society. Apart from organizations for bridges, ferries, pavilions, roads, and irrigation works, private groups and institutions also included clans, temples, industrial and commercial associations, and financial, cultural, entertainment, and sports organizations, academies and free schools, charitable organizations, among others. All such organizations were backed by stable assets and continuous fund sources. They formed sophisticated organizational institutions and governance structures to maintain independence and develop sustainably.

Farmers' independence lies in their ownership of land or farms.[31] Similarly, ownership by legal entities is the institutional foundation for private organizations to operate and develop. Private self-organizing groups assumed various tasks at the grassroots level and operated independently. They formed various ties with the government to maintain social order in the traditional society. Ostrom[32] explained that stakeholder groups may self-organize to achieve lasting common interests through self-management rather than

---

29. While free ferry dominated the middle and upper reaches of the Hanjiang River basin, private ferry services prevailed in the lower reach where the market was more prosperous. See Li Jian, "Ferry Ports in Hanjiang River Basin in the Qing Dynasty," *National Maritime Research*, no.11 (2015).

30. Qu Tongzu, *Local Governments in the Qing Dynasty. Translated by Fan Zhongxin and Yan Feng* (Beijing: Law Press China, 2011).

31. Long Denggao, *China's Traditional Land Ownership System and Transformation* (Beijing: China Social Sciences Press, 2018).

32. E. Ostrom, J. Walker, and R. Gardner, "Covenants With and Without a Sword: Self-Governance Is Possible," *American Political Science Review*, no 2 (1992); E. Ostrom, W. F. Lam, and M. Lee, "The Performance of Self-Governing Irrigation Systems in Nepal," *Human Systems Management*, no. 3 (1994).

government diktats and verified the possibility and achievements of such a self-governance model. In traditional China, this self-governance model found varied expressions.

Theoretically, the Qing Government was only responsible for financing major water conservancy projects for the Yellow River and the Grand Canal and the construction and maintenance of critical riverbanks and irrigation works. Smaller water conservancy projects were financed and administered by local private groups.[33] In 19th century China,[34] water conservancy programs were effectively implemented by private groups. In Hunan and Hubei provinces, private groups constructed river courses and levees across three counties, demonstrating effective organization and management.[35] Similar undertakings also existed in northern China. For instance, "floodgate councils" were created to coordinate irrigation and flood control affairs across villages, townships, and counties.

Charitable and social relief institutions, such as life-saving associations, orphanages, the poorhouse, and charitable granaries, maintained closer ties with the government. Similar to disaster relief programs, life-saving associations were often supported and partially funded by the government and received private donations. Life-saving institutions funded free ferry expenses from rents from their land and housing properties.[36] The "Ten Completions Society" (十全会), a charitable organization in Sichuan, played a significant role in water conservancy and social relief programs.[37] Private non-religious groups became principal, enduring, and well-organized actors in promoting charitable causes and were also recognized and encouraged by the Qing Government.[38]

Land owned by the lineage (族田) and ancestral halls (祠堂) were the most common properties owned by legal entities. The proportion of inherited land by lineage was the highest in Guangdong and Fujian, accounting for 33% and 29%, respectively, prior to the land reform in the 1950s. This ratio averaged 15% in the central and southern parts of China

---

33. He Wenkai, "Public Interest and the Financing of Local Water Control in Qing China, 1750–1850," *Social Science History*, no. 3 (2015).

34. Sen (2008) discussed the management of private public facilities such as levees and dredging operations in Jiangsu, Zhejiang, and Zhili provinces. See Sen Tianming, *Water Conservancy and Regional Society in the Qing Dynasty* (Jinan: Shandong Pictorial Publishing House, 2008).

35. Yang Guo'an, *Study on the Grassroots Organizations and Rural Society in Hunan and Hubei Regions in the Ming and Qing Dynasties* (Wuhan: Wuhan University Press, 2004).

36. Lan Yong, "Study on Lifesaving Boats in the Upper Stream of the Yangtze River in the Qing Dynasty," *The Journal of Chinese Social and Economic History*, no. 3 (2005).

37. Xu Yue, "The Ten Completions Society: A Private Charitable Organization in Sichuan Province in the Late Qing Dynasty and the Republican Period," in "Collected Papers of the Seventh International Seminar on the History of Late Qing Dynasty. Research on Modern China's Institutional Systems. Ideologies and Figures," 888–924, ed. editorial dept. of *Journal of Tsinghua University (Philosophy and Social Sciences)*, 2016.

38. Liang Qizi, *Philanthropy and Moral Teachings, Charitable Organizations in Ming and Qing Dynasties* (Beijing Normal University Press, 2013).

(Jiangxi, Hunan, Hubei, Guangxi, Henan).[39] This land inheritance system had a profound influence on the land ownership system and grassroots society. Clans played a pivotal role in the management of various local public affairs. The land transaction contracts in the collections of Tsinghua University contain such names as "Wufu Hall" (五福堂) in Jiaohe County of Zhili Province, "Zhuiyuan Hall" (追远堂) in Xiangheng County of Shanxi Province, "Yongde Hall" (永德堂) in Wenshui County of Shanxi Province, and "Jihou Hall" (积厚堂) of Lingshi County of Shanxi Province, among many others.[40] In Emperor Qianlong Era, "there were over a hundred associations, each earning 10,000 gold taels."[41]

Temple lands also existed extensively. Apart from Buddhism and Taoism, there were private faith groups across various regions. Some of them were small groups consisting of a few individuals. Others were the village and even provincial-wide groups. Some private faiths received government recognition, and their figures of worship became deified. In the Song Dynasty, monks in Fujian chaired the donation and construction of bridges.[42] Temples had a long history of lending and other financial and economic activities.[43]

Academies, free and private schools assumed the responsibility of providing intermediate and elementary education in the heritage era. Private schools were funded by wealthy families who hired teachers to teach their children at the elementary education level in their family ancestral halls. The rise of academies was spearheaded by private groups.[44] Similar to the Yuelu Academy (岳麓书院), they all possessed lands, including a certain amount of funds and lands granted by the government. The legendary beggar Wu Xun (武训) founded free schools, purchased the lands, and raised donations under the banner of *"Yi Xue Zheng"* (义学正), meaning "official free school"—an honorary title granted by Emperor Guangxu. Ownership of assets supported the land operation of the three free schools.[45]

Backed by assets and cash reserves, private associations had played an important role since the Song Dynasty (960–1279). Societies and associations of various sizes and types existed in different social realms and groups. Industrial and commercial associations, chambers of

39. Long Denggao and He Guoqin, "Inspection and Interpretation of Distribution of Land Ownership on the Eve of Land Reform," *Southeast Academic Research*, no. 4 (2018).

40. Contracts in the collections of Tsinghua University, No. T0032-42, T0086, T1025, and T1153.

41. (Qing Dynasty) Qian Yong, *Court Historian in Zhiyan*, vol. 6 of *Collected Talks of Lü Garden* (Beijing: Chung Hwa Book Company, December 1979), 156.

42. Yang Guo'an, *Study on the Grassroots Organizations and Rural Society in Hunan and Hubei Regions in the Ming and Qing Dynasties* (Wuhan: Wuhan University Press, 2004).

43. Zhou Jianbo and Sun Shengmin, "Buddhist Faiths, Commercial Credibility, and Institutional Transformation: Analysis on the Rise and Fall of Temple Finance in the Middle Ages," *Journal of Economic Research*, no. 6 (2018).

44. Deng Hongbo, *History of Academies in China* (Wuhan: Wuhan University Press, 2012).

45. Long Denggao and Wang Miao, "Wu Xun Making Finance for the Setting up of Schools," *Researches In Chinese Economic History*, no. 3 (2018).

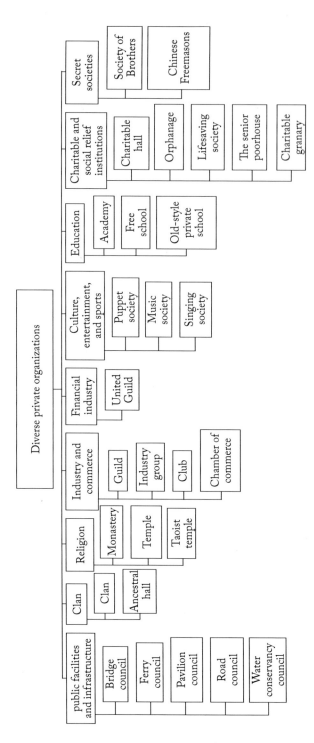

Figure 5 Composition of Private Organizations

trade, and other organizations formulated and maintained industry rules. Financial mutual assistance organizations offered flexible options to meet the financing needs of individuals or social groups. Since the Song Dynasty, sports, cultural, and entertainment organizations funded by private groups had thrived.[46]

Secret societies such as the "Society of Brothers" (哥老会), "Chinese Freemasons" (洪门), and Chee Kung Tong (致公堂) also played a prominent role in modern China. These societies all had steady sources of income to finance their various activities and adopted internal rules.[47] In Huizhou Prefecture, public societies, associations, and clan institutions made profits from lending, pawnshops, and other financial services to finance their operations.[48] Most societies and associations owned land and engaged in land transactions.[49]

5.2 Government and the Legal Entity

Charity land, land owned by the lineage, academy land, temple land, and association land were among the "legal entity properties" owned by charitable organizations, clans, academies, temples, associations, and other organizations, similar to bridge land and ferry land. Their shop properties and funds were owned by legal entities[50] and recognized and protected by the government and the laws. They had special "property certificates" sealed and archived by the government and were independent transaction entities.

Ownership of legal-entity properties and stable incomes became the cornerstone for the independence and sustainability of private self-organizing groups. The Regulations on the Local Self-Governance of Cities, Towns, and Villages enacted in the 34th year of Emperor Guangxu Era (1908) merely recognized and standardized what was already in existence as a traditional practice. Paragraph 8 of Article 5, "Self-Governance of Cities, Towns and Villages," stipulates that cities, towns, and villages should be responsible for their "road works, including road renovation, repair, bridge construction, channel dredging, public houses,

---

46. Long Denggao, "The Entertainment Market in Lin'an during the Southern Song Dynasty," *Historical Research*, no. 5 (2002).

47. Chen Baoliang, *Private Groups and Associations in Chinese Society* (Hangzhou: Zhejiang People's Press, 1996).

48. Lin Shiyun, "Study on Bridges and Ferry Ports in Southeast Guangxi in Qing Dynasty" (M. A. diss., Guangxi Normal University, 2013).

49. Zhang Yi and Ran Tingting, "Search for Publicness. Private Groups and Associations in Shicang Deeds in the Qing Dynasty," *Journal of Shanghai University (Social Science Edition)*, no. 6 (2011).

50. Xu (2013) refers to such ownership as land ownership by social groups, and demonstrates land ownership represented by charitable lands in the Qing Dynasty widely existed among clans, academies, and temples. They were of significant value to social stability in the Qing Dynasty. See Xu Guangxian, "Discussions on Land Ownership by Private Groups: Evidence from the Charity Land System," *Journal of Northwest University (Philosophy and Social Sciences Edition)*, no. 3 (2013).

and road lamps," and "charitable programs, including poverty assistance, care for widows, chastity memorials, nurseries, charitable clothing and food, charitable granaries, recruitment of four workers in factories, life-saving groups, firefighting groups, charitable coffins and tombs, and preservation of ancient relics," as well as "various fundraising activities under this clause" and "other matters that fall into the responsibility of local gentry following local customs." Most of these affairs had been the responsibilities of private groups before the enactment of the regulations. Other undertakings such as education, healthcare, agriculture, industry, commerce, and public programs had a self-governance tradition.

Self-organizing groups took varied forms. As legal entities, they possessed properties under different types of ownership. As public-interest legal entities, bridge councils, ferry councils, and charitable institutions could use their properties and revenues only for public-interest or charitable programs. Such properties and revenues could not be distributed internally among their directors and members.

Self-organizing groups played a pivotal role in maintaining social order at the grassroots level in traditional China, supplementing government functions. Rural gentry served as government proxies to perform certain government functions at the local level.[51] The development of the market system and social groups in the Qing Dynasty strengthened the grassroots society, linking it to the government through market-based actors.[52] Private groups, such as councils, societies, and associations, operated as legal entities recognized and protected by the government. In the grassroots society, they served as self-governing entities or organizers in different realms[53] and cooperated with the government in managing local affairs.

6   Conclusions

In traditional China, private groups constructed most public facilities and infrastructures at the grassroots level. Free ferry and lounge bridges were often built for public interest

---

51. See Wang Rigen, *Social Order in the Ming and Qing Dynasties* (Hunan: Yuelu Books Co., Ltd., 2003); Yang Guo'an, *State Power and Civil Order: A Multi-Perspective Study on the History of Rural Society in Hunan and Hubei in the Ming and Qing Dynasties* (Wuhan: Wuhan University Press. 2012); Wu Xuemei, "Mutually Embedded Multi-hubs: Another Type of Rural Social Order," *Guang Ming Daily*, December 15, 2011.

52. Duara (1996) refers to them as for-profit agents. See Prasenjit Duara, *Culture, Power, and the State Rural North China, 1900–1942* (Nanjing: Jiangsu People's Press, 1996); Hu (2015) argues that in the Qing Dynasty, county governments appointed households to perform certain administrative functions at the grassroots level on their behalf. See Hu Tieqiu, *Research on Official Go-betweens in Ming and Qing Dynasties* (Shanghai: Shanghai Ancient Books Press, 2015).

53. As the government increasingly exercised direct administration over grassroots communities, these private self-organizations morphed from government intermediaries into part of the government bureaucracy in the modern era.

and offered services free of charge. This chapter offers a comprehensive discussion of the organizational model and governance structure of public infrastructure construction by private groups in traditional China. For the first time, this chapter uncovers the types of ownership by legal entities in China's history and systematically reveals the property ownership system of private self-organizing groups. Such revelations provide insights on how grassroots society operated in traditional China.

First, the construction of public infrastructures was underpinned by sophisticated organizations and governance structures. Private groups took the initiative to form a council to raise funds for the construction, maintenance, and operation of bridges and free ferry ports. The councils operated with great transparency, coordinated between various jurisdictions, liaised with the government, and mediated disputes.

Second, bridge councils and free ferry services operated as non-profit and non-governmental institutions. In the era of a shortage economy, their mobilization and organization capabilities reflected the institutional creativity of private groups. Despite the noble public-interest service, these institutions had their intrinsic limitations compared with profit-driven companies.

Third, such social organizations possessed independent properties, particularly land plots and funds that could generate incomes and appreciate in value. Ownership by legal entities was exclusive, indivisible, and protected by the government and laws.

In addition to bridge councils and free ferry services, other legal entities also possessed revenue-generating properties that financed their independent and sustained development; such legal entities include water conservancy councils, industrial and commercial associations, guilds, secret societies, clans, temples, academies, and charitable institutions.

Fourth, Self-organizing groups played their respective roles in various dimensions of economic and social life at the grassroots level. They served as a link of liaison and coordination with the government and the institutional foundation for grassroots governance at low cost in traditional China as a large unified country.

We may draw the following implications from the self-governance of local affairs in traditional China:

(1) The argument that the Chinese people are inept at self-organization is a misunderstanding and bias. The truth is that China's grassroots society has a naivete democratic tradition: In traditional China, people elected council members to manage local affairs and developed sophisticated institutional arrangements.

(2) Social organizations possessed revenue-generating properties, and the government recognized and protected ownership of such properties. Steady sources of income underpinned their independent and sustained development.

(3) They formed effective organizational systems and governance structures with an open and transparent operation. They were responsible for communities and stakeholders and adopted clear-cut rules and charters.

(4) Religion, ethics, and moral principles played a part in forming effective incentives and restraints apart from economic interests, ensuring that council members wholeheartedly devoted themselves to public service.

Such social organizations were characterized by independent legal entity ownership, explicit rules and charters, effective governance structure, transparent operations, social and economic incentives, and public supervision and restraints. We may draw a great deal of wisdom and inspiration from the success of social organizations in building and managing local facilities in traditional China.

References

Chang, Chung-Li. *The Chinese Gentry, Studies on Their Role in Nineteenth-Century Chinese Society (Chinese translation edition)*. Shanghai: Shanghai Academy of Social Sciences Press, 1991.

Duara, Prasenjit. *Culture, Power, and the State Rural North China, 1900–1942*. Nanjing: Jiangsu People's Press, 1996.

Han, Qiming. *Construction in America*. Beijing: China Economic Press, 2004.

He, Wenkai. "Public Interest and the Financing of Local Water Control in Qing China, 1750–1850." *Social Science History*, no. 3 (2015).

Hong, Ziya, and Wu Tao. "Bridge and Ferry Services: Control and Management of Transportation Routes during the Development of Wuning in Ming and Qing Dynasties." *Local Culture Research*, no. 4 (2015).

Hu, Tieqiu. *Research on Official Go-betweens in Ming and Qing Dynasties*. Shanghai: Shanghai Ancient Books Press, 2015.

Jia, Misen. "Report on Fiscal Incomes and Expenditures in the Chinese Empire." In *The Cambridge History of China Late Ch'ing, 1800–1911*. Edited by John King Fairbank and Liu Guangjing. Beijing: China Social Sciences Press, 1993.

Lan, Yong. "Study on Lifesaving Boats in the Upper Stream of the Yangtze River in the Qing Dynasty." *The Journal of Chinese Social and Economic History*, no. 3 (2005).

Li, Jian. "Ferry Ports in Hanjiang River Basin in the Qing Dynasty." *National Maritime Research*, no. 11 (2015).

Liang, Qizi. *Philanthropy and Moral Teachings, Charitable Organizations in Ming and Qing Dynasties*. Beijing Normal University Press, 2013.

Lin, Lijin. "History and Culture of Lounge Bridges and Land Bridges in Northeast Fujian." *History of Heilongjiang*, no. 5 (2015).

Lin, Shiyun. "Study on Bridges and Ferry Ports in Southeast Guangxi in Qing Dynasty." M. A. diss., Guangxi Normal University, 2013.

Liu, Daosheng. "Interests on Private Assets and Economic Mutual Assistance in Huizhou Prefecture in Ming and Qing Dynasties." *History Studies Monthly*, no. 12 (2013).

Long, Denggao, Gong Ning, and Meng Dewang. "The Institutional Innovation of Public Service: Public Interest Organizational Mode of Various Related Parties: Study based on Chinese and Foreign-Language Archives of Haiho Conservancy Commission." *Journal of Tsinghua University (Philosophy and Social Sciences)*, no. 6 (2017).

Long, Denggao, and He Guoqin. "Inspection and Interpretation of Distribution of Land Ownership on the Eve of Land Reform." *Southeast Academic Research*, no. 4 (2018).

Long, Denggao, and Wang Miao. "Wu Xun Making Finance for the Setting up of Schools." *Researches in Chinese Economic History*, no. 3 (2018).

Long, Denggao. "The Entertainment Market in Lin'an during the Southern Song Dynasty." *Historical Research*, no. 5 (2002).

Long, Denggao. "Liberalist Traditions of China's Private Economy in History." *The Ideological Front*, no. 3 (2012).

Long, Denggao. *China's Traditional Land Ownership System and Transformation.* Beijing: China Social Sciences Press, 2018.

Ostrom, E., J. Walker, and R. Gardner. "Covenants With and Without a Sword: Self-Governance Is Possible." *American Political Science Review*, no. 2 (1992).

Ostrom, E., W. F. Lam, and M. Lee. "The Performance of Self-Governing Irrigation Systems in Nepal." *Human Systems Management*, no. 3 (1994).

Ostrom, V., and E. Ostrom. "Legal and Political Conditions of Water Resource Development." *Land Economics*, no.1 (1972).

Qu Tongzu. 2011. *Local Governments in the Qing Dynasty.* Translated by Fan Zhongxin and Yan Feng. Beijing: Law Press China.

Sen Tianming. 2008. *Water Conservancy and Regional Society in the Qing Dynasty.* Jinan: Shandong Pictorial Publishing House.

Shen Qi. 2018. "18th Century Transportation Revolution. a New Direction for the Research of Britain's Transportation History." *Guang Ming Daily*, June 18.

Wang Rigen. 1993. "On the Development of Social Undertakings in Fujian in the Ming and Qing Dynasties." *Research in Chinese Economic History*, No.3.

Wang Rigen. 2003. *Social Order in the Ming and Qing Dynasties.* Hunan: Yuelu Books Co., Ltd.

Wittfogel, Karl August. *Oriental Despotism: A Comparative Study of Total Power (Chinese translation edition).* Beijing: China Social Sciences Press, 1989.

Wu, Jilei. "Historical Contracts for Wooden Lounge Bridge Construction." *Lantai World*, no. 13 (2012).

Wu, Xuemei. "Mutually Embedded Multi-hubs: Another Type of Rural Social Order." *Guang Ming Daily*, December 15, 2011.

Xiao, Ben. "Free Ferry Service in Huna, Perspective from Ferry Logs in the Qing Dynasty and the Nationalist Period." M. A. diss., Hunan Normal University, 2014.

Xu, Guangxian. "Discussions on Land Ownership by Private Groups: Evidence from the Charity Land System." *Journal of Northwest University (Philosophy and Social Sciences Edition)*, no. 3 (2013).

Xu, Yue. "The Ten Completions Society: A Private Charitable Organization in Sichuan Province in the Late Qing Dynasty and the Republican Period." In *Collected Papers of the Seventh International*

Seminar on the History of Late Qing Dynasty. Research on Modern China's Institutional Systems. Ideologies and Figures, 888–924. Edited by editorial dept. of *Journal of Tsinghua University (Philosophy and Social Sciences)*, 2016.

Yang, Guo'an. *Study on the Grassroots Organizations and Rural Society in Hunan and Hubei Regions in the Ming and Qing Dynasties.* Wuhan: Wuhan University Press, 2004.

Yang, Guo'an. *State Power and Civil Order: A Multi-Perspective Study on the History of Rural Society in Hunan and Hubei in the Ming and Qing Dynasties.* Wuhan: Wuhan University Press, 2012.

Yang, Liansheng. *Comments on Chinese History.* Beijing: New Star Press, 2005.

Yang, Wenhua. "Integration of Social Functions by Private Free Ferry Services in Sichuan in the Qing Dynasty." *Seeking Truth*, no. 7 (2016).

Yu, Xiqiang. "Memories Evoked at the Ancient Ferry Port in Guazhou: Stories of My Grandfather at Shuzi and Zhenjiang Guazhou Free Ferry Council." *Zhenjiang Daily*, August 5, 2011.

Yu, Zucheng. "Japan's Public-Interest Legal Entity Recognition Systems and Inspirations." *Journal of Tsinghua University (Philosophy and Social Sciences)*, no. 6 (2017).

Zhang, Jun. "Study on the Construction and Management of Bridges and Ferry Ports in Hubei in the Qing Dynasty." *Theory Monthly*, no. 3 (2004).

Zhang, Shidai. "Wooden Arch Bridge Stele in Northeast Fujian." *Popular Archaeology*, no. 9 (2015).

Zhang, Yan, and Niu Guanjie. *Evolution in Dual Governance Pattern in the 19th Century China.* Beijing: Renmin University Press, 2002.

Zhang, Yi, and Ran Tingting. "Search for Publicness. Private Groups and Associations in Shicang Deeds in the Qing Dynasty." *Journal of Shanghai University (Social Science Edition)*, no. 6 (2011).

Zhou, Jianbo, and Sun Shengmin. "Buddhist Faiths, Commercial Credibility, and Institutional Transformation: Analysis on the Rise and Fall of Temple Finance in the Middle Ages." *Journal of Economic Research*, no. 6 (2018).

Zhu, Ruihong, Pang Xun, and Zhang Zhengrong. "Jingkou Life-Saving Society and Zhenjiang Free Ferry Council." *Southeast Culture*, no. 6 (2005).

PART TWO

Overseas Development

Beyond Culture: Economic Analysis of the Characteristics of Overseas Chinese Business*

1 Introduction

It has been argued that no matter where they live, whether in China, Southeast Asia, or America, ethnic Chinese have always demonstrated a strong desire to become their own bosses or business owners than people from other countries and areas. Such a widespread phenomenon has been conventionally and conveniently attributed to the unique Chinese culture or cultural tradition. Overseas Chinese[1] (sometimes also known as ethnic Chinese, Diaspora Chinese, Chinese overseas, and Chinese abroad) build family-run enterprises with capital raised largely from clans or pan-families and establish complex and intricate social networks that are based on pan-family ties of bloodline and locality. According to this line of reasoning, the utilization of family/ethnic clans and social networks is a reflection of Chinese culture in general and Diaspora culture in particular. Furthermore, these Chinese business entrepreneurs are shrewd in exploring new and existing opportunities to make profits, even though they do not possess strong brand names and advanced technology like most of their western counterparts.

* Long Denggao and Han Qingming, "Beyond Culture: Economic Analysis of the Characteristics of Overseas Chinese Business," in *Chinese Entrepreneurship in a Global Era* (Routledge, 2008). Han Qingming, Head of Library Information System, Housatonic Community College, Bridgeport, Connecticut, USA.

Similarly, when people talk about distinctive and unique characteristics of Chinese business practices, they tend to attribute such phenomena to the *unique* Chinese cultural influences. As Hodder[1] summarized, "it is commonly believed that the most important determinant [in shaping Chinese business practices] is [their] culture." Yao further pointed out that the concept of Confucian capitalism has been crucial in shaping our understanding of the economic success of the Chinese Diaspora.[2]

Although this line of reasoning may seem logical and reasonable, some scholars argue that it is *not* sufficient to draw the above conclusions about the origins of overseas Chinese business management practices. While some critics argue that the influence of Chinese culture has probably been exaggerated[3] or misinterpreted and misunderstood,[4] others even argue that many of the so-called unique characteristics may have never existed. Although these criticisms cast some doubts or even reject outright the view of cultural determination, their narrow and delimited inquiries *within* the cultural context are certainly restrictive and unfortunate. For example, most previous studies ignore similarities between Chinese and non-Chinese business practices. Hodder's study of Overseas Chinese business is probably an exception where he investigates cultural factors as well as economic, sociological, and psychological forces. In particular, he found that the success of overseas Chinese is not an outcome of Chineseness but rather of "multidimensional values, institutions, and actions which have been consciously manipulated by the Chinese and 'turned' towards the extension and institutionalization of trade."[5]

This chapter aims to extend this particular line of reasoning further to explain Chinese business characteristics from an economic perspective. We contend that the characteristics of Chinese business entrepreneurship, if not all but surely a large majority, should be viewed as one form or another of *personalized transactions* that can be accounted for under the institutional economics theory. According to Douglas North,[6] one of the most important economic transformations in a modern economy is the gradual replacement of personalized transactions with non-personalized transactions. Personalized transactions are often based on personal ties such as bloodline (consanguinity), common locality, common unit and

1. R. Hodder, *Merchant Princes of the East: Cultural Delusions, Economic Success and the Overseas Chinese in Southeast Asia* (Chichester, UK: John Wiley & Sons, 1996), 187.

2. Yao S. C., *Confucian Capitalism: Discourse, Practice and the Myth of Chinese Enterprise* (London: Routledge Curzon, 2002).

3. Li P. S., "Chinese Canadians in Business," *Asian and Pacific Migration Journal* 10 (2001): 99–121.

4. Chan K. B., *The Chinese Diaspora (World Diasporas)* (London: Routledge, 1998).

5. R. Hodder, *Merchant Princes of the East: Cultural Delusions, Economic Success and the Overseas Chinese in Southeast Asia* (Chichester, UK: John Wiley & Sons, 1996), xi.

6. D. North, "Big-Bang Transformations of Economic Systems: An Introductory Note," *Journal of Institutional and Theoretical Economics* 156 (2000): 3–8.

organization, friendship, and classmates. Non-personalized transactions, on the other hand, refer to socialized or institutionalized transactions that are frequently based on modern institutions and laws.

Under a non-personal environment, the principal-agent plays an important role in the conduct of business. For example, a public company with shares of its stock distributed among many owners in which the owners do not take an active part in the daily management of the company. Instead, they entrust professional managers to be their agents to direct and administer company resources. The principal-agent also represents legal ties or basic elements of financial instruments, such as security markets, mutual funds, and pension funds. With the help of principal-agent, companies and financial markets are able to rapidly raise capital and human resources anywhere, without geographic and other restrictions. Inevitably, this arrangement costs businesses huge sums of money for the professional services of agent organizations such as accounting and legal firms. In return, these companies are able to raise capital effectively and efficiently in the market and receive higher liquidity and better performance of their stocks.

On the other hand, personalized transactions, which are based on special personal ties without relying on the principal-agents services, incur much less cost. At the same time, personalized transactions have little effect beyond their personal ties and cannot reach outside of their personal networks to raise capital, human resources, and management skills. Under such a non-institutional environment, the ability to raise large capital and human resources for expansion is extremely limited and prohibitively expensive. Under this institutional economic framework, this chapter will try to re-interpret the origins of overseas Chinese enterprise management style and to investigate how factors such as the local and global economic surroundings influence how overseas Chinese entrepreneurs operate their businesses.

2   Chinese Culture and Chinese Business

As noted earlier, many scholars attribute the reason why many Chinese prefer to be their own boss and operate their own business is an outcome that is directly or indirectly influenced by Chinese culture. Can "Chinese culture" really lead many Chinese at home or abroad to become business owners? Our response below will begin with China's experience and then proceed with the discussion of other countries.

Indeed, there are many small business owners on China's mainland today. Since China's economy is still at an early stage of economic development with rapid growth and the transition from a planned/command economy to a market-oriented economy, there are numerous and increasing opportunities for people to set up small enterprises. In fact, we would argue that it probably is easier for small business owners than large corporations to make good profits in such a burgeoning environment. However, as the scale of economy and efficiency weigh more and more in conducting business in China, the opportunities and space for people to become business owners would become less in the future, similar to the experiences of the United States and other developed countries in the past century.

What about Chinese businesses in Hong Kong, Taiwan region, and Southeast Asia? They all experienced rapid economic growth during the past several decades, and the role of small-scale enterprises seemed to dominate in major industries and fields. To keep things in proper perspective, it is important to consider significant differences between these economies and China's mainland economy. Most of these areas have small economies with limited internal consumer demand and market. They are driven largely by export industries, with brands and technologies supplied by western multinational corporations. Many Chinese enterprises are manufacturing factories in the putting-out system of multinational corporations and occupy middling positions in the production/supply chain of the global economy. Although the export industry also constitutes an important component of the Chinese economy, its level of dependency is much lower, and the potential for expansion in the internal market is significantly greater.

While it is probably true that the prevalence of entrepreneurship and small business among ethnic Chinese in Southeast Asia and China is higher than in Europe and America, it probably reflects more on the economic conditions under which overseas Chinese operate their business rather than inherent cultural influences. Undoubtedly, the Western economy is at a higher and more mature stage of market development and technology advancement, where many industries have undergone repeated industrial integrations and consolidations. As a result, a few corporate giants dominate their respective businesses with unsurpassed economies of scale and high value-added products and/or services. They create significant barriers and thresholds for new enterprises to cross and enter. For instance, giant supermarket chain stores such as Wal-Mart, Shaws, and Walgreens in the United States all seized sizable shares in their respective sectors at the national level, making it extremely difficult for small, independent supermarkets and grocery stores to compete directly. In the manufacturing industry, big corporations generate large profits by relying on strong brand names and core technology with high value-added products and services. Some industries, especially those with low value-added products and services, have increasingly moved their operation to developing countries and areas such as China and Southeast Asia. As a result, with the exception of a few "new" markets, it has become harder and harder for Americans with small means to start their own businesses as well.

Paradoxically, these "sunset" industries with low value-added products and services and low thresholds to enter relinquish ample business opportunities for Chinese entrepreneurs. They provide a large, private market space and opportunities for the Chinese to operate their own businesses throughout Southeast Asia and China. Under this new arrangement, Americans and Europeans still have their chances to carry out their dreams of investment. Even though they may not be able to become their own boss directly, they can share corporate profits via the securities market, which is already fully developed in the West. Furthermore, because wages are higher in Western countries than in Southeast Asia and China, the start-up cost is higher in the former, whereas the incentives to operate their own businesses are higher in the latter.

While there are more business owners of Chinese descent than local natives and other ethnic groups in a number of Southeast Asian countries, this can be partly attributable to their historical intermediary or go-between status in their adopted countries instead. Chinese merchants had served as the middle agents between then-developed China and underdeveloped Southeast Asia long before the arrival of Westerners who built the colonial commercial systems. Later, Chinese merchants became intermediaries between local natives and western colonists during their long, mutual interactions, where most natives continued to make their living in agriculture.[7]

We contend that the lack of development of an economy of scale in these countries contributes to the encouragement of ethnic Chinese to be their own boss either in China or abroad. Closely related is our further argument that there has been a lack of principal agents that are rested on modern institutions in these places. There has been relatively weak development of the principal-agent in Southeast Asia and China's mainland in the past two decades. Given existing constraints, full development of such a system to help the expansion of enterprises in China and Southeast Asia may not be forthcoming in the foreseeable future. Without the institution-based principal-agents, business entrepreneurs have limited ways to raise capital beyond their immediately controlled enterprises or to entrust professional managers to help manage their businesses. This is in sharp contrast with the myriad financial instruments that American and European companies can utilize to raise capital from security markets, mutual and pension funds, trusts and foundations, and venture capitals.

Our discussion so far focuses on why Chinese businesses tend to differ from Western businesses in operation in China and Southeast Asia. What about their operations in North America and Western Europe? In those places, many Chinese immigrants have

---

7. Long Denggao, "Keynote Address: Overseas Chinese Businessman in the History of Globalization," Conference on Globalization and Overseas Chinese, Kobe, Japan. 2002.

become small grocery store and restaurant owners, while a few, mostly coming from Hong Kong, Taiwan, and Southeast Asia, venture outside and engage in other business endeavors. The explanations here only differ slightly from the discussion earlier. First, like most other immigrants, many Chinese felt less competitive in the American labor market as they might not be proficient at the English language, their skills and professional/academic credentials from their home country may not be recognized, and/or they are not familiar with the local culture. The existence of an invisible "glass ceiling" in the corporate hierarchy and obstacles to upward mobility for ethnic minorities certainly encourage many to seek alternative routes to economic success.[8] Their route to ownership usually began as workers in Chinatowns or Chinese restaurants somewhere in the country. Eventually, after accumulating sufficient capital, they then strike it out on their own, opening their own grocery stores and restaurants. Most owner-operators, together with their employees, work 12 hours a day and seven days a week, a working condition that average Americans either do not like or even cannot endure. The situation, however, is not unique but very common in other ethnic businesses as well.

Many are able to establish niche markets within the Chinese American communities and fill the void for the demands of certain services. The intercity bus services between Chinatowns in New York, Boston, Philadelphia, and Washington, DC, offer a perfect example. These inter-Chinatown buses are operated mainly by Chinese immigrants. The fares are extremely cheap, costing only a fraction of the regular costs of its national competitor, Greyhound. These intercity bus services cannot only take advantage of the frequent movement of the Chinese population among the nation's major metropolitan areas, but their successful operations have also attracted non-Chinese travelers.

Recently, because of a booming Chinese economy and its related trade opportunities, a number of first and second generation immigrant entrepreneurs used their connections in China and knowledge of Asian markets to conduct business between Asia and America, thus transcending the traditional local boundary limitations. They fly frequently across the Pacific to conduct business and maintain multiple residences and personal identities.

Chinese business entrepreneurs in America used to pursue opportunities in marginal areas outside of the mainstream economy; they include laundry shops, restaurants, and grocery stores. Only in the past two decades did they turn their attention to a few forefronts and nascent technology areas. The most notable example, of course, is the activities of

---

8. Wong B. P., "Culture and Work: The Chinese Professionals in Silicon Valley," Paper presented at the 5th Conference of the International Society for the Study of Chinese Overseas, University of Copenhagen, May 10–14, 2004.; A. L. Saxenian, Motoyama, Y., and Quan X. H., "Local and Global Networks of Immigrant Professionals in Silicon Valley, San Francisco," CA: Public Policy Institute of California, 2002.

some high-caliber business entrepreneurs, including new immigrants, and their venture companies in Silicon Valley (see Table 2). Several important characteristics of this "new" form of investment strategy are that the technology is relatively new, rapidly evolving, knowledge-based, and no one can hold absolute monopoly power. The development of a "new economy" driven largely by information technology and biotechnology in the 1990s provided many new opportunities for Chinese entrepreneurs and others to forge ahead into some important areas of American mainstream industries. According to one calculation, the number of Chinese who have occupations in the high-technology industries located in Silicon Valley more than doubled in less than ten years, from 19,218 in 1990 to 41,684 in 1998. Many of them were employed or directly engaged in new start-up activities. Start-up firms are important sources of new ideas and innovations. They have advantages over larger established firms in emerging areas where the new technology has yet to be worked out, and the demand patterns are unclear and risky. By assuming higher risks, these entrepreneurs, if successful, could receive handsome rewards as well. It is, therefore, of little surprise that ethnic minorities who possess technical skills and training find the "new economy" particularly attractive. In fact, the proportional share of start-up firms by ethnic Chinese in Silicon Valley skyrocketed from 9% in 1980–84 to about 20% in 1995–98. The increased share of ethnic Indians was equally impressive, from 3% to 9% over the same period.[9]

3   Family Firms and Social Networks

It is widely held that family operation and extensive business networks among Overseas Chinese are the most visible and defining characteristics of Chinese business enterprises. Their origins are believed to derive from Chinese culture, particularly Confucianism. In reality, family-run firms are common everywhere in the world and are not restricted to Chinese *per se*.[10] For instance, family-run businesses account for more than 85% of all firms in OECD countries and approximately 30 to 40% of the Fortune 500 companies in the United States.[11]

---

9. A. L. Saxenian, *Silicon Valley's New Immigrant Entrepreneurs* (San Francisco: Public Policy Institute of California, 1999).

10. K. E. Gersick, J. A. Davis, M. M. Hampton, and I. Lansberg, "Generation to Generation: Life Cycles of the Family Business" (Cambridge, M. A. diss., Harvard Business School Press, 1997).

11. OECD, *OECD Observer*, no. 234, October 2002.

Table 2 Sales and Employment of Silicon Valley High-technology Chinese Firms in 1998

	Number of firms	*Total sales ($m)*	*Total employment*
Number of Chinese share	2,001	13,237	41,684
of Silicon Valley high-tech	17.3%	13.4%	10%
firms			

Source: Dun & Bradstreet database, 1998.

Note: Statistics are for firms started by Chinese between 1980 and 1998.

Similarly, the prevalence of business connections and networks is not just widespread among overseas Chinese. Still, it is also equally common among other Diaspora groups such as Jews and Overseas Indians. For instance, through intricate and diverse merchant networks, capital, goods, and human flows that originated from the Indian sub-continent are linked to other countries of the world. Indian merchants who need help at every step can find contacts and services these networks provide.[12] Many of these overseas Chinese business networks were formed in their respective host countries rather than originated from China. In fact, we would further argue that the development of an elaborate and sophisticated business network was only a recent one, a reflection of changing business and economic environment rather than some stable cultural dispositions.

In sum, both business networks and family operations are not just confined to overseas Chinese groups but are characteristics of Diasporas. They represent necessary and conscious choices made by different ethnic groups in order to survive in the host economy. These relatively weak ethnic groups face significant barriers and obstacles in language, culture, and skills for economic advancement and therefore are more prone to seek resources internally. The only difference is that in Southeast Asia, the capital market is either undeveloped or underdeveloped and protection from legal institutions is rather limited. The opportunity structure and capital markets are more structured and mature in North America and Europe.

It should be noted that some family enterprises, particularly those in developed countries, gradually transformed into companies with share capital and managed by professional managers. These companies frequently acquired capital and management talents outside the family and clan networks. However, similar transformation proves to be rather difficult in Southeast Asia, where the capital markets are still underdeveloped. Of course, this is not to deny the possibility of a few successful companies. Rather, it points out that the

---

12. C. Markovits, "Indian Merchant Networks Outside India in the Nineteenth and Twentieth Centuries: A Preliminary Survey," *Modern Asian Studies* 33 (1999): 883–991.

general condition and environment slow down the transformation process. Without an encouraging environment and suitable conditions, Chinese family enterprises may hesitate to break up family ownership, install professional management, and tap outside capital, even though the owners themselves fully understand that they would contribute to the long-term vitality and viability of their businesses.

On the other hand, it will be difficult for enterprises to expand if they continue to restrict their options exclusively among their own family or clan. Non-personifications come into existence in modern society through the establishment of law and order. Unfortunately, the relative paucity of capital and management resources in Southeast Asia imposes severe constraints on using such non-personal, institutional means. Their available options are rather limited locally. This helps to explain why a number of Southeast Asian Chinese entrepreneurs gradually shifted some, if not a significant proportion, of their capital to places like Singapore and Hong Kong, where the supply of qualified managerial personnel is abundant and capital markets are well established and institutionalized. In sum, the lack of an adequate legal system in many Southeastern Asian countries contributes to the importance of personal factors in resource distribution and allocation. Trust in business transactions is still based on personal relationships[13] or personal trust,[14] as opposed to institutional trust, which is based on contractual and legal agreements. Of course, the fact that the Chinese population has been singled out as a discriminating target by the indigenous majority group further limits their willingness to enlarge their trust beyond one's ethnicity, but note the latest development in Malaysia as documented in the chapter by Gomez.[15] Finally, it should be noted that the exclusion of Chinese immigrants also occurred in North America, Australia, and elsewhere.[16] The extent of such barriers is much narrower and more subtle and has been reduced over time, though they never completely disappear.

Why do Chinese choose to operate the family-run business and utilize personal social networks in business? Our tentative answers above outline two interrelated factors: the lack of institutions and the early stages of economic development. The former implies a general lack of principal-agency, whereas the latter implies the lack of an economy of scale.

---

13. T. Menkhoff, "Trade Routes, Trust and Tactics: Chinese Trader in Singapore," in *The Moral Economy of Trade: Ethnicity and Developing Markets*, eds. H. D. Evers and H. Schrader (London: Routledge, 1994).

14. Long Denggao, "A Sociological Analysis of Overseas Chinese Businessman of Operation and Management," *Sociological Research* 2 (1998): 75–82; Long Denggao, *On Overseas Chinese Business (in Chinese)* (Hong Kong Social Sciences Press, 2003).

15. E. T. Gomez, *Chinese Business in Malaysia: Accumulation, Ascendance, Accommodation* (London: Curzon Press, 1999).

16. D. Chirot and R. Reid, *Essential Outsiders: Chinese and Jews in the Modern Transformation of Southeast Asia and Central Europe* (Seattle, WA: University of Washington Press, 1997).

They both explain why existing Chinese family enterprises tend to be of small scale. More importantly, they also point to the limits of further growth of Chinese enterprises unless these constraints can be transformed and lifted.

4 Characteristics of Chinese Entrepreneurs

Overseas Chinese business entrepreneurs are often characterized as bold and good at taking risks in a rapidly changing market. They venture into emerging markets with significant risks of failure, though the promises of rewards are also high. Can one really relate such opportunistic moves to the encouragement of Chinese culture? Or, are Chinese entrepreneurs culturally more endowed to spot new business opportunities? To answer these questions, perhaps we may also want to step back and consider differences. Still, related questions: if culture is really the key, is there anything *inherent* in Chinese culture that would make Chinese entrepreneurs lag behind their western counterparts in technology and brand name creation? Or, why do they concentrate on specific service sectors and continually strive to diversify their portfolios into related or unrelated businesses?

Indeed, many Overseas Chinese entrepreneurs are able to reap handsome profits from taking substantial risks by entering and opening up new and emerging markets. They represent markets that many multinational corporations (MNCs) initially tried to avoid either because of perceived high risk or unstable markets with weak demands. For instance, Overseas Chinese were the first to enter untested new markets in Southeast Asia, China's east coastal areas in the 1980s and then recently moved inland to Central and Western China, Vietnam, and Burma.[17] Western multinational corporations soon followed suit, but only after these markets showed enduring signs of success and stability, long after the pioneering work of Overseas Chinese entrepreneurs. Similar situations can be observed in the once red-hot but highly risky information technology (IT) industry in Silicon Valley during the 1990s. During that period, many Chinese and Indian venture capitalists took great risks investing in nascent technologies. Many of these small ventured firms were later merged with or bought out by big corporations, though a substantial number failed miserably as well.

With the exception of the Silicon Valley case, however, most Chinese entrepreneurs rely upon low cost factors to make their firms competitive and reap profits through sales volume rather than upon brand names and advanced technology. While it proves to be advantageous in numerous situations, the strategy of reliance or over-reliance upon low

---

17. Long Denggao, *On Overseas Chinese Business (in Chinese)* (Hong Kong Social Sciences Press, 2003).

cost factors also poses major weaknesses for Chinese businesses and hinders their future expansions. Although similar observation has been echoed in a number of theoretical and empirical works, it would be inappropriate and wrong to conclude that the development is inherent in or attributable to Chinese culture.

In order to be successful, many Chinese entrepreneurs, just like their counterparts elsewhere, understand the importance of technologies in economic activities. Yet, the core technology has been tightly controlled or dominated by western MNCs. These large corporations provide and control necessary production facilities and installation services. They entrust only their production lines to certain companies, particularly those owned by Chinese entrepreneurs in East and Southeast Asia. Under such an arrangement, Chinese manufacturing companies can only compete in the cost of production: an abundant supply of cheap labor and lands in underdeveloped areas, particularly within China, and to scourge all over the world for cheap raw materials. From the perspective of MNCs, it is far more convenient and economical to outsource their production functions to the Chinese than to manufacture products themselves, particularly when they would be subjected to much more stringent labor regulations than their Chinese counterparts.

This division of labor works well for both sides, especially the latter, since the Chinese would not be able to manufacture these products without the technology transfer from their western counterparts. Under existing arrangements, they would have to rely on the brand names of western corporations to sell their products globally and locally. According to this interpretation, nothing inherent within Chinese culture would imply that Chinese are weak in technology. Rather, the outcome is due to their adopted economic role and conscious economic choices in a highly competitive global market. The phenomenon reflects the strategic division of labor and specialization in the global economy, given that Chinese enterprises are still in a weak position and dependent on western technologies. At the current stage, it is rational that Chinese entrepreneurs pay little attention to technological innovations but devote their energy to reducing production costs to generate profits instead. As one Chinese Malaysian businessman once told the author in Kuala Lumpur before the 1997 Asian economic crisis, "We need not promote technological skill with a huge cost. We simply buy innovations from the West."

The perception that it is cheaper for Chinese entrepreneurs to buy innovations from the West rather than to conduct their own research and development is quite widespread. At the same time, an increasing number of Chinese entrepreneurs realize that they should change their dependent status or secondary role in the world economy and start investing more resources in research and development (R&D) to enhance their technological competitiveness in the future. Nonetheless, R&D requires an enormous amount of investment in capital, human talents, and other supporting resources. One manager of a big television manufacturer in Jiangmen, Guangdong, once told the author in 2000 that individual corporations currently cannot directly challenge their Western counterparts in R&D spending because the latter continues to hold core technologies and has deep pockets. Instead, he suggested that the Chinese government should invest in and coordinate manufacturers' efforts in R&D of core technology. This, of course, is not a farfetched idea and follows the past successful experiences of some Japanese and Korean companies.

This point can be further illustrated by another example: the Tsann Kuen International Group. Tsann Kuen is a multinational enterprise based in Taiwan. It was once the model of original equipment manufacturer (OEM) in the manufacturing of electrical appliances. Over time, the company grew and became an original design manufacturer (ODM) in Xiamen, China. It then started to develop and market its brand name products under the EUPA label. According to the Shanghai Economic Information Research Center, EUPA was the second best-known household electrical appliance brand in Shanghai in 1996. In particular, EUPA's flat iron was the number one brand in China, with approximately 33% market share. Wu Tsann Kuen, the company owner, once hoped to capitalize on the brand popularity and grow his company by using an aggressive brand promotion strategy. However, after a careful study of the failed experience of some less-successful Korean companies to gain world market share by drastically reducing prices and giving up profits, Mr. Wu became hesitated to pursue such an expansion strategy. He recognized that it is extremely difficult to develop and promote *new* brand names to the world markets that have been traditionally dominated by the West, particularly the hegemonic American culture, in shaping consumer taste and demand worldwide. In the end, Tsann Kuen International decided to focus on the company's core competitiveness in the global chain of industrial production by utilizing cheap labor in China, low-cost raw materials from the world, and the higher selling price in Western markets. It was also practical to cooperate with Western corporations in design development that has already been outsourced to various designing companies in Europe and America. This division of labor enables Tsann Kuen International to catch up with the technological and market trends in western countries while maintaining lower production costs and stable profit margins.

Overseas Chinese businesses are also good at service industries such as real estate, hotels, and financial services. These sectors share the following common characteristics: their prosperity is not determined by technology, the barrier of entrance is relatively low, and brand name recognition is not critical. In addition, the performance of these industries is more likely to be decided by non-technical market factors such as price fluctuations and information availability.

Another successful "trait" of overseas Chinese businessmen is that they are flexible in making constant adjustments according to the changing demand in the market. Their flexibility is reflected in the constant shift from one industry to another or an expansion from a single industry into multiple industries. This explains why many Chinese businesses eventually become diversified business groups. In Malaysia, for example, nine out of ten of the top tycoons are ethnic Chinese; they all own holding companies with interests in real estate and infrastructure properties, hotels, recreation, and banking.[18] Similarly, Ling[19] found that twenty-seven business groups in Malaysia have a common characteristic of investment holding companies with diversified investment portfolios. Among the top twenty-four Chinese business groups in the Philippines, twenty are engaged in property, construction, and hotels either as their core businesses or as diversified subsidiaries, sixteen in banking and financial services, and fourteen in trading or retailing.[20] Only a handful of them is in the manufacturing sector. Whereas western business groups are more specialized in one or two industries and frequently dominate in their respective industry on the basis of their superior technology and strong brand names, Chinese business entrepreneurs opt for diversification with well-mixed portfolios.

Again, the decision to adopt such an economical mode should be interpreted as a *conscious* economic choice in the rapidly changing global market, which may, on the surface at least, make the Chinese practices seem unique and different from their western counterparts. Such practices also reflect long historical adaptations from the precarious and sometimes volatile positions that the Chinese population occupied in these economies. Although they once led Asian trade until the 1800s, their role was subjugated as secondary to the Western colonial capitalists as middlemen and intermediaries, particularly in Southeast Asia. Today, they become business partners in the global economy and may soon poise to become competitors with western multinationals in the near future.[21] However, under existing global trade arrangements, the factors of production flow into different areas according to their capital priority. Through their domination of superior technology and business innovations, Western multinational corporations control and lead changes in the marketplace and will probably continue to do so in the near future. While these MNCs can extract huge profits through brand recognition and advanced technology, overseas Chinese entrepreneurs have to rely on unconventional but pragmatic ways to make their business competitive and successful.

Because of its relative success, it is understandable why "Chinese culture" leaves some marks on overseas Chinese business practices. But this shrewdness is the result of

18. Malaysian Business. *Malaysian Business*, February, 2001.

19. Ling W. G., "Public-Listed Chinese Company in Malaysia (in Chinese)," in *Encyclopedia of Overseas Chinese (Economy Volume)*, ed. Zhou N. J. (Beijing: Press of Overseas Chinese, 2000).

20. Jiang X. D., "Philippians Chinese Economy (in Chinese)," in *Encyclopedia of Overseas Chinese (Economy Volume)*, ed. Zhou N. J. (Beijing: Press of Overseas Chinese, 2000), 120.

21. Long Denggao, "Keynote Address: Overseas Chinese Businessman in the History of Globalization," Conference on Globalization and Overseas Chinese, Kobe, Japan, 2002.

conscious manipulations of existing constraints. The so-called unique Chinese business style is definitely not determined by Chinese culture in general or Diaspora culture in specific. As the chapter illustrates, overseas Chinese are highly flexible and adaptable. In their business pursuits, they do what they see fit in the marketplace and in the local social, legal, economic, and cultural systems of their adopted countries. They would fully utilize their own advantages, cultural or non-cultural, and minimize their disadvantages to try to fit into the local and global business environment.

5   Conclusion

This chapter argues that many of the so-called characteristics of Overseas Chinese entrepreneurs are rooted in economic considerations rather than cultural predispositions. Firstly, most Chinese entrepreneurs, particularly those in Southeast Asia, conduct their business in an environment with a relatively lower economic development stage. They are largely small-scale, with no brand name recognition and core technology. Secondly, without a well-established principal-agent system that is based on modern legal and economic institutions and sophisticated financial instruments, Chinese entrepreneurs are trapped. They cannot enlarge their scale, area, and field of economic activities. In a sense, they are forced, either voluntarily or involuntarily, to rely on personal or family ties, which in turn impose limits on the size of their firms and operations. Thirdly, Chinese-owned businesses currently occupy the lower rung (low-value links) of the commodity production/supply chains in the global economy. They are largely dependent on multinational corporations in core technology. Finally, it is not because of cultural factors that American Chinese are engaged in marginal areas of the U.S. economy or their recent participation in the frontiers of the "New Economy." In fact, they have long been interested in and will continue to search and develop niche markets within the local Chinatown economy. At the same time, they would also explore high-risk and high-reward opportunities in the new economy, just like any other entrepreneurs.

References

Chan, K. B. *The Chinese Diaspora (World Diasporas)*. London: Routledge, 1998.
Chirot, D., and R. Reid. *Essential Outsiders: Chinese and Jews in the Modern Transformation of Southeast Asia and Central Europe*. Seattle, WA: University of Washington Press, 1997.

Gersick, K. E., J. A. Davis, M. M. Hampton, and I. Lansberg. *Generation to Generation: Life Cycles of the Family Business*, Cambridge. MA: Harvard Business School Press, 1997.

Gomez, E. T. *Chinese Business in Malaysia: Accumulation, Ascendance, Accommodation*. London: Curzon Press, 1999.

Hamilton, G. G. *Cosmopolitan Capitalists: Hong Kong and the Chinese Diaspora at the End of the 20th Century*. Seattle, WA: University of Washington Press, 1999.

Hodder, R. *Merchant Princes of the East: Cultural Delusions, Economic Success and the Overseas Chinese in Southeast Asia*. Chichester, UK: John Wiley & Sons, 1996.

Jiang, X. D. "Philippians Chinese Economy (in Chinese)." In *Encyclopedia of Overseas Chinese (Economy Volume)*. Edited by Zhou N. J. Beijing: Press of Overseas Chinese, 2000.

Li, P. S. "Chinese Canadians in Business." *Asian and Pacific Migration Journal* 10 (2001): 99–121.

Ling, W. G. "Public-Listed Chinese Company in Malaysia (in Chinese)." In *Encyclopedia of Overseas Chinese (Economy Volume)*. Edited by Zhou N. J. Beijing: Press of Overseas Chinese, 2000.

Long, Denggao. "A Sociological Analysis of Overseas Chinese Businessman of Operation and Management." *Sociological Research* 2 (1998): 75–82.

―――. "Keynote Address: Overseas Chinese Businessman in the History of Globalization." Conference on Globalization and Overseas Chinese, Kobe, Japan. 2002.

―――. *On Overseas Chinese Business (in Chinese)*. Hong Kong Social Sciences Press, 2003.

Malaysian Business. *Malaysian Business*, February, 2001.

Markovits, C. "Indian Merchant Networks Outside India in the Nineteenth and Twentieth Centuries: A Preliminary Survey." *Modern Asian Studies* 33 (1999): 883–991.

Menkhoff, T. "Trade Routes, Trust and Tactics: Chinese Trader in Singapore." In *The Moral Economy of Trade: Ethnicity and Developing Markets*. Edited by H. D. Evers and H. Schrader. London: Routledge. 1994.

North, D. "Big-bang Transformations of Economic Systems: An Introductory Note." *Journal of Institutional and Theoretical Economics* 156 (2000): 3–8.

OECD. *OECD Observer*, no. 234, October 2002.

Saxenian, A. L., Motoyama Y., and Quan X. H. *Local and Global Networks of Immigrant Professionals in Silicon Valley*. San Francisco, CA: Public Policy Institute of California, 2002.

Saxenian, A. L. *Silicon Valley's New Immigrant Entrepreneurs*. San Francisco: Public Policy Institute of California, 1999.

Wong, B. P. "Culture and Work: The Chinese Professionals in Silicon Valley." Paper presented at the 5th Conference of the International Society for the Study of Chinese Overseas, University of Copenhagen, May 10–14, 2004.

Yao, S. C. *Confucian Capitalism: Discourse, Practice and the Myth of Chinese Enterprise*. London: Routledge Curzon, 2002.

CHAPTER 5

Re-generating the Cultural Identity and Social Network Abroad*

It is ignored by a lot of researchers in China that the cultural identity and social network were re-generated overseas, not originally from the homeland, such as the networks of Chinese from Indo-China, and the multi-name clan associations outside China. The Chinese Christian networks in North America even surmounted some obstacles to religious belief from the homeland. Similar experiences and backgrounds shaped the identity of Chinese immigrant groups. The common origin, common pursuits, interests, and beliefs all play a role in one way or another in forming mutual trust and setting certain restraints within networks. The mechanism of credibility is strengthened in repeat games inside the business networks or the economic activities of the ethnic Chinese. Actually, almost every ethnic Diaspora forms social networks of one kind or another based on their new-found identities overseas.

More and more recent immigrants from China are becoming involved in the Chinese Christian networks in North America. Such Christian networks do not pre-exist in their home country. On the contrary, their cultural identities and social networks were regenerated in Canada and USA by overcoming cultural barriers derived from their homeland. Other social networks, such as Indo-Chinese refugees' networks and numerous clan or kinship associations, also originated overseas, whereas they are almost non-existent

* Long Denggao and Han Qingming, "Re-generating the Cultural Identity and Social Network Abroad," 2014. Han Qingming: Head of Library Information System, Housatonic Community College, Bridgeport, Connecticut, USA.

in China. It is certainly not an adequate explanation that Chinese immigrants rebuild their social networks overseas because they share a common language and cultural background. As this chapter will demonstrate, It is also their common experiences overseas, interests, and welfare that give rise to the regeneration of Chinese immigrants' identity and networks in faraway lands.

1 Chinese Christian Networks: Obstacles to Religious Belief from Homeland Are Surmounted

It is very difficult for non-religious Chinese immigrants from China to become religious believers and subsequently pay their reverence for a supernatural power or power, i.e., "god," as their creator and the governor of the universe. It is equally difficult for the Chinese to make transitions from the Confucian influence in their traditional culture to the Christian beliefs that were of Western origin.[1]

However, more and more Chinese in North America are converted into Christians, with an increasing number of Chinese Christian churches in the U.S. and Canada. Christianity has become the most practiced religion among Chinese immigrants in America. However, there is very little scholarly research on Chinese Christians and their churches in North America.[2] This chapter will reveal the underlying reasons why Chinese immigrants reconstruct their identity and social/religious networks abroad.

Chinese Christians congregate in a big metropolis with a sizable Chinese population. Most of the Chinese immigrants' churches are located in the five biggest metropolises with the largest Chinese population in North America. They are Toronto, Vancouver, New York, Los Angeles, and San Francisco. There are also a great number of Chinese churches in other metropolitan areas. While the Chinese population in Canada is 1.5 million, their churches number 276, 78% of which are located in only two provinces, Ontario and British Columbia. 25% and 16% of the churches are located in the cities of Toronto and Vancouver, respectively.

---

1. Many Chinese people associate Christianity with "western religion." Actually, Christianity originated from the Middle East, not from Europe. It is not a religion of Western origin, although many Chinese people think that is the case. According to some Chinese Christians, Christianity reached China and took root there much earlier than in North America (at least as early as 9th century). However, Christians were persecuted. The news about Jesus Christ and the Bible could only be spread quietly and privately throughout most of China's history. In Europe and later in North America, the news about Jesus Christ and the Bible could be spread more freely. That is the reason why Christianity has had stronger influence in the west, according to Ms Eva, a Chinese Christians in MA.

2. Yang Fenggang, "Chinese Christians in America, Conversion, Assimilation, and Adhesive Identities," August, 1999.

Table 3 Top 5 Metropolis with Chinese Churches in North America

New York	Toronto and Scarborough	San Francisco	Vancouver	Los Angeles and Monterey Park
76	59	55	46	34

Source: www.immanuel.net.

Table 4 Number of Chinese Churches in Canada

Province	Churches	%	Churches of metropolis
British Columbia	81	29.3	Vancouver, 44
			Victoria, 3
Alberta	37	13.4	Calgary, 18
			Edmonton, 11
Saskatchewan	5	1.8	Regina, 3
			Saskatoon, 2
Manitoba	8	3	Winnipeg, 7
Ontario	134	48.6	Toronto, 69
			Ottawa, 6
			Windsor, 3
Quebec	11	4	Montreal, 5
			Halifax, 2
Total	276	100	

Table 5 Number of Chinese Churches in Greater Boston

Language	Mandarin/Chinese	Cantonese	English	Taiwanese
Churches	15	12	8	3
Originate	China's Mainland and Taiwan region	Hong Kong, Canton, Southeast Asia	Native	Taiwan

There are 27 Chinese churches in Massachusetts. Among them, 22 are in the Greater Boston Area, where over 100,000 Chinese live. Fifteen churches conduct their services in Mandarin (Putonghua), 12 in Cantonese, 8 in English, and 3 in Taiwanese. 13 churches conduct their services in two or three different local dialects or languages mentioned above. The first Chinese immigrant church in Boston was established in the 1940s, followed by the second and the third in the 1960s. The core members of the early churches are from Taiwan and Hong Kong. Most of them are pre-1980s immigrants to the Boston area. Since the early 1990s, the majority of church members are recent professional immigrants from China.

Chinese churches have expanded over the years with the influx of newly-arrived immigrants from China. Boston Chinese Evangelical Church (BCEC) is the second oldest Chinese church in Massachusetts. It was established in Chinatown in 1961 with only 18 members. Now BCEC has become the largest congregation, with almost 1000 worshippers every Sunday. The Mandarin and Cantonese services occur in the main church building, while the English service is at an elementary school right behind it. The BCEC launched a new campus in 2003 in Newton, about 15 minutes by car from downtown Boston. It is BCEC's vision to branch out its services and locations closer to the expanding Chinese population in the Boston suburbs as their Christian outreach. The Newton campus is located in a newly purchased 100-plus-year-old former church. Most fellowship groups are combined with the Chinatown campus in order to share resources.

Chinese Bible Church in Greater Boston (CBCGB), established in the 1970s, is the third oldest Chinese church in Massachusetts. CBCGB now has almost 1000 parishioners. Many of its members are Chinese or Chinese-American professionals with newly-mint U.S. university degrees. In October 2006, CBCGB launched its offshoot site Metro-west Church in the western part of the Greater Boston area.

Chinese immigrants are attracted to the Christian church for a number of reasons. First, the church provides a welcoming and warm social environment with interesting and appealing activities to the immigrants who, far away from their homeland, often feel socially isolated. Most of them need help to acclimatize themselves to the new country. Churches such as CBCGB provide many community programs designed to promote socialization and friendship among Chinese immigrants. They also offer training and services for young children and junior and senior high school students through a variety of educational, inspirational, recreational, and community service programs. For many college students, young couples, and professionals, the Chinese church represents a warm, friendly and caring community. Church activities and congregations such as women's fellowship are popular among young couples, families, and especially women who share the same life stages in an environment of different languages, cultures, and customs.

Second, Chinese immigrant churches are also engaged in its missionary works as part of the global Christian forces. The development of the Chinese churches in North America testifies to the glory of Christ in Chinese Christians' minds. In their early existence, the Chinese churches had difficulties financially supporting themselves and were hardly involved in missionary outreach works. By the late 1960s, with the increase of Chinese professionals in North America, the financial status of Chinese churches has been greatly improved. The Chinese churches operating with "three-self principles"[3] began to appear in North America.[4]

Gospel Carrier International Inc. (GCI) is an evangelical organization established solely to spread the Christian faith. Its source of financial support comes from churches and individuals in North America and other parts of the world. GCI, established in 1993, is based in Maryland to promote preaching and provide discipleship assistance to distant areas. The organization's support includes a ministry staff, aircraft operations and maintenance, office building and equipments, evangelical outreach, general funding, and other most-needed areas. GCI acquired its first gospel aircraft in 1995 and another eight-seat gospel plane in1998. They used aircraft as a convenient means of transportation for missionary workers to reach out to distant towns, cities, and counties.[5] GCI, in its mission statement, indicates that "We use literature, multi-media, and modern transportation to overcome geographical barriers for advancing the Lord's Great Commission to bring the gospel of the salvation of Jesus Christ and his love to the needy in distant towns, cities, and counties."[6] GCI also helps the Chinese Christians maintain close ties with one another in various North American cities, especially among those in Toronto, Chicago, and Cleveland in the Greater Lakes area, as well as New England.

It is no surprise that North America has become the center of the Chinese Christian world. From there, the Chinese Christian churches dispatch mission groups to other parts of the world to spread the Christian faith. They do that by providing the areas they had reached with educational, medical, and other services.

CBCGB, a Chinese Bible Church in Greater Boston, supports over 30 missionaries working in five continents, including North America, South America, Europe, Africa, and Asia. U.S. ministries include working with college students and immigrants. Overseas ministries include Bible translation, church-building friendship outreach, evangelism, and pastoral training. In BCEC or Boston Chinese Evangelical Church, 19 evangelists are working in different parts of the world, including 7 in China, 3 in Hong Kong, 1 in the Philippines, 1 in Mongolia, plus several others in America, Africa, the Middle East, and Central Asia.

---

3. Self-government, self-support, and self-propagation.

4. Wang Zhongxin, "The Chinese Church Experience in North America," accessed February 15, 2006, www.cwts .edu.

5. Light aircraft operates efficiently for remote outreach rather than long-distance driving. Flight schedule is flexible and the aircraft may be utilized on an as-needed basis. There is no check-in and boarding procedure for aircraft passengers. This saves time and it is a convenient tool for advancing a series of outreach meetings in various distant areas.

6. http://www.gcigospel.org/eng_mission.html.

The Short-Term Missions subcommittee at CBCGB is created primarily to promote partnership with and provide training to those potential short-term missionaries who intend to participate in either domestic or international cross-cultural ministries or both. The churches strive to provide resources, mentoring, and prayer support for those individuals participating in short-term missions. From BCEC, 22 Short-Term Missions were sent all over the world between 1987 to 2005. Individual members/missionaries were supported in 25 countries and some U.S. cities.

Some Chinese evangelists from North America traveled to Europe, where they found more and more Chinese and new immigrants as their Gospel preaching audience.[7] Most of the evangelists are returning to the Chinese Christian's homeland, where the early Chinese Christian ministers once left and emigrated overseas.

These newly-established Chinese social networks are built upon Christianity. They do not pre-exist in the Chinese Christians' homeland. Once settled in their adopted countries, some Chinese immigrants gradually broke away from their homeland's ideological/ psychological/cultural baggage, and reconstructed their cultural identities and social networks through Christianity in Canada and the United States.

There are two major obstacles for the immigrants from China in their transformation to Christianity. The first is atheism and the theory of evolution, which are deeply rooted in the socialist ideology and education among the Chinese people since 1949. It is a thorough transformation when the Chinese immigrants turn to a Christian God for their life's guidance.

The second is the unique traditional Chinese culture which, inclusive of Buddhism, Taoism, and Confucianism, is quite different from Christianity in both form and content. The transformation to Christianity also means for many Chinese an evolution in their system of thinking and expression. The Chinese version of the Bible is not easy to read; the translation is stiff and rough. In many cases, there are no proper Chinese terms that correspond to the concepts in the Bible. A lack of familiarity with Christian backgrounds and stories among Chinese readers also makes the Bible foreign, confusing, and difficult to comprehend. In one example, when the term "sin" is translated into Chinese as *zui* (罪), it is equal to the meaning of "crime" (罪) in Chinese. There is no specialized term in Chinese that contains the meaning of "sin" as in the Bible. In another example, God in Chinese means Shang Di (上帝), which is also different from the meaning of God in the Christian world. On the contrary, Buddhism has a long history in China, and its scripture has become part of the Chinese culture and even vocabulary.

---

7. Chinese Overseas Christian Mission, Headquarters in UK.

Many Chinese immigrants are intellectuals with advanced degrees such as PhDs in sciences and engineering. Some have previously argued with the ministers and their Christian friends and resisted the religion for years due to their prior education in the theory of evolution and sciences. It took many of them a long time to finally become Christians. It is even more difficult for intellectuals with a background in humanities and social sciences to embrace Christianity as their religion. They bear stronger Chinese cultural influences. When they read the Bible in Chinese, they found it hard to understand due to different ways of thinking and language expressions. In addition, the meaning of the terms and concepts in the Bible are foreign to traditional Chinese culture. Unlike Buddhism, which has become part of Chinese history and culture for many centuries, there are no Bible stories and characters pre-existing in Chinese culture.

Figure 6 The Church in Chinese Building in Chicago Chinatown
(August 2006 Photograph by Long Denggao)

When Chinese immigrants become Christians, a social network is formed with religion as the conduit. God, Christ, and the Bible became the guiding faith and the governor for those who joined the Christian community. The tenet, church, famous minister, and popular readings become their symbols to identify the denomination.

The social networks of the Chinese Christians formed in North America also strive to extend their social impacts all over the world, especially in their homeland China. They also reached the rising Chinese population in Europe, where Christianity was first established and later spread out. The basis of their new identity and social networks does not originate from their homeland. On the contrary, their new-found religious affiliations tie them together after overcoming the ideological/psychological/cultural barriers brought with them from their homeland.

2 Reconstruct the Identity Abroad: Other Chinese Networks

The Chinese Christian network is not an isolated phenomenon of immigrants from China's mainland or Taiwan region. In this chapter, there will be a brief survey of other overseas Chinese networks as well.

The first example is the networks of those ethnic Chinese who migrated from Indo-China. They immigrated from several countries in that region, including Vietnam (both South and North), Cambodia, and Laos. Their Chinese ancestors originally emigrated from Teochew, Canton, Hakka, Fukien, and Hainan of China. They were scattered around in various countries and subdivided into different dialectical groups. Most of them had little contact with one another when they were in Indo-China. While in Europe and America, they came together and formed their own unique Indo-Chinese networks based on their common life experiences nonetheless. These ethnic Chinese were persecuted in the socialist revolution of Indo-China during the 1970s. They had to escape as refugees and settle in strange cities. Many of them finally established their new lives in western countries. They are Chinese and Vietnamese/Cambodian/Laotian in identity. Being both Chinese descendants and Indo-China immigrants, they formed their own social networks as a subgroup of ethnic Chinese in America rather than being amalgamated into other subgroups of Chinese-Americans.[8] Meanwhile, they have maintained their identity as a subgroup of Vietnamese, Cambodian, or Laotian-Americans.

Some of them settled in Chinatown or in other Chinese communities in America. Many Vietnamese immigrants of ethnic Chinese origin also tend to own their own businesses as other Chinese immigrants usually do. There are many Chinese-Vietnamese-owned supermarkets, restaurants, beauty parlors, and auto repair shops in the main general mixed-Chinese commercial thoroughfares in Chinatown, as in the case of Monterey Park, California. The cases studied by Chan, meanwhile, include the various volunteer associations of Chinese-Vietnamese, Chinese-Cambodian, and Chinese-Laotians in Montreal, Canada.[9]

---

8. "The Adaptation of Ethnic Vietnamese Chinese in America," *Huaqiao Huaren Lishi Yanjiu,* Jan, 2007.

9. Chan Kwok-bun, Migration, *Ethnic Relations and Chinese Business* (London and New York: Routledge, 2005), 100.

Some Chinese-Vietnamese mixed together with other Vietnamese refugees in the well-known Vietnamese-American communities called "Little Saigon." Ethnic Vietnamese are the predominant population in Little Saigon, where, in many cases, a large number of Chinese-Vietnamese from Indo-China also choose to live. Many of the Chinese-Vietnamese arrived in North America during the second refugee wave in 1980. They own a large share of businesses in Little Saigon today.[10] Viet Wah Supermarket, a business on 1035 S. Jackson St., Seattle, was first established in 1988 by Duc Tran, a Chinese refugee from Vietnam. It is now the largest Southeast Asian-owned supermarket in Seattle, Washington. Situated in "Little Saigon," the supermarket is a thriving cluster of shops and restaurants that make up the heaviest single concentration of Vietnamese businesses in that state.[11]

The worldwide associations established by the Chinese from Vietnam, Laos, and Cambodia span North America, Europe, Australia, and Southeast Asia. They hold worldwide conferences in different locations across the globe once a year.

The second example is the Chinese immigrants' clan or kinship associations. Clan Associations (宗亲会) are formed by Chinese immigrants on the basis of the same family names among their members. Early Chinese immigrants were used to band together with those who shared the same surnames to form mutual help associations. The clan associations are still widespread among overseas Chinese. It is mainly for the clan to look after its fellow members. Interestingly, there are multi-name clan associations outside China.

For instance, Lung Kong Tin Yee Association (龙冈亲义公所) is composed of 4 clans: Liu, Guan, Zhang, and Zhao. Its origin may be traced back to a legendary story of friendship almost two thousand years ago. Long-gang temple, an ancient temple set up in 1662, is located in Kaiping, Guangdong, a famous *qiaoxiang* 侨乡 (homeland of overseas Chinese) in southern China. The first overseas Long-gang temple was set up in San Francisco in 1876. Thereafter, Lung Kong Tin Yee Association was formed one after another in countries around the world like Canada, Mexico, Cuba, Peru, Australia, Thailand, Japan, Korea, Malaysia, and Singapore. The Global Lung Kong Tin Yee Association came into existence in 1963. The total number of its member associations in the world reaches 143, with only one temple in the homeland.

Traditionally in China, the clan associations limit their members to not only the same surname but also the same or a single ancestry. That same surname or common ancestry usually is shared by only a small portion of the Chinese population at different locations overseas, however. It is, therefore, helpful and beneficial for several surname clans to come together to form one large association. In a number of cases, some clans can even find a

---

10. www.answers.com/topic/little-saigon.

11. http://seattlepi.nwsource.com/neighbors/id/todo.html.

historical story to connect one another and justify the formation of a multi-clan association. The global organizations of multi-clan associations first appeared in the 1960s. They have been spread widely since the 1970s.

Chew Lun Association(Chau Luen Towe 昭伦公所)is composed of 4 surnames (谈、谭、许、谢). Toronto Chew Lun Association added one more surname Ruan (阮) and became an association with five surnames. (Note: Chew Lun Assoc was established in SF in 1896; therefore, multi-surname clan associations have a long history in North America—U.S., Canada.)

Liu Kwee Tang (六桂堂) is composed of 6 clans, Hong, Jiang, Wen, Fang, Gong, Wang(洪、江、翁、方、龚、汪)。It is believed by the clan members that the six surnames in Fukien of Southern China were from the same Wen family. The historical story is that Mr. Wen's six sons fled from the North to Fukien in Song Dynasty. Later on, they all became officeholders by passing the imperial examinations together.

Gee De clan association (至德宗亲会) includes five surnames: Wu, Zhou, Cai, Wen, Cao (吴、周、蔡、翁、曹). It is believed by the clan members that they all originated from one common ancestry. Its global clan association was established in 1974.

Gee How Oak Tin Association (至孝笃亲公所) includes Chan, Woo, and Yuen (陈、胡、袁). Some of its branch associations even include six surnames, adding Tian, Sun, and Lu (田、孙、陆) three more surnames. With 27 branch associations in the U.S, Canada, and Mexico, Gee How Oak Tin Family Association is the largest Chinese family association in Washington State. Individuals with the surnames Chin, Woo, and Yuen belong to this organization. It provides housing, cultural activities, and other services to its members. The Oak Tin Association was first formed in Seattle in 1900.[12]

The association with the most surnames is the one with ten surnames, and all are believed to be descended from Shun (舜), the second great emperor in ancient China. The ten surnames are Chan, Woo, Yuen, Yao, Yu, Tian, Sun, Lu, Wang, and Che (陈、胡、袁、姚、虞、田、孙、陆、王、车) with a total population around 150 million all over the world. There are more than 100 associates of ten Shun's descendants in the world. The international sodality has been held in different cities around the world since 1982.

Some other clan associations have also merged together. The Zhuang clan association and Yan clan association in Singapore were combined in 1990. The two surnames Zhuang (庄) and Yan (严)were said to be originally from the same clan centuries ago. A global clan association of Zhuang and Yan came into existence afterwards. Lai (赖), Luo (罗), and Fu (傅) clan associations joined together too.

Most observers ignore that these networks are formed overseas, not brought from the homeland. The historical stories and legends have had little influence at home. Nonetheless,

---

12. http://seattlepi.nwsource.com/neighbors/id/todo.html.

they exerted profound influences upon the ethnic Chinese after their emigration overseas. The Chinese immigrants saw the need for a ligament of common surnames, ancestors, or even common locality of origins, to connect them into closer groups to help one another while overseas. The need in their lives and businesses drives the Chinese immigrants to seek some common links by forming clan societies. The historical stories and legends that provided shared family roots are usually serving as a convenient and useful conduit to establish clan-based organizations overseas.

In fact, the associations of those dialectal groups are not transplanted overseas by the Chinese immigrants from their homeland. While in their home country, conflicts of interest in various dialectal areas were frequent. While abroad, common dialects become easily helpful ligaments that can tie the Chinese immigrants into clan groups or networks.

Associations based on shared dialectal backgrounds also exist among Chinese immigrants. These associations, too, are formed outside of China, not imported from the immigrant's homeland. While inside China, disputes among groups speaking the same dialect often led to severe regional conflicts, it is not evident among the share-dialect group overseas. In fact, the common dialect becomes the catalyst that binds these immigrants together in a manner no different from the clan-based associations.

3   Why Are the Cultural Identity and Network Formed Abroad?

Why did legends and historical stories become the identities of immigrants abroad while they had no influence in the homeland? What functions do these identities serve in the formation of overseas Chinese social networks while such identities were not part of their lives back in China?

3.1 Similar Experiences and Shared Backgrounds Shape the Identity of Chinese Immigrant Groups

Before emigration, some immigrants were young college students in China. Others may simply come from the same regions sharing a similar local dialect. When the immigrants try to make a living in a different and foreign environment from their adopted country, they often harbor certain similar interests and pursuits. Numerous young Chinese college students have come to North America to pursue advanced studies and remained there after graduation. When those Chinese immigrants forsook their upbringing in atheism, communism, or even Confucianism, and turned to Christianity, they transformed themselves thoroughly after enduring a painful spiritual realignment. As newly-converted

Christians, they show happiness in learning the teachings of the Bible and are not shy of sharing their life's testimonials about God's grace with one another.

3.2 Social Networks and Personal Trust

The common origin, similar experiences, common pursuits, interests, and beliefs all play a role in one way or in forming mutual trust and setting certain boundaries within networks. The mechanism of credibility and trust is strengthened in repeat games inside the business networks or the economic activities of the ethnic Chinese. It is not a formal institutional credit system and is not to be substituted with any other institutional arrangements. The religious networks are based on faith, which is rooted in Christianity. When a member fails in his or her true religious belief, it is believed that the divine judgment from God will befall upon the person, and fellow parishioners will assist him or her in the spiritual healing from the misdeeds. Religious networks with a large number of followers can provide an appealing and inspirational environment, which, in turn, re-enforces the parishioners' common beliefs and faith. Even for Zen Buddhism, its followers still like to gather together even though the Zen practitioners need only to show or practice their beliefs according to the Zen tenet without frequent congregating. Once away from the environment or the net, however, the belief may gradually diminish, as told to me by a famous scholar's wife. She was once a Christian in Australia. After moving to Singapore and away from her Christian network, she is no longer an active church-goer. The followers of religion need either formal or informal networks to connect with one another. The church communities are the basis of such social networks, which further provide support to and supervision of their members.

Inside the language-dialect associations, the restraints for trust or credibility are invisible and ubiquity. If a member's credibility or reputation were in doubt, the negative image would not be limited inside the overseas networks. It will spread all the way back to the member's local communities in their homeland. The negative feelings will linger well into the future. It also means huge losses for the offenders of valuable information shared within the network and opportunities inside and outside. Perhaps we could say that he may gain some instant cash or benefits but lose the trust and credibility for a longer term. Being a good member of the network, he will feel proud, safe, mentally, and spiritually satisfactory, and enjoy potential benefits in business and life. No one can afford to lose his credibility within his own network. Once that happens, the loss of current benefits and future opportunities will surely follow.

The common origins and experiences make the Chinese immigrants closer to one another. The common pursuits and interests make the network take shape. The credibility and associated benefits make the network a potent force and last long. The common language, customs, and culture are also parts of the background influences that help form the networks in a different environment. However, they are not the determining factors.[13] It is not the clan's common dialect and shared historical story that serve as the primary bonds to tie the Chinese immigrants together. It is due to their interests in spiritual needs and satisfactions, as well as the realities of life in foreign lands. The common pursuits and similar experiences can also serve as bonding factors. The phenomenon of social networking is not particular for Chinese immigrants. Almost all ethnic emigrant groups form social networks of one kind or another based on their new-found identities overseas.

References

Chan, Kwok-bun. *Migration, Ethnic Relations and Chinese Business*. London and New York: Routledge, 2005: 100.

Long, Denggao, and Han Qiming. "Beyond Culture: Economic Analysis of the Characteristics of Overseas Chinese Business." In *The Chinese Entrepreneurship in a Global Era (Asian Studies Series)*. Routledge, 2008.

"The Adaptation of Ethnic Vietnamese Chinese in America." *Huaqiao Huaren Lishi Yanjiu*, Jan, 2007.

Wang, Zhongxin." The Chinese Church Experience in North America." Accessed February 15, 2006. www.cwts.edu.

Yang, Fenggang. "Chinese Christians in America, Conversion, Assimilation, and Adhesive Identities." August, 1999.

---

13. Long Denggao and Han Qiming, "Beyond culture: Economic Analysis of the Characteristics of Overseas Chinese Business," in *The Chinese Entrepreneurship in a Global Era (Asian Studies Series)* (Routledge, 2008).

CHAPTER 6

The Growth of Chinatown Bus: Beyond Ethnic Enclave Economy in America*

The popular Chinatown inter-city bus services among major U.S. cities were almost non-existence ten years or so ago. They began as a response to the transportation needs of the ever-growing Chinese immigrant population in this country. It was chaotic, ruthless in competition and price wars, unregulated, and even unsafe in some instances at its beginning and early years. Over time, the services and safety records have been steadily improved. Their operations have become subject to local and state regulations and are better managed professionally. The popularity and acceptance of Chinatown buses by travelers from many different walks of life have stimulated the growth of inter-city bus services and helped revitalize the ailing bus transportation industry in the U.S. They intensified the competition with Greyhound Bus Line and Peter Pan Bus, the dominant forces in the long-distance bus transportation market, as well as the competitions among themselves. The outlook of the bus transportation landscape amid intense competition and ongoing mergers and acquisitions remains to be fully revealed.

* Long Denggao and Han Qingming, "The Growth of Chinatown Bus: Beyond Ethnic Enclave Economy in America," 2013. Han Qingming: Head of Library Information System, Housatonic Community College, Bridgeport, Connecticut, USA.

1   Chaotic Beginning: Meeting the Transportation Needs of Chinese Immigrants

It is a well-known fact that many Diaspora are extremely creative in establishing niche markets from within the ethnic communities and filling the void for the service and product needs of immigrants in their adopted countries. The intercity bus services between Chinatowns in New York City, Boston, Philadelphia, and Washington, DC areas offer a perfect example. The Chinese immigrants created a new business opportunity, formed a unique transportation market, and later expanded the service into the mainstream.

Since the 1990s, more and more Chinese immigrants have come to the U.S. On the east coast, the population of Chinese immigrants in NYC, Boston, Philadelphia, Washington DC, and other major metropolitan centers grew exponentially. Chinese communities also emerged in numerous small and medium size towns throughout the area and beyond. As a result, the commercial ties and the movements of the population among the Chinese communities, especially among Chinatowns in major Metro centers, increased dramatically, which no doubt drew the attention of Chinese entrepreneurs to the transportation needs of burgeoning Chinese communities.

In the beginning, Asian goods, especially food products and kitchenware, were carried from NY Chinatowns to other states via commercial trucks and vans. Occasionally, some immigrants were transported along the way. As time passed, independent long-distance Chinatown bus services emerged (NYT 2002). The Chinatown buses, first established in 1998, primarily transporting restaurant workers to and from Chinatowns across the East Coast—have gradually become the popular choice among students and other budget-conscious travelers looking for a cheap way to get from city to city.

The operations of Chinatown bus lines were very chaotic at the beginning, featuring super-cheap fares along the Eastern seaboard, erratic schedules, and cutthroat competitions. When the Fung Wah bus line launched its first services in 1998, it was the only company that offered inter-city Chinatown-to-Chinatown long-distance bus services. Between NYC and Boston, Fung Wah offered the customers a super low fare of $25 for a one-way trip. Another bus line, Lucky Star, after launching its bus line, soon knocked down the one-way fare to $10 during the fabled bus wars of August 2002 and 2003. The $10 fare ultimately proved untenable for both companies—it was a "suicide amount." The prices later settled at $15 each way for a pre-bought Internet ticket, still astonishingly cheap. Other bus routes between New York, Washington DC, and other areas had their shares of periodical price wars too. Many of those price wars could not last for more than two months though. Due to chaotic competition, some bus lines like Sunshine had to abandon certain bus routes. Others were closed or folded into the businesses of their stronger competitors. A number of violent activities were reported regarding Chinatown buses and their owners. The eruption of violence went away around 2004 while competition among Chinatown bus lines continued.

The targeted market of Chinatown bus lines were those Asian immigrants who wanted to shop or visit relatives between major metro centers and needed cheap and convenient transportation. Although the buses were modern and comfortable, the services were bare bones. No advertising, customer services, and even no bus stations. Customers simply went to the designated bus stops, waited for the bus, and paid the driver upon boarding. For those willing to do without frills, these companies offered virtually the same service as Greyhound and other established bus and rail lines but at a substantially lower price.[1] For instance, it costs $50 one way by Greyhound traveling between NYC and Boston, far above those charged by the emerging Chinatown bus lines. Before long, words were spread about the availability of the deep discount transportation services of Chinatown buses, and travelers from different walks of life started using the service. The service became especially popular among young college students, budget travelers, or people for whom the service was simply more convenient.

There were a number of reasons for the unbelievably low fares of Chinatown bus services. The bus lines provided direct, non-stop transportation for those who travel between Chinatowns in major metro centers without the need to make frequent stops at small towns and cities along the routes, which not only cut down the traveling time but reduced the operating costs considerably. The lower cost was also the result of irregular and flexible operations. For instance, the Fung Wah bus line featured curbside pick-up and drop-off points in Chinatowns and occasionally at other locations in the cities. They operated no full-service stations and had small overhead costs. The new and existing immigrants in major cities provided ample sources of cheap labor. The drivers' wages are generally very low. The convenience of non-stop transportation and the low price attracted a growing number of Chinese immigrants, young college students, and other ethnic travelers to Chinatown bus lines, which in turn, allowed them to operate their services on the basis of smaller profits but larger customer volumes. For instance, Chinatown buses were often fully or at least 3/4 seated, while Greyhound had a much lower seating rate.

---

1. The air shuttle from New York to Washington can cost more than $300, and, while the flight takes less than 90 minutes, there's that pesky ride to and from the airports. The same-day fare on Amtrak between New York and Washington ranges from $103 to beyond $200, depending on the time of day.

2   Rapid Growth and Challenges to the Established Bus Lines

Initially, the newly emerged intercity bus lines were based in Chinatowns along the east coast. They took advantage of the frequent movement of the Chinese population among the nation's major metropolitan areas. The concentration of Chinese immigrants in Chinatowns and their expanding population formed a steady stream of basic customers for inter-city bus traveling services. Some Chinese entrepreneurs saw the opportunity and plunged themselves into the new venture.

The Chinatown bus lines spread gradually into other areas and functions. Some bus lines are special tourist or leisure buses that transport large groups of mainly Chinese and Vietnamese immigrants to and from casino establishments such as Foxwoods Casino and Mohegan Sun Casino in Connecticut. These gambling buses are modeled after the popular older Atlantic City bus routes, which also target Asian American customers.

Beyond the Northeast corridor, Chinatown buses rolled out a number of new travel routes. Down to the south, the services reached as far as the major southern transportation hubs, Atlanta and Orlando. They even opened limited services routes to a few medium size cities like Rockville, Maryland, Richmond, and Norfolk, Virginia.

In other parts of the country, cities like Chicago and Detroit, which also saw their Chinese population growth in recent decades, attracted Chinese entrepreneurs to open similar bus services there too. Chinatown bus lines are undoubtedly catching on at the traditional centers of ethnic Chinese immigrants in Los Angeles and San Francisco on the west coast.

Overall, Chinatown buses now travel around 30 cities. There are more than 40 such companies in operation across the country.[2]

The attractiveness of low-cost and non-stop direct travel increased the popularity of Chinatown buses among Chinese immigrants as well as other budget-conscious travelers. According to one report of Eastern Travel, 30% of its customers were students; another 30% were returning customers; nearly 40% were customers coming from bus line giant Greyhound. Chinatown buses cost only a fraction of the regular expenses of its national competitors Greyhound Bus Lines and Peter Pan Bus Lines. As the words spread about their services, the 40-plus Chinatown bus companies posed a growing threat and challenge to the established national bus lines.

In May 2004, Peter Pan Bus Lines sued Fung Wah and Kristine Travel for violating regulations of the Federal Motor Carrier Safety Administration. According to Kim

---

2. Lionel Beehner, "Chinatown Buses Unveiling New Routes," *New York Times In Transit Blog*, acessed 9 June 2010, http://intransit.blogs.nytimes.com/2010/06/09/chinatown-buses-unveiling-new-routes.

Plaskett, a Greyhound spokeswoman, the two Chinatown lines named in the suit had only charter authority, which does not permit hourly departures and arrivals. "We have no objection to competition, as long as it's on a level playing field," Plaskett said. "[In the lawsuit], we asserted that Fung Wah and Kristine were operating under charter authority." However, the judge, in that case, allowed Fung Wah to continue operation as long as it applied for proper registration.[3]

According to *The Boston Globe*, the lawsuit against Chinatown buses was motivated by Peter Pan's and Greyhound's interest in maintaining their monopoly on the NY-Boston bus route. Timothy Shevlin said: "The big dog out there, Peter Pan, is dead set against [Chinatown bus lines]. They don't want that kind of competition."

The other attack was the discrimination case against Fung Wah (2004–2007). The State of Massachusetts Commission Against Discrimination ordered a New York-based bus line, Fung Wah, to pay a blind couple more than $60,000 for refusing them to carry their service dog aboard the bus. Fung Wah had a policy that pets were not allowed because of allergies and other health concerns. Most Asian travelers do not have pets.

3   Streamlining Operations and Improvement of Services

Whether various lawsuits and customer complaints were fair or not, Chinatown bus lines had no choice but to improve their operations and service quality, enforce strict safety measures to meet government regulations, and attract new customers.

In the summer of 2005, a serious accident changed the fate of many Chinatown bus owners. A bus from one of the major Chinatown bus lines caught fire on I-91 while traveling in Connecticut.[4] Fortunately, all passengers were safely evacuated before the fire got worse.[5] Local and state governments in New York, led by senator Schumer, started to impose strict regulations on Chinatown bus lines, including surprise inspections and forced disclosures, among others. Even under massive media coverage of the police crackdown, consumers continued to endorse Chinatown bus lines. This was evidenced by the rising online ticketing traffic by the largest bus ticketing service gotobus.com.

---

3. Beendan R. Linn, "Chinatown Bus Hikes Tickets to $15: Popular, Cheap Student Transport Changes Route to Dock at South Station," *Harvard Crimson*, October 6, 2004.

4. Several well-publicized incidents and accidents: in 2005, one of Fung Wah's buses caught fire in Connecticut; in 2006 another Fung Wah coach overturned in Massachusetts. In 2006, the Federal Motor Carrier Safety Administration (FMCSA) announced more than $44,000 in fines against Fung Wah for violating safety regulations.

5. In fact, Greyhound's fatigued driver crashed a bus and killed two people in California around the Thanksgiving holiday.

However, after the incidents, Chinatown buses implemented better safety measures and drastically improved their safety records. Major Bus lines Fung Wah, Lucky River, Lucky Star, and USAsia are currently all listed by the government regulators as "satisfactory" except Megabus' Chicago as "conditional." According to U.S. Department of Transportation, the out-of-service rates due to safety and operation concerns for Greyhound is 7%, Eastern travel at 9%, and the current average is 25%.

Increased popularity led to increasing regulatory interest. In September 2004, the City of Boston required all regularly-scheduled intercity bus services to operate exclusively to and from the South Station transportation terminal instead of dangerous curbside pick-ups and drop-offs. There had been conflicts for limited curbside spaces among Chinatown buses, for instance, Eastern, Today' and New Century bus lines. They had to rely on the local leaders of the Chinese community to help coordinate the usage of curbside space issues and services.

The competition for the neighborhood's limited curb space was ferocious. In addition to the coordinating efforts by local leaders, Chinatown bus operators had also lobbied the city governments to establish designated pick-up and drop-off locations. The buses, which provide the cheap and convenient transportation service to and from Chinatowns across the East Coast, currently still do not have set depots or stops in the Manhattan area where passengers have to get on and off the buses from curbsides. Drivers claim they have no choice but to illegally park their large vehicles on congested neighborhood streets. "We need regulations, but the regulations for bus stations do not exist. And I don't think we are in a position to evaluate who gets limited curb space," said CB3's transportation committee chairman, David Crane.[6]

The competition among various bus lines was another factor forcing Chinatown bus lines to streamline their operations and improve their services. A customer once said in his travel diary, "The bus was a little warm, and the air circulation wasn't top-notch, creating that familiar sickly, stale bus smell that makes even the most iron-stomached traveler worry she'll succumb to carsickness." To maintain the popularity among their regular customers and attract new travelers, Chinatown buses added some individual touches to their services. At the South Station of Boston, hand-drawn maps were taped up to the windows with labels in both Chinese and English. On some buses, they provided punch-colored personal trash bags affixed to the arm of each seat, a surprisingly efficient method of keeping the bus

---

6. Ma Suzanne, "Chinatown Buses, Long Denied Legal Drop-off Zones, Lobby for Downtown Curb Space," DNAinfo Reporter/Producer2010-03-18.

tidy. On Eastern Travel, the neatly dressed driver, speaking good English, politely collected the tickets.

Another noticeable improvement was online booking and scheduling using gotobus .com, a nationwide online bus ticketing service, and chinatownbus.org. The bus operators increased the number of buses in operation and the frequency of trips each day and week. For instance, Fung Wah has maintained a reliable schedule, departing from New York every hour from 7 a.m. to 11 p.m., with additional departures on a half-hour basis during peak afternoon hours.

The new bus lines even brought other feeding businesses for Chinese entrepreneurs along the busy bus routes. Chinese restaurants were opened along the routes to accommodate travelers' lunch or dinner breaks during the journey. In 2003, the bus the author took at that time stopped at a MacDonald's for a short break. Three years later, as expected, when the author took the bus again on the same routes, the bus stopped at a newly opened Chinese buffet restaurant staffed with Mexican immigrants as waiters. It is a natural fit between Chinese restaurants and Chinatown bus lines to complement one another's services along the traveling routes since most bus travelers are Chinese or other Asian immigrants.

4   Beyond Chinatown: From the Margin to the Mainstream

The success increased Chinatown bus operators' confidence in doing business in a previously unfamiliar land. Some entrepreneurs thought the discount bus services could do a lot better by cutting across the ethnic lines and venturing beyond Chinatowns. David Wong, a native of Nanjing, China, literally took his bus company to the heart of Manhattan to attract non-Chinese travelers. Instead of operating in traffic-clogged Chinatown, Wong chose Penn Station, a major Manhattan transportation hub, as the base for his Eastern Travel. In an interview with *Asian Weekly*, Wong's partner and co-owner of Eastern Travel, Zhen Yongming, said, "This is America. We should do more business with Americans." According to its records, 95% of Eastern Travel customers are non-Chinese travelers. It serves its customers in three different languages of English, Chinese, and Spanish. Even half of its bus drivers are of Hispanic origins.

Other Chinatown bus lines are not far behind in expanding into the areas of non-Chinese communities. They travel across eastern seaboard cities and other areas ranging from the immigrant center like New York City to some small to medium size cities with a small number of ethnic Chinese. For instance, travelers are set to benefit from a new daily bus service between New York City and Allentown, PA, which started on October 10,

2009. This service is provided by Sky Line Bus and is a welcome addition to their already popular service route between the State College in PA and New York City.

Clearly, Chinatown buses have become a viable and even favorable long-distance inter-city travel vehicle welcomed by not only ethnic Chinese but increasingly acceptable by African Americans, Hispanics, other Asian immigrants, and even Caucasians. They attracted many low-income and middle-class travelers. To further their entry into the mainstream, Chinatown bus lines also joined U.S. Bus associations UMA and ABA.

The very existence and the growth of the Chinatown bus lines reflect the demand for this type of service. They have outgrown their humble and chaotic origins and become more professional, contending successfully in the U.S. inter-city bus service industry.

5 Competition and Emulation: Chinatown Bus Wave

The rapid growth of Chinatown bus lines intensified the competition among the existing inter-city bus lines and attracted newcomers. Greyhound, the largest bus line in the U.S., dropped its prices, offering a familiar name-brand alternative to the increasingly popular low-cost Chinatown coaches.

Dozens of new competitors emerged. Hasidic Jews from Brooklyn founded the Washington Deluxe and Vamoose Bus. A former Marriott executive founded DC2NY, a bus line between Washington and NY that guarantees customers seats if booked online and charges only slightly more than the Chinatown buses (a \$40 round-trip versus \$35). It also offers free bottles of water and Wi-Fi internet access.[7]

To promote their service, the newcomers offered customers brand new buses with comfortable leather seats, a perfectly calibrated air-conditioning system, a clean bathroom, and even electrical outlets as well as wireless connection. Given their relatively competitive fares to the mainstream Greyhound Lines, they have also become popular among non-Chinese customers, especially among young students.

In 2008, after a long and exhausting lobbying battle against curbside bus companies, two motor-coach heavyweights, Greyhound and Peter Pan, reversed their position and jointly formed their own curbside bus line, BoltBus, in the hope of recovering some lost market share to Chinatown buses and to fender off the anticipated entry of MegaBus that competes with Greyhound in the Mid-West region. BoltBus (boltbus.com) currently serves five destinations between Boston and Washington, D.C., and offers Wi-Fi access, power plug-ins, other amenities, and even a frequent rider program.

---

7. "The Chinatown Express," *The Economist*, October 25, 2007.

The same year, another motor-coach heavyweight, Coach USA entered the low-fare fray. The British transportation conglomerate launched Megabus (megabus.com/us) on the U.S east coast. It currently serves the domestic market of approximately 30 major cities in North America. Both BoltBus and MegaBus tried 'From $1' as the marketing tool to attract customers. Some Chinatown bus lines matched the 'From $1' pricing model head-on, while others continued their fixed price model. A dynamic price war started among all bus service providers.

Ten years ago, Chinatown buses were lesser known and little noticed. Nowadays, they have clearly become a dynamic force in the American long-distance bus transportation industry. A competitive marketplace emerged following the Chinatown bus wave, offering the customers an alternative money-saving and convenient travel vehicle.

6   The Renaissance of Intercity Bus Service and Industrial Integration

The convenience of Chinatown buses stimulated the demand for inter-city bus services. A satisfied student traveler wrote in her BLOG that it cost only a small sum of $15 to ride the Chinatown bus to New York City for a fun day visiting friends and shopping at her favorite stores. In 2006, the author had an opportunity to interview an Egyptian woman who sat beside the author when both of us were on our way from NYC to Boston via a Chinatown bus. The woman is a Math teacher in NYC, while her husband works in Boston. The couple could afford only to meet one another once every month before. But now, they can afford to meet each other once every week, thanks to the low cost and convenience of Chinatown buses. According to *Business Week*, "Travelers who wouldn't have given a thought to bus travel before are now stepping on board."[8] "I've become a complete convert to bus travel," said Sue T. Cohen, a psychotherapist waiting in line to board a Vamoose Bus on the street near Penn Station. "I used to think buses were terrible." Now she says there is less wear and tear in getting to the bus. It actually takes less time and is easier than facing the congestion and confusion of train stations or airports.[9]

The no-frills, low-cost bus lines buzzing along highways in every region of the United States are causing more Americans to reconsider intercity bus travel as a viable alternative. They helped revitalize a long-forgotten yet important part of the U.S. transportation industry. The seating rate of the bus lines has increased by 6.9%, one report indicated.

---

8. Brian Burnsed and Joseph Damian, "Suddenly, It's Cool to Take the Bus," *Business Week*, no. 4101 (2008): 64.

9. Bruce W. Fraser, "Bus Wars Ease Travel for New Yorkers," accessed March 21, 2010, www.chinatown-bus.org/ps/p1/6565.html.

A recent study by the Chaddick Institute for Metropolitan Development at DePaul University in Chicago, which tracked down the industry performances, concluded that "The renaissance of intercity bus service dates to May 1, 2006, when Megabus introduced to service." In fact, that bus line's traffic grew by 97% between 2007 and 2008, and this January, Megabus boarded its two millionth customer. As for its competitor BoltBus, the study noted that it has not released its traffic statistics but has reported profitability and steady growth.

According to BTS, more Americans travel more miles by bus, and those numbers have been steadily increasing in recent years. Scheduled bus services rose by 8.1% in 2007 and again by 9.8% in 2008 (BTS). Also, according to the Chaddick Study, bus ridership has gone up 13 percent since 2006—the first increase in 40 years.[10]

"Nationally, intercity buses today carry more people in two weeks than Amtrak carries coast-to-coast in a year," said Robert Schwarz, executive vice president of Peter Pan, citing a 2009 study by the American Bus Association. "Bus travel is a better deal, and people today are looking for deals." Long-distance bus ridership in the United States expanded by nearly 5% last year over 2008 levels, according to Joseph Schwieterman, director of the Chaddick Institute and the conductor of the Chaddick Study. The bus industry has outperformed all other modes of transportation, according to professor Schwieterman.[11]

Buses are the most eco-friendly mode of transportation on certain routes. And there is no contest if you compare the carbon footprints of buses to cars. In fact, a recent study from the American Bus Association found motor coaches provide 206.6 passenger miles per gallon of fuel, compared to 92.4 for commuter rail and just 27.2 for single passenger cars. The Chaddick Institute estimates these new low-fare bus lines reduce carbon dioxide emissions by an estimated 36,000 tons a year.[12] The emergency of Chinatown bus services and the revitalization of bus transportation benefit the nation as a whole in terms of saving energy and environmental protection.

Inevitably, as more players are chasing the same customers and markets, industry consolidation happens via mergers and acquisitions. In fall 2008, shortly after Eastern began offering Wi-Fi on its coaches, Coach USA purchased the bus line using the operating authority of a then-inactive company whose operations were sold to Peter Pan in the early 2000s. It gave Coach USA its first foothold in the Chinatown bus market.

In 2009, Coach USA purchased Today's, placing Coach USA right in the busy Chinatown bus market in the Philadelphia area. Earlier in 2008, Coach USA had

---

10. Tracie Rozhon, "Jet Set, Meet the Bus Bunch," *New York Times*, September 26, 2008, P. F1.

11. Bruce W. Fraser, "Bus Wars Ease Travel for New Yorkers," accessed March 21, 2010, www.chinatown-bus.org/ps/p1/6565.html.

12. Bill McGee, "Are Buses the New Way to Go?" *USA TODAY*, April 30, 2009.

introduced its Megabus service into the northeastern U.S out of a hub near Penn Station in Manhattan, which competed at the time with two of the companies purchased by Stagecoach to form what is now Eastern Shuttle. With the acquisition of Eastern and Today's, Coach USA significantly expanded its Megabus service to Philadelphia and D.C. However, in August 2009, Coach USA divested itself of Eastern Shuttle operations, and the two lines are no longer affiliated with each other.

How the mergers and acquisitions will continue to evolve remain to be seen. The impact of the industrial consolidation on Chinatown bus lines is also hard to predict. No doubt, however, being born out of a limited niche market serving Chinese immigrants' transportation needs, Chinatown buses have grown into a major force in the inter-city bus transportation market in the U.S. Their unexpected emergence and growth, without exaggeration, have helped revitalize America's ailing bus transportation industry.

References

Beehner, Lionel. "Chinatown Buses Unveiling New Routes." *New York Times In Transit Blog.* Acessed 9 June 2010. http://intransit.blogs.nytimes.com/2010/06/09/chinatown-buses-unveiling-new -routes.

Burnsed, Brian, and Joseph Damian. "Suddenly, It's Cool to Take the Bus." *Business Week*, no. 4101 (2008): 64.

Fraser, Bruce W. "Bus Wars Ease Travel for New Yorkers." Accessed March 21, 2010. www .chinatown-bus.org/ps/p1/6565.html.

Linn, Beendan R. "Chinatown Bus Hikes Tickets to $15: Popular, Cheap Student Transport Changes Route to Dock at South Station." *Harvard Crimson*, October 06, 2004.

Ma, Suzanne. Chinatown Buses, Long Denied Legal Drop-off Zones, Lobby for Downtown Curb Space." DNAinfo Reporter/Producer2010-03-18.

McGee, Bill. "Are Buses the New Way to Go?" *USA TODAY*, April 30, 2009.

Rozhon, Tracie. "Jet Set, Meet the Bus Bunch." *New York Times*, September 26, 2008, P. F1.

"The Chinatown Express." *The Economist*, October 25, 2007.

PART THREE

Blend and Contrast

CHAPTER 7

New Explorations in the Comparative Study of Economic History in China and the West*

Based on the new academic achievements of the California School scholars, this chapter aims to introduce the new progress in comparative studies on the socioeconomic developments in China and the West. It also tries, with breakthroughs in methodology and challenges to European centrism, to analyze and summarize the changes and trends of research paradigms in the field of world economic history.

Comparative studies of economic development in China and the West have always been a hot topic that strongly attracted scholars at home and abroad. Yet, a new generation of economic historians, called the California School, has brought into view another huge wave in international academia. Works such as *One Quarter of Humanity: Malthusian Mythology and China Realities* by James Z. Lee and Wang Feng, *China Transformed: Historical Change and the Limits of European Experience* by R. Bin Wong, *Re-Orient: Global Economy in the Asian Age* by Andre Gunder Frank, and *The Great Divergence: China, Europe, and the Making of the Modern World Economy* by Kenneth

* Long Denggao, "New Explorations in the Comparative Study of Economic History in China and the West," *Chinese Studies in History* 45, no. 1 (2011): 7–27.

Pomeranz[1] have all had a certain impact with their brand new perspectives, methods, and achievements, and most of these scholars have won scholarly awards in the United States.[2] Represented by the above-mentioned scholars, this newly rising group earned the name of the "California School"[3] as most of the representative members of the group came from California. However, they are not a regional or sectional academic clique but a group emphasizing similar academic ideas.[4] This California School consists of young and energetic socioeconomic historians. With their research interests overlapping each other, as well as their constant communication, nonstop discussions, and idea exchanges, they have had a huge impact on the discipline of economic history in the world.

Generally speaking, the California School possesses the following characteristics: first, in terms of research paradigm, they have a strong tendency to reevaluate theories and methods based on European centrism; second, they stressed that the global economic system and the idea of globalization were neither first established nor promoted in Europe; third, they pay great attention to China studies, placing China in the context of world history to explore the relations between China and the outside world to demonstrate China's importance, and at the same time, to examine the views and theories of Western history; fourth, they place emphasis on comparative studies, with their perspectives turning away from the traditional study of cultural differences to the economic developments in China and the West so as to reexamine traditional theories. Based on the achievements of the scholars of the California School, this chapter will try to comment on their main viewpoints and new ideas, as well as explore their breakthroughs in a new research paradigm.

---

1. See the Chinese versions of the book by James Lee and Wang Feng (trans. Chen Wei, Yao Yuan, et al., Sanlian Press, 2000); R. Bin Wong's book (trans. Li Bozhong et al., Jiangsu People's Press, 1998); Andre Gunder Frank's book (trans. Liu Beicheng et al., Zhongyang Bianyi Press, 2011); and Kenneth Poweranz's book (Princeton: Princeton University Press, 2000). The Chinese translation of Pomeranz's book has recently been published (trans. Shi Jianyun, Jiangsu People's Press, 2003), and comments in this chapter regarding his theories mainly come from this translation. Only the author's name will be mentioned when citations from the above books appear later in the chapter.

2. For example, James Lee's book won the 2000 Alan Sharlin Award for Best Book in Social Science History and the 2000 Otis Dudley Duncan Award for distinguished scholarship in social demography. Pomeranz's new book was the winner of the 2000 John K. Fairbank Prize of the American Historical Association, co-winner of the 2001 World History Association Book Prize, and one of Choice's Outstanding Academic books of 2000.

3. Besides these scholars, the California School also includes Richard Von Glahn, Dennis O. Flynn, Arturo Giraldez, Tolbert Marks, Cameron D. Campbell, Jack A. Goldstone, and so on, each of them a leading figure in their own field.

4. Andre Gunder Frank of the University of Miami felt pretty honored when admitted to the group. Chinese scholar Li Bozhong, because of his many visits and long-time studies in California and his similar academic ideas, also became one of the leading members of the California School. Philip C.C. Huang is also considered a member of the group because he shares some of the basic ideals, though he disagrees with other members on certain positions.

1   The Great Divergence

Works by James Lee, Wang Feng, R. Bin Wong, and Andre Gunder Frank have all seen their Chinese translations published with huge influence in China. Although Philip C.C. Huang's book[5] had a much earlier circulation in China, we are not going to discuss that one in particular. This chapter will only briefly introduce the newly published Chinese translation of Pomeranz's book and the academic debate it caused among scholars.

Like R. Bin Wong and Li Bozhong, Kenneth Pomeranz also maintains that China's Jiangnan area in the eighteenth century shared similar economic growth to that in Britain—both belong to the same "Smithian growth" model. Pomeranz also holds that it was the same for Jiangnan in China, Japan, India, and Southeast Asia, without exception. His original idea is that throughout the eighteenth century, all major economic centers in the world faced the same problem: a shortage in intensively land-based products. The ecosystems in China and Japan were not necessarily worse than those in Europe. The only difference was that the Europeans, because of their overseas colonies and the development of new energy resources, were able to avoid the ecological confinement of the "Malthusian constraints" on their own countries, while the Chinese and other Asian nations could not. If the Europeans had failed to profit from their underground discoveries and overseas resources, they would have followed the same old path of development themselves. Combining his studies in economic history and ecology, Pomeranz has also tried to assess the value systems of different regions in the world regarding their social, political, and cultural developments and appraise the historical significance of the relations among these regions. He stresses that the global economy originated from the mutual influence of the economies of different regions and was not something that was forced upon other regions by a more "advanced" Europe. His point obviously is inspired by Gunder Frank: It is not Europe that made the world; it is the world that made Europe.

The processes of industrialization in China and the West differ, and efforts to study such differences in geographic environment, society, economy, ideology, culture, and ethnical psychology have been carried out by scholars at home and abroad. The conventional view maintained that the European economy had already developed very fast, even before industrialization. In contrast, China's economy stagnated or remained in recession, and there are huge differences between the economic development models of the two regions. Pomeranz refutes other Western scholars' theories on such differences and European

---

5. Philip C.C. Huang, *Small Farmers' Family and the Rural Development in the Yangzi Delta: 1368–1988* (Beijing: Zhonghua Book Company, 1992).

superiority. He insists that there are actually many similarities between China and the West in terms of living standards, consumption, development in agriculture and industry, and the "de facto market." At least until 1750, Europe was not more advanced than China. In reality, he holds, the Jiangnan area in China was more developed; its economic and political systems were more efficient than those in Europe of the time. Comparing the two, he concludes that there was no such superiority or inferiority between China and Europe before industrialization in economic development and economic growth models. That is to say, the level of economic development and growth models are not the causes of industrialization.

What caused the divergence of economic developments in China and Europe then? This question means we must reevaluate our comparative studies of China and the West and our viewpoints and research paradigm. To further his studies, Pomeranz focused on Jiangnan and England. The traditional mainstream view was that the English model of economic development and social evolution would inevitably lead to industrialization and that such a model is universally applicable. However, recent research results in European economic history have proved that industrialization is not necessarily the inexorable result of traditional English economic evolution. Actually, the Jiangnan model and the Dutch model are more universal, while the English model is more particular. So it makes more sense to compare the Jiangnan area with England and Europe. Both growth models of Jiangnan and Britain belong to the same "Smithian dynamics," which are said to have led to the realization of the division of labor, advantage of specialization, and enhanced profits. The more the market expands, the greater the space for economic growth. The traditional mainstream view also holds that the market and the development of the commercial economy, along with the enlargement of specialization and division of labor they bring about, are the basic factors in England's industrialization, and the huge British colonial market provided a strong stimulus for its expansion. Based upon such a premise, this view logically leads to the conclusion that industrialization did not happen in China because China did not have a developed market and lacked an overseas market like the British one. Li Bozhong challenged this viewpoint. He pointed out that a "national market,"[6] which had already come into being during the Ming and Qing dynasties in China, provided a huge market for Jiangnan as the country's economic center. Even the whole of the British overseas market fails to match it. The traditional theory obviously collapsed in front of this challenge because there are no essential differences between the British overseas market and Jiangnan's outside market. Besides,

---

6. Li Bozhong, "The Formation of China's National Market, 1500–1850," keynote address at the Eighth Annual World History Association International Congress, Canada, June 27, 1999.

Jiangnan, as the economic center of Southeast Asia, also possessed a pretty large overseas market of its own.

Pomeranz insisted that the major role the overseas colonies played was not as markets of British manufacturing products as described in the traditional view. In talking about the market itself, the Chinese market actually looks more similar to the "Smithian" model of free competition. Productive elements like land, the flow of labor force, and so on simply could not find any challengers among Western European nations of the time. Other scholars in Europe and America shared Pomeranz's theory or held similar opinions even before he did. Mark Elvin and Evelyn Rawski even pointed out that the Chinese market during Ming and Qing China was an over-heated competition.[7] With such arguments here, the market-promotes-industrialization theory could no longer hold water. Since Jiangnan's domestic market was even greater than Britain's domestic and overseas markets combined, with much more free competition, Jiangnan should have had the advantage over England if the "Smithian dynamics," which were supposed to lead to industrialization, still stood. The market factor was not where the two models differed. Instead, it is where they shared similarities. What, then, were their differences?

Pomeranz believes that Western Europe did not possess any innate advantage in terms of various economic indexes. The only advantage it had was coal. Coal mines in England are located in economic development centers, unlike Jiangnan in China, where the coal mines are far away. The geological conditions of English coal mines also differ greatly from those of the coal-producing Shanxi Province in China, as British coal mines contain high water levels. The invention of the steam engine came along with the demand for pumping out water while mining, thus leading to the birth of the most important power machines. On the other hand, Coal mines in Shanxi are relatively dry, and the technology born out of this situation was air circulation, not the great invention of the steam engine and its wide use. England's industrialization stimulated by coal mining did not occur in China. It did not happen in India, where coal is in short supply, nor did it take place in Holland. The modern economic system actually experienced a transition from the traditional "advanced organic economy" toward an "economy based on fossil energy." England's industrialization just came from this great development of mining in coal, iron, and other minerals.

It was not the market but the mining of coal, iron, and other minerals, as well as the different industrial structures that followed, that led to the great divergence between Jiangnan and Britain. At first glance, such a point seems skeptical. Yet it is logical. That is because natural resources and geographic conditions are the most important factors

---

7. Mark Elvin thinks the village life during Ming and Qing China had already become too commercialized; see *The Pattern of the Chinese Past* (Stanford University Press, 1973).

in deciding the region's industrial structure. Europe is lucky to have rich coal deposits that made it possible for fossil fuel–intensive industries to develop, although there is still another major contributing factor—trade with the New World.

The traditional view holds that the role played by colonies is that they open a market for the mother country's industrial products. Pomeranz, however, insists that such colonies supplied Britain with rich natural resources. So, even if these colonies did not promote industrialization through the market, they produced another important cause for such industrialization. Large quantities of cheap cotton, wheat, meat, and lumber, as well as other land-intensive products, helped save the land and forests in Europe, so the Europeans could concentrate on energy development and other production. It also enabled the Europeans to reduce geological restraints and move forward with their industrial revolution. At the same time, colonies also helped to absorb about 60 million surplus populations, moving labor-intensive industries from Europe to overseas colonies. These changes also led to the rapid population increase in Western and Northern European countries, where people were increasingly moving away from the countryside and focusing on further industrial development instead of holding onto the traditional effort to promote the maximum production of the organic economy. Coal and the New World made it possible for Europe to move on to energy-intensive, labor-efficient development. Europe greatly benefited from obtaining rich primary products through international trade. In sharp contrast, none of the peripheral areas in Asia could do the same. Although the interior parts of Asia saw great population growth and industrial prosperity after 1750, such development prevented these areas from supplying important resources for the industrial center in the Yangzi Delta. Such peripheral areas in inner China were always able to find some imported substitutes, thus relatively reducing the market of China's central commercial market and raising the price of materials that the industrial center had to import from inland China.[8] At the same time, demand for land-intensive products in industrialized areas continued to grow, and such areas could only follow the path of labor-intensive and resource-saving development. If Europe had not been able to have the resources from underground and overseas, it could have only followed that same path.

2   The Great Debate

The scholars of the California School challenged traditional mainstream thinking. Each of their works, such as those by James Lee and Andre Gunder Frank, has always caused

---

8. Pomeranz had been considering this problem for quite a while. See *The Making of a Hinterland: State, Society, and Economy in Inland North China* (University of California Press, 1993).

heated debate within international academic circles. Pomeranz's works have also led to a debate among scholars of the California School itself and strongly impacted Western scholars. Many scholars in the fields of China studies, European studies, ecological history, and others have published their introductions, comments, and discussions on his work.[9] Debates caused by Pomeranz's ideas have actually extended far beyond his works. They have touched on the research results and analyses he cited in his works, especially those by Li Bozhong and James Lee, with their emphasis on comparative studies on China and the West in general and Britain and Jiangnan in particular, among many other topics. James Lee's work had caused quite a lot of comment and discussion, and the impact could still be felt. Today, it has become the focal point of this new debate again, which can be described as a great parade of the research works of California School scholars.

On June 3, 2002, a spectacular forum was held at the Social Theories and Comparative History Center of the University of California, Los Angeles. Its theme was "The Great Divergence? The Roots of Economic Development and Underdevelopment in China and Europe." More than a hundred people attended the meeting, almost all of them scholars of the California School, and heated debates were conducted on works by Pomeranz and James Lee. The meeting began with brief introductions by the two authors, Pomeranz and Lee (and Lee's coauthors Wang Feng and Cameron D. Campbell), followed by critiques from Philip C.C. Huang, Arthur Wolf, Robert Brenner, and Chris Isett. Then Pomeranz and Lee responded, followed by another round of critique and response.[10] Nine papers were presented at the conference, and the major debating points were as summarized in the following.

In his paper, "Development or Involution in Eighteenth-Century Britain and China,"[11] Huang pointed out that Pomeranz's theory was very attractive, as it not only commented on European centrist scholars' interpretations of why China failed to develop like Britain but also explained why Britain avoided following the same "intensive content-type"

---

9. Besides the following citation, there are others: Jack Goody, "Falling Fortune of the Lands of the Rising Sun," *Times Higher Education Supplement*, no. 1460 (November 3, 2000); P.H.H. Vries, "Are Coal and Colonies Really Crucial? Kenneth Pomeranz and the Great Divergence," *Journal of World History* 12, no. 2 (Fall 2001); Graeme Lang, "Geography as Destiny?" *Science* 288, no. 5468 (May 12, 2000). There are still many others. We can see what intense critical reaction his work has caused.

10. "The Great Divergence? The Roots of Economic Development and Underdevelopment in China and Europe," conference proceedings. Some of the papers had already been published in *Journal of Asian Studies* 2 (May 2002).

11. Philip C.C. Huang, "Development or Involution in Eighteenth-Century Britain and China," *Journal of Asian Studies* 2 (May 2002). The Chinese translation can be found in *Historical Studies*, no. 4 (2002). As for the word "involution," Huang translated it as 内卷化 and for a while he also translated it as 过密化. I prefer to translate it as 内涵化, as 内涵 (connotation or content) easily pairs up with 外延 (extension), not only following the rules in Chinese language but also fitting into Huang's original meaning. Fang Xing, while discussing in 2001 the Chinese land market during the Ming and Qing dynasties, used the phrase 内涵 (development).

development as China did. But the problem with Pomeranz's theory is that he failed to rely on the examination of primary sources. Instead, he depended much on secondary sources and others' research results. Pomeranz stated that there were no major differences between Britain and China's Yangzi Delta in terms of development before 1800. Huang's criticism was that Pomeranz obviously ignored the theory of the eighteenth-century agricultural revolution in Britain. The degree of intensivity of labor in the Yangzi Delta was higher than that in Britain because the character of its agrarian economy decided that. Such content-oriented agriculture killed the possibility of capitalizing on large-scale, labor-efficient farms and developing economies of scale. At the same time, the production units of family farms/family-based industries also suppressed the capitalization of primitive and labor-efficient modern industries. Apparently, Pomeranz was wrong when he stated that the pressure of population and resources in the Yangzi Delta was not worse than in Britain. It was just this kind of pressure that actually caused the "content-oriented" development in the Delta. Huang also challenged the population theory of James Lee.

Huang summarized his paper by pointing out that eighteenth-century Britain and Jiangnan (Yangzi Delta) represented European development and China's "content-type" development models. Compared with agriculture in the Yangzi Delta, the British labor input per unit of land was much lower, with its average farms a hundred times larger than Jiangnan farms and forty-five times larger in terms of land use for agricultural purposes. As a result, the British productivity per unit of labor/time was also much higher. Such improvement in agricultural productivity, in turn, promoted the development of the handicraft industry in urban areas of Britain. Britain in 1800, therefore, had more advantageous conditions than any other region in the world to move toward modern agriculture and industry. Jiangnan tells a different story, with its labor-intensive, content-oriented development reaching its maximum. This "content-type growth" means the realization of an absolute increase in output at the cost of a progressive decrease of reward per unit of labor. It also reflects the high output per unit of land and capability of supporting urban networks.

In their article, "England's Divergence from China's Yangzi Delta: Property Relations, Microeconomics, and Patterns of Development," European historians Robert Bremer and Chris Isett used Bremer's previous work on the uniqueness of British agricultural capitalism to compare grain production in both Britain and Jiangnan. Their major points were: Between 1500 to 1750, the different development models in England and the Yangzi Delta led to the divergence between these two great economic systems, with Britain becoming the most economically advanced and prosperous region in the world while the Yangzi Delta increasingly declined. Colonies in America contributed greatly to Britain's prosperity, but this was not the major reason for its success. They concluded that the major reason for this great divergence was the unique structures of social and property relations in Britain. Such relations differed from those in the Yangzi Delta and medieval England and those in other European regions between 1500 and 1800. In the above three cases, their economies followed the old Malthusian model of growth, in which the land owners and the ruling class dominated the agricultural section of the economy. Through its compulsory exploitation of the poor peasantry, the ruling class was able to continue its self-reproduction. The common development of such economic entities usually led to a decline in productivity and living standards. England, however, avoided such a fate during the initial stage of its contemporary history. That is because its economy was no longer led by peasants and landlords. In their places, the controlling forces came from the "direct producers" in agricultural and nonagricultural sectors. On the one hand, such forces could get rid of compulsory exploitation economically; on the other hand, they could also avoid nonmarket means to obtain their subsistence directly. Therefore, the British economy (unique as it was in Europe) became a sharp contrast to that of China's Yangzi Delta: from the early seventeenth century to the 1850s, British productivity in agriculture rose, and the gross domestic product (GDP) per capita also grew. Britain finally advanced into its industrial revolution, following the Smithian path.

Pomeranz responded with his article, "Beyond the East-West Binary: Resituating Development Paths in the Eighteenth-Century World." He also drafted another long article to respond to Robert Brenner and Chris Isett.[12] Pomeranz thought that, in the first place, Huang's comments distorted his basic points and their supporting evidence. Second, the major points of Huang's comments also failed to realize that Pomeranz's 1990 book, in which the Yangzi Delta economy was described as the best system of the time, had received a lot of criticism, and Huang obviously ignored a lot of new developments in European and Asian studies. Third, Pomeranz pointed out that Huang himself barely had any data on the eighteenth century and generally relied on inference based on the time, while neglecting the differences between the eighteenth and nineteenth centuries and later regarding population growth, political stability, and geological crisis, as well as any new technological development. In his lengthy response to Robert Brenner and Chris Isett, Pomeranz held to his former conclusion: The great divergence between England and Jiangnan did not happen in the eighteenth century but in the following century; it did not happen on the farmland but came from underground and overseas.

---

12. Kenneth Pomeranz, "Beyond the East-West Binary: Resituating Development Paths in the Eighteenth-Century World," *Journal of Asian Studies* 2 (May 2002); Pomeranz, "Jiangnan in the Contemporary World Economic History: Comparison and Comprehensive Observation—In Response to Mr. Philip Huang," *Historical Studies*, no. 4 (2003); Pomeranz, "Reponses to Robert Brenner and Christopher Isett" (unpublished paper).

Jack Goldstone, in his paper "Missing the Forest for the Trees: A Comment on the Huang-Pomeranz-Brenner and Isett Exchange,"[13] agreed on the following points: During the eighteenth century, as late as 1750, the Chinese economy was equal to Europe's or even better, and its economic center was more advanced than that in England. As for the view of Philip C.C. Huang, Robert Brenner, and Chris Isett held that the high agricultural productivity in nineteenth-century England led to industrialization, while the low agricultural productivity in China caused stagnation and "content-type" development. Goldstone attempted to prove that such a view was wrong or at least had shortcomings. He compared England and Jiangnan by pairing up the two parties' population growth, living standards and poverty levels, productivity, and development trends. He emphasized that even if we had all the details in front of us, we still needed to understand the nature and core meaning of industrialization: the basic changes in technological innovation, represented by the steam engine's invention, caused the development in the mining industry. Of course, providing capital and market demand for manufactured goods was the necessary and basic condition. To truly understand the divergence between the British agricultural economy and other economies, one must pay great attention to factors such as technology and science, especially the role played by the steam engine, and not simply focus on agriculture and natural resources because scientific development in Europe was something lacking in other regions. The implication is that the outbreak of revolution could not be stopped even in a backward economy so long as certain conditions were present. It does not matter whether economic development is advanced or not.

Pomeranz's published works cover a wide range of topics, so his works also received more critiques from many other scholars. For example, Alan Macfarlane has two articles regarding the great divergence.[14] He deemed the differences between the two extremes of Europe and Asia to be much larger than Pomeranz's observations of the span of 200 years. They were not confined to economic and social factors only; factors such as politics, ideology, and culture should also be included. He compared the family demographic structures of India, England, Japan, and China, finding that China and England had huge differences. Such differences existed for many centuries, not only during those 200 years. He worried that people's overemphasis on the eighteenth century might prevent us from seeing the real differences.

---

13. Jack A. Goldstone, "Missing the Forest for the Trees: A Comment on the Huang-Pomeranz-Brenner and Isett Exchange" (unpublished paper, 2002).

14. Alan Macfarlane, "Reflections on 'The Great Divergence': Reliable Knowledge of the World" and "Reflections on 'The Great Divergence': Demographic and Social Structures." These two commentaries were presented at Tsinghua University of Beijing and Nankai University of Tianjin in August 2000. His comments on the family lives of different countries were challenged at the International Conference of Family History of China.

James Lee's major point was that there was no Malthusian distinction between China and the West regarding demographic history and pattern. Just like the Europeans, the Chinese followed their "fertility-driven" model through the "preventive checks" instead of a "death-driven" model through "positive checks." There has been a long tradition among the Chinese, one with a "collective restraint" that can be traced back from the ancient tradition of clan-controlled family planning to contemporary, state-controlled family planning. This has been Pomeranz's major supporting evidence for his explanation of demographic changes. Huang has his arguments on the phenomenon of infanticide (especially among female babies). He insisted that such a phenomenon resulted from poverty and the pressure of survival. The Qing dynasty in China was precisely the period in which population pressure and social commercialization were becoming increasingly dominant; thus, infanticide became one of the major signs of the social crisis of the time. Huang criticized his opponents for their demographic interpretations, arguing that they were actually trying to find a European counterpart in China. Lee and others responded to Huang's criticism with their article, "Positive Checks or Chinese Checks?"[15] The research of James Lee and Li Bozhong has shown that population pressure did not exist during the Qing dynasty. As the richest region in China, Jiangnan, during the early and middle Qing, actually had a little lower birth rate than the Ming and much lower than the national average of the time. The phenomenon of infanticide was recorded during the Song Dynasty, and it was not because of a hard-living environment but because it was a traditional means of birth control. As for Huang's misunderstanding of finding "a European counterpart in China," Lee made it clear by using the phrase "Chinese checks" to defend his original argument.

Arthur Wolf, in his paper, "Is There Evidence of Birth Control in Late Imperial China?" demonstrated his doubts about James Lee's research results and those of Zhao Zhongwei. His major evidence consisted of the data he collected between 1980 and 1981. He used these numbers to challenge his opponents' statistical basis of the low marriage and birth rates in late imperial China. Besides, Wolf believed that there should be some more reasonable explanations than his opponents' so-called planned birth control ("start late, stop early, long intervals" and "postpartum abortion"). He also insisted that the low rates of marriage and birth in imperial China were not the result of birth control but of poverty and the pressure of survival. He held that "most Chinese couples simply hoped the more sons they had, the better," and his studies conducted that there was actually "high fertility" in China. But Wolf may not have noticed while arguing his case that he had unintentionally proved James Lee's viewpoints. That is because Wolf's research objects lived in a true "fault period" where the old traditions were falling apart. At the same time, a new one

---

15. James Lee et al., "Positive Checks or Chinese Checks?" *Journal of Asian Studies* 2 (May 2002).

(state policy of birth control) had not been established, which means there was actually no collectively sponsored restraint on fertility policy at the time. On the contrary, there was collective encouragement for giving birth to more children. As a result, the birth rate during that period was high, without any effective control. No wonder Cameron Campbell and others hesitated quite a while about whether they needed to respond to Wolf's critique. Finally, in their paper, "Pre-transition Fertility in China,"[16] they replied to the three major points in Wolf's critique: the level of pre-transition fertility, the demographic model of reproduction, and the low marital birth rate. James Lee also gave a brief response with a short paper, "Fertility Control in the Past: A Reply to Arthur Wolf."[17] Besides insistence on the accuracy of his data and pointing out Wolf's misunderstanding and mistakes in interpreting the data, Lee also stressed that Chinese scholars and officials had already shown concern over China's population more than 2,000 years before. However, it is also important to note that there have always been different voices and practices through time, although traditional thought in China always promoted more sons in a family. It is not wise to speculate that the Chinese had always tried to have more babies and never worried about fertility control. We should point out here that the strong desire of Chinese peasants to have more children under the pressure of the state-sponsored birth-control policy today may help mislead people in their ideas about China's traditional view of fertility. Lee's painstaking effort is not unnecessary.

During the several rounds of exchanges, the tendency to argue for argument's sake also occurred from time to time. Distorting the other party's point of view and focusing on the other party's minor errors or details while neglecting the whole picture all showed that bias was present. There were also different interpretations of some of the data. For example, Pomeranz and Huang used Fang Xing's research results on the consumption of the Jiangnan farmers[18] to support their own positions. It is also true that both parties relied heavily on the research results of Li Bozhong. Still, they just used what they considered useful in supporting their views without looking at the development of Li's theory in its early and late periods. However, all these petty problems cannot tarnish this fruitful scholarly debate. The comparisons between Britain and Jiangnan, in particular, can be said to have successfully reviewed, summarized, and elevated the studies on this topic throughout academic circles.

---

16. Cameron D. Campbell et al., "Pre-transition Fertility in China: Old Wine in New Bottles," *Population and Development Review* (2002).

17. James Lee, "Fertility Control of the Past: A Reply to Arthur Wolf" (unpublished paper, 2002).

18. Fang Xing, "The Consumption of Farmers in the Yangzi Delta during the Qing Dynasty," *Chinese Economic History Studies*, no. 3 (1996).

3   The Change of Research Paradigm

The greatest obstacle confronting comparative studies in the new environment today is Western-centrism. Such Western-centrism is the reflection of the reality that scholarly circles in the world have long been dominated by the West. It divided the world into "the West and the rest," believing that the European experience of development represented the whole of humankind's evolution. All others from different regions in the world have been following the development track of the European model, and they will continue to follow this track in the future. In academic circles, European models have also been used to apply to the observations of social and economic developments in China and other regions in the world. This is decided by the reality that the contemporary social sciences are built upon the European experience regarding the scope of research and study systems, just as Frank described: "an observation always under the European light." Some scholars have opposed to this Eurocentrism in concept, but in theory and methodology, they still cannot take themselves off this old academic track. Suppose we fail to have a theoretical reevaluation and restructuring of research paradigms and systems. In that case, the idea of anti-Eurocentrism can only result in the form of lip service, or even worse, continued practice of the old way. But we must also realize that any breakthrough in the research paradigm will be very difficult.

According to Thomas Kuhn's definition, A paradigm consists of the basis and principle of research that is followed according to consensus by scholars in one or more disciplines. It may include the concept, theory, methods, standards of evaluation, value system, operational procedures, and ways of solving problems. It may be labeled as an academic platform guiding research activities and scientific exploration. Such a paradigm also has the directional effect that may help establish certain mindsets. Different paradigms can produce different research results for the same topic. Just as Huang commented, a "standard paradigm" has a subtle yet extensive effect on people, guiding them to what they should consider but, more important, what they should not think about. The standard paradigm also sets any debate's tone and starting point. But this universal "standard paradigm" may not be correct because it should evolve along with academic competition. It should be challenged, revised, and even replaced by new paradigms, hence the scientific revolution.[19] The California School made a lot of breakthroughs against traditional bias and hopefully will promote the birth of even more new paradigms. This is obvious in the following points.

---

19. Thomas S. Kuhn, *The Structure of Scientific Revolutions*, 3rd ed (University of Chicago Press, 1996).; Thomas S. Kuhn, "What Are Scientific Revolutions?" in *The Road Since Structure: Philosophical Essays, 1970–1993*, with an autobiographical interview, eds. James Conant and John Haugeland (University of Chicago Press, 2000).

4   Challenges to the Euro-Centered Theory

The Development of a Non-European Center in Economic Geography ·Fernand Braudel and other historians all agreed that Europe had established a world economic system, with Europe itself as the center. Immanuel Maurice Wallerstein stated that such a European-centered economic system spread from Europe and gradually included all other regions in the world. However, the California School and some other scholars insist that the world economic system was not promoted by the West.

Pomeranz once pointed out that the global economy originated from the mutual influence between the economies in different regions. It was not something that Europe forced upon the rest of the world. Most regions that were populous and commercially developed usually also had some geological restraints that Europe successfully avoided because of the favorable conditions in its New World colonies and its advantages in natural resources. By combining the comparative histories of economy and geology, he also attempted to evaluate the social, political, and cultural developments in several different regions. Andre Gunder Frank went even further, "From Karl Marx and Max Webber to Fernand Braudel and Immanuel Wallerstein, almost all theorists in history and sociology have distorted Europe's participation in the world economy and the key factors of economic development in Europe." He mercilessly overthrew his own old theory. Earlier, he had described capitalism as an exchange system with a "core-periphery" model20 in which underdeveloped nations were located on the periphery and relied heavily on the system's core, which is Western capitalism. As a result, they could not develop independently and were exploited by Western monopolies in their exchanges. After 1500, Western Europe moved first toward capitalism, making itself the world's economic center. This idea was greatly changed in his 1998 book, *Re-Orient: The Global Economy in the Asian Age.* The contemporary world was not promoted by Europe. Instead, it was shaped by a global economic system that had been running for quite a long time. The 300 years in which Europe began its rise was interpreted by Frank as the time of Asian hegemony. If there was indeed a center during that time, then it had to be China, whose development is closely linked to the global economy. By participating in the Asian trade, Europeans benefited greatly from the more productive and wealthier Asian economies.

Frank proposed a new "holistic" global view of world history. In his eyes, the evolution of world history was the shifting of the world's center and the exchange of positions between the center and periphery. In *Re-Orient*, his historical perspective was the inevitable extension of his own theory of a global system. It should be pointed out here that Frank's idea is actually based on the theories developed by Takeshi Hamashita and other scholars.[20] A group of scholars from Australia and Europe, digging into historical records in English, Dutch, Spanish, and Portuguese, has reevaluated nineteenth-century Southeast Asia's economic development. They concluded that people underestimated development in the region, and one of the major contributing factors was that the Chinese government did not pay much attention to foreign trade. Foreign trade records in the Chinese language are very limited, so Chinese overseas trade especially that conducted by individuals, has been greatly underestimated. At the same time, the eighteenth-century trade in Southeast Asia, led mainly by Chinese merchants, has also been underestimated.[21] All these research results coincided with the views of scholars of the California School, and at least one point cries out for the attention of Chinese scholars: dependence on neglected and limited Chinese sources will not enable us to comprehensively understand the international trade by Ming-Qing China and overseas Chinese.

5   Challenge to European-Centered Theory: Plural Centers Replacing the Monocenter

The theory that the non-European center helped promote the global economy is greatly limited by historical reality, at least in modern history. In contrast, the plural-center theory holds more in its effort to replace Euro-centered theories. Actually, it is also a more realistic challenge. The monocenter theory of Western centrism holds that the socioeconomic development of all the people and all the regions follows natural law and a path based on the European model. In other words, the European model has been proved true universally, and there is no exception among other people. Western scholars' "impact-response" model holds that regions beyond the Western world industrialized and modernized as a response to the challenge from the West. Such a view neglects the history and culture of such regions as a whole and their individual evolution tracks. Many theoretical models in Western Sinology are actually a repetition of the "universal model" that changes in non-Western societies are simply the realization of Western experience in these regions. General

---

20. Takeshi Hamashita, *Modern China's International Opportunity: Tribute Trade System and Modern East Asian Economic Circle* (China Social Sciences Press, 1999); "China's Absorption of Silver and Its Tribute Trade System," in *Asian Trade Circle and Japan's Industrialization*, ed. Takeshi Hamashita (Fujiwara Bookstore, 2001); Quan Hansheng, "American Silver and Overseas Trade," in *Modern China Economic History Forum* (Taipei: Daoxiang Press, 1996).

21. Some recent publications include L. Blussé, Zhuang Guotu, et al., *Batavian-Chinese and Chinese-Dutch Trade* (Guangxi People's Press, 1997); Adam Mckeown, "From Opium Farmer to Astronaut: A Global History of Diasporic Chinese Business," *Diaspora* (2002).

application of Western experience, theories, and research methods, without limitation and careful examination, is exactly the core of Western centrism.[22]

Our opposition to this Eurocentrism does not mean we cannot use European standards for comparison. Instead, we should expand such comparisons, especially using Chinese standards to observe and evaluate Europe in many different respects, thus forming a more comprehensive understanding. R. Bin Wong insisted that our effort in overcoming Eurocentrism should take the European experience "as a historical process instead of some abstract theoretical modes." If we take it as an abstract theoretical mode, it should have some universal value, not just the monist phenomenon in which non-Western regions "responded" to the impact of the West. However, as a real course of history, it will enrich historical content through comparative studies of complete societies with their cultures and histories. So pluralism should be the starting point of our comparative history studies.

The focus of the California School's scholars is that the realities of Chinese socioeconomic history should be applied to correct theories based on Eurocentrism. In modern times, the world's academic circles were generally led by Western scholars, while there was not much scholarly achievement in China. This is the result of the decline of the Chinese economy. According to the statistical calculations and theories of James Lee, Angus Madison, and Andre Gunder Frank, the Chinese population, throughout most of human history, was a little more than one-quarter of the world's total population. Regarding economic scale, China's GDP was 23.1 percent to 32.4 percent of the world's total from 1700 to 1820.[23] Before 1800, China had been the economic center of the world, with extraordinarily competitive capacity in the world market. Such development in China did not happen by itself but was due to close links with the outside world— its integration with economies in Southeast Asia had reached very high levels. Any neglect of this Chinese experience will lead to incomplete and biased theories. Since the Chinese economy before the nineteenth century occupied an unmatched position in the world's economic history, academic achievement commensurate with such a position should be produced so as to reevaluate the development of world socioeconomic history and to prove and correct the theories as well as the methods of social science based on the Western experience. There seems to be some continuity between neo-Confucianism and the California School in their theories. If Tu Weiming, Yu Ying-shih, and others

22. Li Bozhong, "Jiangnan Model and British Capitalism," *Historical Studies*, and "Beyond Sinology," *Horizon* (2002).

23. Angus Madison, *Chinese Economic Performance in the Long Run* (Xinhua Press, 1999).

have tried to explain that Confucian ideals were not barriers to capitalism in China, thus revising Max Weber's points,[24] then the California School has enriched and perfected the academic theories in the world by summing up the Chinese experience through its economic development.

The achievement in demographic studies by James Lee and Wang Feng stands out sharply. With eye-catching titles and fresh ideas, they promoted the most direct and fruitful challenges to Western-centered classical theory, the Malthusian theory of population, and supplied a replacement theory built on the Chinese experience. Based on the scope of their own concepts about population and society in the West, Malthus and his followers observed and interpreted what they saw in China and other regions beyond the West in world history. They believed that the population in those regions experienced unlimited growth. Such a passive process of population growth and decline inevitably led to poverty, and only Western Europeans could establish certain control mechanisms. As Adrian C. Hayes pointed out, Malthus's points relied heavily on descriptions by Western travelers and other scattered information sources, so there is no way he could understand, not to mention interpret, the Chinese experience.[25] The analysis done by Lee and Wang, however, insists that the collective culture in China helped to establish an automatic, internal balancing mechanism in population control, which was very different from that in Western Europe, and such a mechanism played an important role in avoiding food shortages, poverty, and a worsening living environment.

The emphasis on conducting research by putting Chinese history into the larger world spectrum will greatly highlight the importance and character of China, thus enriching the theoretical origins and academic content of our studies. Of course, the California School has no intention of building "Sinocentrism" or establishing a new academic system to rival the contemporary academic world. Instead, it is using the reasonable and scientific parts of the old system to improve those that are not reasonable.

---

24. In his famous book, *The Protestant Ethic and the Spirit of Capitalism* (Sichuan People's Press, 1986), Max Weber states that the Protestant ethic and the spirit of capitalism are compatible with each other and are mutually promoting, and this is not necessarily true in other religions and cultures. In his later works, he also mentioned the conflicts between Confucian ideas and capitalism. The neo-Confucian school, however, holds the opposite opinion. For example, *Religious Ethics and Modern China Merchants Spirit* (Lianjing Press, 1987); *Neo-Confucian Ethics and the Spirit of Enterprise* (Sanlian Press, 1989); *Religious Ethics and the Modernization of China* (Shangwu Press, 1991), and so on. After these publications, "Confucian capitalism" dominated the debate for quite a while.

25. Adrian C. Hayes, "Was Malthus Right about China?" *China Journal* 47 (January 2002).

6   Breakthrough in Research Paradigm: Innovative Methods in Comparative Studies

Based on their pluralist views, California School scholars, in terms of epistemology, abandoned logical positivism, which has been very popular in the United States since the 1950s and has become a major research method that derives predictive conclusions from general premises and initial conditions. People have always been trying to establish certain independent and universal values. Such efforts are inspiring, though hopeless or impossible.[26] With their new beliefs, California School scholars have started some very fruitful activities establishing new comparative study methods. In summary, the standards of universal values usually require some monist preconditions, such as inevitability and the uniqueness of historical developments; in contrast, California School scholars put a lot of emphasis on the inference of probability and examined accidental events and their impacts very carefully. To bypass the limits of retrospective analysis, that tie researchers to the inevitability of historical development and consequences, California School scholars adopted the methods of prospective analysis to help examine the diversity of historical development. To conquer the a priori confinement of Euro-centered standards, scholars of the California School adopted the research methods of comparative studies based on the respective experience of both Europe and Africa so that the two could mutually prove each other. Though far from perfect or even too delicate or biased, All these creative research methods have provided some new research tools and means for our studies, thus helping to build new perspectives with attractive results.

• *The Combination of Retrospective Analysis and Prospective Analysis*

Retrospective analysis is one of the major methods in historical studies, which traces back from the situation today to the past event to prove what actually happened is the inevitable prospect. On the other hand, the prospective analysis starts at a certain point in history and explores the possible prospects. Retrospective analysis, because we know the consequences already, often leads to predestination and teleology. In contrast, the prospective analysis will try to design certain possibilities of all kinds of changes under certain conditions and then observe the effects and changes of all the variables. As Charles Tilly pointed out, "If we assume we were back in 1750," we will never be able to predict modern industrialization

---

26. Evelyn Rawski holds that the decline of China's sugar and tea exports was caused by excessive competition; see "Competitive Markets as an Obstacle to Economic Development: China's Market in Transition," *Academic Sinica* (1990).

either in Europe or China's Jiangnan. The economic developments in China and Europe before the mid-eighteenth century were similar, with the same power behind them, and they may have had the same destination. The such prospective analysis demonstrates that European development during Adam Smith's time would not necessarily have evolved into nineteenth-century industrial capitalism. By applying prospective analysis, Li Bozhong's new work[27] presents a fresh view regarding a possible prospect of early industrialization in Jiangnan.

- *The Combination of Examinations Based on Both Inevitability and Contingency*

The development of human society as a very complicated process of history has all kinds of contingencies and accidents that would make late developments occur in new forms. What happened in history is not necessarily what would most possibly happen or should happen, nor is it even something inevitable. The sense of historical inevitability obscures many possibilities of certain specific historical moments in history. Therefore, comparative studies in history contribute a lot to people's understanding of the universal meaning of history, because they help discover similar historical moments that are consistent with expectations in the law of causality but with different outcomes, and contribute to the accumulation of historical phenomena in a much wider range. Such thinking by R. Bin Wong is exactly what is new about the California School. Observations by Wong, Li Bozhong, and Kenneth Pomeranz, all based on the development of human history, have demonstrated that the British model was not inexorable and the Industrial Revolution, to a certain degree, was accidental. Therefore, people's efforts to measure the economic developments in Jiangnan and other regions using the British model would lead them to the wrong conclusions.

- *Comparison and Examination with Each Other as a Subject: Using the European Experience to Evaluate Chinese History and Using the Chinese Experience to Evaluate European History*

This comparison of intersubjectivity helps create some new patterns of behavior and values. Such a research method was summarized and upgraded by R. Bin Wong. Wu Chengming called it "a two-track" system and also pointed out that such a method seems simple but not so in practice. Li Bozhong and Pomeranz conducted their studies comparing the Jiangnan model and the British model using this method of intersubjectivity. They achieved many innovative breakthroughs.

---

27. Li Bozhong, *Early Industrialization in Jiangnan, 1550–1850* (Social Science Academic Press, 2000).

Previous historians usually followed the European standards of economic development to query why the same phenomenon did not happen in China. They only focused on the differences but neglected the basic commonalities of the two. For example, Carlo M. Cipolla once pointed out, "It is already obvious to everyone that industrialization is fundamentally a sociocultural phenomenon rather than a purely technical phenomenon. People have noticed that those earliest industrialized nations all shared some similarities with England in terms of culture and society" (Frank, 47). Andre Gunder Frank first proposed that differences in culture and society between the East and the West were just a myth, though he did not discuss it in detail. However, research works by Pomeranz and others have helped prove such bold assumptions. For that reason, Frank enjoyed Cipolla's book and never tried to hide his feelings by enthusiastically cherishing it.[28]

We are not saying there is no difference between the East and the West. However, if we fail to find the similarities between them, we will not be able to identify what differences deserve more of our attention. Therefore, paying attention to finding common ground between the two has become the focal point of the comparative studies of the California School. From the perspective of economic history, there is no big difference between the Chinese economy and that in the West before British Industrialization, as both were based on Smith's economic growth model. R. Bin Wong once mentioned that there were indeed some differences between these two economies during the sixteenth to the eighteenth century, though they were not as great as those in the nineteenth century. If we just look at the nineteenth century, then we must notice that apparent differences indeed existed between the two during this time. But we should not allow such attention to these differences to affect our understanding of the earlier times. Economic levels and structures in China and Europe were similar to each other, but the political systems differed greatly. Wong considers it inappropriate to label these differences as being more advanced or backward. He even believes that political and economic organizations are relatively simpler and, therefore, easier to evolve into newer sets of relations. The developments in Europe and China are the results of their own historical evolution or, say, the results of creation from their own historical possibilities.[29] Built upon such innovative research results, comparative studies on the economic developments in the West and China have entered a brand new realm.

---

28. Andre Gunder Frank, "Review of The Great Divergence," *Journal of Asian Studies* 60, no. 1 (February 2001).
29. R. Bin Wong's speech and exchange at Tsinghua University's Chinese Economic History Research Center.

7   Methodological Breakthrough: Scientific History and Modern Technological Means

Scientific studies in history, especially economic history, mean the wide application of economic theory and method. The next step would be the social scientific transition of history or the penetration of all kinds of theories and methods adopted in the social sciences into historical studies. Next still is the reference to natural science methods. James Lee and others have started some very valuable experiments. Through cross-border cooperation in academic research, they have established large-scale data integrations by introducing new technologies like computer simulation and other technical means and achieved remarkable results in their comparative studies.

Scientific studies in history will make our research more precise and meticulous, and the introduction of new research methods will also lead to changes in analytical tools and research paths; some old consensuses will be reexamined, and some phenomena and fields that used to be unsolvable will have new hope while some new theoretical frameworks will be established. As James Lee once said, their large-scale data collection and analysis of human population will become a microscope for social scientific studies, which will change some old views that have been taken for granted and make it possible for some new understandings that were not accessible in the past.[30] Mathematical models as an analytical tool, though not suitable for direct application in analyses of history and reality, possess some of the most rigorous logic. They can help reduce the pitfalls and errors of other analytical methods. At the same time, existing mathematical models can also be used to derive some new results, discover some problems that are hard to find using other methods, seek the relations between some seemingly unrelated phenomena and structures, and thus derive some new results that can provide historical studies with more empirical proofs.

The California School has presented a lot of refreshing ideas, which are very different from the ones long held by mainstream scholars. Such new ideas force us to reexamine and further study those old conclusions and long-neglected biases. However, there are still some issues worth discussing, new research perspectives open for development, and new research methods and theories waiting for us to improve and perfect. That is because the comparison of economic development in the East and the West is indeed a huge and complex issue, and more in-depth investigations are called for.

---

30. From James Lee's lectures and exchanges, as a special visiting professor in the graduate studies department of China's Economic History Studies Center.

The differences between the societies in the East and the West, as well as their modern variations, have been a very important theme that has attracted numerous schools into the field. From Max Weber's idea about religious differences and the capitalist spirit to the opposing neo-Confucianism led by Tu Weiming, from the institutional change theory of the New Economic History School represented by Douglas North to Samuel Huntington's cultural differences and conflicts, we have seen many masters coming out one after another to join the debate. From assumption to analysis, from inference to proof by evidence, from Western-centered perspective to Eastern perspective, the range of our research is expanding, our research paradigms are repeatedly being challenged, and it is the California School that has promoted and furthered all these happenings. From their comparative studies on the development of socioeconomic structures, the California School scholars have creatively proposed that industrialization and the great divergence between China and the West are not the results of differences between two different cultures and systems. Instead, we should try to seek answers by looking into issues such as ecological constraints, industrial structures, and so on. Such efforts will lead our research works to a new realm and hopefully promote a revolution in new research paradigms.

However, our reevaluation of views and theories that have become consensus needs to build upon more solid and more challenging as well as more specific research, and purely ideological paradigm shifts can only turn out ambiguously. The successful challenges of the California School to the conventional paradigm come out of these scholars' hard work and academic reflection in each of their study fields. In this regard, James Lee's theoretical models built upon empirical analysis and R. Bin Wong's comparative study theory have all given us inspiration and encouragement. Similarly, Pomeranz works like a hard-working architect while Frank, with his unique personality, works more like a promoter of passion. Meanwhile, a paradigm shift is painful, like a phoenix rising from the ashes. Actually, the new exploration by the scholars of the California School is the result of their continuous reevaluation and dialectical negation of the discipline of international economic history as well as themselves. The revolution in the research paradigm is not something involving a few. It demands the collective efforts of all academic communities.

References

Blussé, L., Zhuang Guotu, et al., *Batavian-Chinese and Chinese-Dutch Trade*. Guangxi People's Press, 1997.

Campbell, Cameron D. et al. "Pre-transition Fertility in China: Old Wine in New Bottles." *Population and Development Review* (2002).

"Competitive Markets as an Obstacle to Economic Development: China's Market in Transition." *Academic Sinica* (1990).

Elvin, Mark. *The Pattern of the Chinese Past*. Stanford University Press, 1973: 27.

Fang, Xing. "The Consumption of Farmers in the Yangzi Delta during the Qing Dynasty." *Chinese Economic History Studies*, no. 3 (1996).

Frank, Andre Gunder. "Review of The Great Divergence." *Journal of Asian Studies* 60, no. 1 (February 2001).

Goody, Jack. "Falling Fortune of the Lands of the Rising Sun." *Times Higher Education Supplement*, no. 1460 (November 3, 2000).

Hamashita, Takeshi. *Modern China's International Opportunity: Tribute Trade System and Modern East Asian Economic Circle*. China Social Sciences Press, 1999.

———. *China's Absorption of Silver and Its Tribute Trade System, in Asian Trade Circle and Japan's Industrialization*. Fujiwara Bookstore, 2001.

Hayes, Adrian C. "Was Malthus Right about China?" *China Journal* 47 (January 2002).

Huang, Philip C.C. *Small Farmers' Family and the Rural Development in the Yangzi Delta: 1368–1988*. Beijing: Zhonghua Book Company, 1992.

———. "Development or Involution in Eighteenth-Century Britain and China." *Journal of Asian Studies* 2 (May 2002).

Kuhn, Thomas S. *The Structure of Scientific Revolutions*. 3d ed. University of Chicago Press, 1996

———. *What Are Scientific Revolutions? The Road Since Structure: Philosophical Essays, 1970–1993*. Edited by James Conant and John Haugeland. University of Chicago Press, 2000.

Lang, Graeme. "Geography as Destiny?" *Science* 288, no. 5468 (May 12, 2000).

Lee, James et al. "Positive Checks or Chinese Checks?" *Journal of Asian Studies* 2 (May 2002).

Li, Bozhong. *Early Industrialization in Jiangnan, 1550–1850* (Social Science Academic Press, 2000).

———. "The Formation of China's National Market, 1500–1850." Keynote address at the Eighth Annual World History Association International Congress, Canada, June 27, 1999.

———. "Jiangnan Model and British Capitalism, Historical Studies, and Beyond Sinology." *Horizon* (2002).

Mckeown, Adam. "From Opium Farmer to Astronaut: A Global History of Diasporic Chinese Business." *Diaspora* (2002).

Pomeranz, Kenneth. "Beyond the East-West Binary: Resituating Development Paths in the Eighteenth-Century World." *Journal of Asian Studies* 2 (May 2002).

Pomeranz. *The Making of a Hinterland: State, Society, and Economy in Inland North China* (University of California Press, 1993).

———. "Jiangnan in the Contemporary World Economic History: Comparison and Comprehensive Observation: In Response to Mr. Philip Huang." *Historical Studies*, no. 4 (2003).

Quan, Hansheng. *American Silver and Overseas Trade, in Modern China Economic History Forum*. Taipei: Daoxiang Press, 1996.

Vries, P.H.H. "Are Coal and Colonies Really Crucial? Kenneth Pomeranz and the Great Divergence." *Journal of World History* 12, no. 2 (Fall 2001).

Wu, Chengming. *New Thoughts on Sino-Western Comparative Studies, in China's Modernization: Market and Society*. Sanlian Press, 2001.

CHAPTER 8

The Role of Engineer-in-Chief and the Introduction of Foreign Hydraulic Dredging Technology and River Conservancy into China, 1890s–1930s*

This chapter discusses studies of the development of river conservancy in modern China and the role of engineers-in-chief in river improvement planning on rivers such as the Hai-ho (Haihe) and the Whangpoo (Huangpu). It discusses the introduction of foreign hydraulic dredging technology and management into two major Chinese ports. It then analyses the process by which two agencies of the Chinese government absorbed and adjusted this technology to suit local circumstances in the treaty ports of Tianjin and Shanghai beginning in the 1890s. Without prior experience in river conservancy, the conservancy boards adopted a range of foreign technologies. This allowed them to develop into major institutions that facilitated increasing trade flows between China and the rest of the world. Of particular significance in this process of technological change was the role of the expatriate engineers-in-chief who were employed as chief executive officers of both agencies. They were responsible for establishing the operations of the agencies, accommodating an increasing range of responsibilities such as financial and human resource

* Yi Wei, Long Denggao, and Pierre van der Eng, "The Role of Engineer-in-Chief and the Introduction of Foreign Hydraulic Dredging Technology and River Conservancy into China, 1890s–1930s," *Frontier of History in China* 15, no. 2 (2020): 34. Pierre van der Eng: Research School of Management, College of Business and Economics, The Australian National University, Canberra ACT 0200, Australia.

management, and training Chinese engineers and managers for senior positions until they were ready to replace the expatriate engineers-in-chief after the 1930s.

1 Introduction

Historical studies of technological change in China generally focus on the autonomous developments of science and technology in imperial China in the distant past. A prominent case is the multivolume work of Joseph Needham.[1] Alternatively, studies assess technological development in communist China after 1949.[2] Fewer studies dwell on the significant technological changes in late imperial China and until the 1940s. Perhaps this is because Needham found that scientific discovery had come to a halt in 16th-century imperial China. Technological applications of scientific results also halted and caused economic stagnation in China.[3] Another possible reason is that the period since the mid-19th century largely involved China adopting foreign technologies rather than generating and applying new technologies.

This perception is now changing. A range of scholarships has emerged over the past few decades. Many cases of the introduction of imported foreign technology—broadly defined as scientific knowledge embodied in equipment and organizational methods—during the 1850s–1940s have been studied in recent years: the telegraph,[4] the post office,[5] the customs service,[6] and the railways.[7] And for the 1880s–1940s, chapters in a recent book edited by Tsu and Elman discussed the introduction of other innovations.[8] Furthermore, more case studies have analyzed the assimilation of science and technology in the Chinese context. Together with Dan Asen's work on forensic sciences,[9] Annie Reinhardt's work on Steam Shipping,[10] Meng Yue's work on the Jiangnan Arsenal,[11] Chiang's work on social

---

1. Gregory Blue, "Joseph Needham: A Publication History," 90–132.

2. Chunjuan Nancy Wei and Darryl E. Brock, eds., *Mr. Science and Chairman Mao's Cultural Revolution: Science and Technology in Modern China*.

3. Justin Lin, "The Needham Puzzle: Why the Industrial Revolution Did Not Originate in China," 269–92.

4. Erik Baark, *Lightning Wires: The Telegraph and China's Technological Modernization, 1860–1890*; Wook Yoon, *Dashed Expectations: Limitations of the Telegraphic Service in the Late Qing*, 832–57.

5. Lane Jeremy Harris, *The Post Office and State Formation in Modern China*, 1896–1949.

6. Hans van de Ven, *Breaking with the Past: The Maritime Customs Service and the Global Origins of Modernity in China*.

7. Elisabeth Köll, *Railroads and the Transformation of China*.

8. Jing Tsu and Benjamin A. Elman, eds., *Science and Technology in Modern China, 1880s–1940s*, 7–8.

9. Daniel Asen, *Death in Beijing: Murder and Forensic Science in Republican China*.

10. Chih-Lung Lin, "Reinhardt, Anne, Navigating Semi-Colonialism: Shipping, Sovereignty, and Nation-Building in China, 1860–1937," 286–89.

11. Meng Yue, "Hybrid Science versus Modernity: The Practice of the Jiangnan Arsenal, 1864–1897," 13–52.

engineering,[12] and Prescott's work on Economic sciences,[13] these cases indicate that the success of imported technologies depended crucially on their adoption and adaptation to suit local circumstances in China.

This chapter discusses a further case of technological change and its organizational dimensions in China during this period. It analyses how foreign hydraulic technology was imported into Qing China and was adapted to suit local circumstances, particularly how hydraulic engineering technology was introduced for river conservancy. River conservancy is a complicated process. Multidisciplinary knowledge of hydraulics, hydrology, and soil geography is required. Hydraulics is a physical science requiring knowledge of fluids' static and dynamic behavior. Hydrology is the study of the interaction between water and the environment. Through testing, analysis, calculation, and simulation, it can predict the change and development of water quantity and quality and provide a scientific basis for developing and utilizing water resources, flood control, and environmental protection. Soil geography studies the spatial distribution and combination of soil and the relationship between its geographical environments. Dredging is the operation of removing material from one part of the water environment and relocating it to another, including winning material, deepening of water, environmental remediation, and civil engineering.

River conservancy technology is a body of knowledge containing technical ideas and solutions, information and data surveys, personal technical skills and expertise, machinery and equipment, etc. As a broad concept, technology transfer may take different forms according to one's motivations and desired outcomes. Technology transfer is the mechanism by which the accumulated knowledge developed by a specific entity is transferred wholly or partially to another, allowing the receiver to benefit from it. Technology transfer plays an important part in industrial development.[14] Workers employed by multinationals acquire knowledge of its superior technologies.[15] Previous studies have examined the implications of technology transfer, identifying the managerial capabilities required to absorb new technology. Particular attention has been paid to intermediary roles in bridging the "managerial gap," the changing nature and scope of services offered by consultants, and the contributions they can make.[16]

Previous studies showed that successive imperial governments accumulated considerable experience with hydraulic technology and the management of hydraulic structures before

12. Yung-Chen Chiang, *Social Engineering and the Social Sciences in China, 1919–1949.*

13. Edward C. Prescott, "The Transformation of Macroeconomic Policy and Research," 3–20.

14. Paiboon Thammarutwasik, "The Food Research Centre—Assisting Small and Medium Sized Industry," in *Case Studies in Food Product Development*, 53–66.

15. Amy Jocelyn Glass and Kamal Saggi, "Multinational Firms and Technology Transfer," 495–513.

16. John Bessant and Howard Rush, "Building Bridges for Innovation: The Role of Consultants in Technology Transfer," 97.

the 16th century.[17] Examples include the construction of the Grand Canal since at least the 6th century, as well as the use of embankments and dams to mitigate damaging river floods. However, the water flows of China's many rivers are very substantial. Their high silt loads resulted in large sediment deposits that caused floods and altered river flows. By the late 19th century, Qing government officials faced major hydraulic issues that they were powerless to resolve using established technology and management.[18] For example, they had no adequate response to the massive 1851–1855 flood of the Yellow River (Huang-he 黄河) in Northern China. Inaction had devastating consequences when the Yellow River flooded again in 1887–1888.

Foreign observers of Chinese hydraulic technology, such as a visiting Dutch civil engineer,[19] were unimpressed by its unscientific and often improvised nature. Western knowledge and technological transfer may date as early as the self-strengthening movement that began in 1861. The various arsenals that were set up focused on supplying weapons for a modern Chinese army, such as cannons, naval vessels, etc., as well as on translating a range of Western knowledge. The guiding philosophy for the movement was to use Western learning while retaining Chinese learning as the basis of the state. To some extent, Western knowledge systems needed to be embraced. Meng Yue's notion of hybrid science as applied to the practice of the Jiangnan Arsenal is an example.[20]

In principle, there was fertile ground in China during the late 19th century for the adoption of foreign methods of scientific engineering to improve China's waterways. However, river conservancy is not controlled by any individual local party. River conservancy was not a duty that the foreign concession areas in the treaty ports could take on. Furthermore, budget shortages made it difficult to engage foreign engineers and use foreign hydraulic technology on a large scale.[21] Consequently, the first breakthroughs in introducing this technology occurred at the interface of the foreign presence and imperial China. In the treaty ports of Tianjin and Shanghai, more specifically, it took the form of river conservancy from the 1890s to the 1930s.

Once the two river conservancy organizations were built, expatriate engineers-in-chief appointed by the two conservancy agencies were crucial to the application and adaptation of the technology. All board members, such as the imperial circuit intendant (*daotai* 道台) and the commissioner of customs, were part-time employees of the conservancy organizations. Therefore, the engineer-in-chief, the highest level full-time employee, was in charge of

---

17. David N. Keightley, "'Benefit of Water': The Approach of Joseph Needham," 367–71.
18. Kenneth Pomeranz, *The Making of a Hinterland*.
19. F. J. Blom, "Hydraulic Engineering in China," 1000–1010.
20. Meng, "Hybrid Science versus Modernity," 13–52.
21. Edward T. Lockwood, "Floods and Flood Prevention in China," 164–68.

overall operations and was responsible for all aspects of the organization's operation, including human resources, financial audits, engineering technology, public announcements, and all the day-to-day work. Meanwhile, the Chief Engineers are the actual leaders, who were effectively the CEOs of two important public agencies that facilitated the navigation and trade of two of China's key river ports. They connected both downstream to the Sea of China and beyond and upstream to the hinterlands, including the capital city Beijing. The agencies sought to tap the expertise of the expatriate engineers—their abilities to organize, manage, expand and diversify the ventures, as well as their contribution to the training of Chinese engineers and managers to replace expatriate staff. This process took place during a period of considerable political change in China, which enhanced the uncertainties with which the engineers-in-chief had to contend.

This chapter closes a gap in the existing literature on dredging and river conservancy histories of China, using a number of unpublished English archival documents from both the Hai-Ho Conservancy Commission (Haihe gongchengju 海河工程局, hereafter HHC) and the Whangpoo Conservancy Board (Junpu Ju 浚浦局, hereafter WCB). Historical studies covered aspects of river conservancy agencies in pre-war China[22] but in relation to state-building, urban planning, and environmental change, not in the context of the introduction of new technology and its adaptation to the Chinese context. The paper's second section explains the emergence of the two conservancy agencies. The third section details their governance, structure, and finance. The fourth section explains the multifaceted role of the engineers-in-chief, their pivotal role in the transfer and adaptation of relevant river conservancy technologies, and how this benefited the development of the Tianjin and Shanghai ports. The last section concludes.

2   China's Treaty Ports and Their Water-Dependent Development

Since the mid-19th century, foreign concessions in the treaty ports of China grew and became important conduits for China's foreign trade.[23] Foreign trading and shipping companies

---

22. See David A. Pietz, *Engineering the State: The Huai River and Reconstruction in Nationalist China, 1927–1937*; "Controlling the Waters in Twentieth-Century China: The Nationalist State and the Huai River," in *A History of Water: Series I, Volume 1: Water Control and River Biographies*, eds. Terje Tvedt and Eva Jakobsson, 92–119; Shirley Ye, "Corrupted Infrastructure: Imperialism and Environmental Sovereignty in Shanghai, 1873–1911," 428–56; "River Conservancy and State-Building in Treaty Port China," in *Treaty Ports in Modern China: Law, Land and Power*, eds. Robert Bickers and Isabella Jackson, 121–38; Wang Ai, *City of the River: The Hai-Ho and the Construction of Tianjin, 1897–1948*.

23. For the emergence and governance of the treaty ports in China, see Bickers and Jackson, eds., *Treaty Ports in Modern China*; on the role of foreign concessions and foreigners in these treaty ports, see Robert Nield, *China's Foreign Places: The Foreign Presence in China in the Treaty Port Era, 1840–1943*.

operating in these concession areas facilitated China's increasing trade relations with the rest of the world. As part of the "Self-Strengthening" (*ziqiang* 自强) or "Westernization Movement" (*Xihua yundong* 西化运动), the imperial Qing government introduced new agencies in attempt to defuse domestic opposition, resolve its role in Chinese society, and accommodate the interests of foreign powers. Examples include China's Imperial Maritime Customs Service in 1861 and the Post Office in 1896. However, the Qing government had little experience with the services that these new agencies were expected to provide or how to establish, structure, manage and grow them. For these purposes, it contracted experienced foreign expatriates to substitute them in due time with suitably trained and experienced Chinese professionals.

Expatriates employed at these Chinese agencies faced uncertainties, particularly in relation to political change in the country. Various forms of resistance against the Qing Dynasty took place in different parts of China, especially after the 1900 Boxer Rebellion. The Qing Dynasty disintegrated and made way in 1912 for the new central government of the Republic of China. A short period with high hopes for accelerating development was quashed when the civil war spread after 1916. Warfare did not directly involve the ports of Tianjin and Shanghai, but it occasionally affected the hinterlands and China's foreign trade relations.

During the 19th century, the establishment and development of several treaty ports facilitated China's increasing foreign trade and economic activity in the port cities and their hinterlands. Several ports were located upriver, including Shanghai (a treaty port in 1842) and Tianjin (a treaty port in 1861). Chinese rivers were navigable for small, traditional Chinese vessels with shallow drafts. However, foreign shipping companies operated increasingly large steamships with deeper drafts, which faced difficulties navigating the ports. In addition, siltation problems increased in the river deltas.

By the late 19th century, the rivers leading to the ports of Tianjin and Shanghai needed conservancy services to improve navigability. River conservancy was not a duty that the foreign concession areas in the treaty ports could take on. International agreements about the treaty ports and the concession areas left the management of rivers under Chinese authority. Requests from the boards of foreign concessions led the Qing government to consider the silting problems and also the implementation of semi-autonomous river conservancy boards. The foreign communities in both cities were keen to expedite the search for solutions. For example, in 1875, the Shanghai consulates commissioned a report on the underwater sandbar at Wusong that affected navigation of the Whangpoo River to Shanghai.

However, Chinese authorities faced various other issues that demanded their attention. As mentioned, they could not respond to the Yellow River's disastrous flooding during

1851–1855. The river's changed course required them to suspend the important Grand Canal and divert grain tax shipments to Beijing via the East China Sea and the port of Tianjin. Accessibility to upstream Tianjin via the Hai-ho River (now Hai-he 海河)— then the main gateway to Beijing—became crucial to the Qing government. Consequently, resolving navigation problems associated with the Taku (now Dagu 大沽) sandbar at the mouth of the river became urgent.

These issues, as well as the lack of success with the recommended dredging of the Wusong sandbar in 1883 and the increasing requirement to accommodate steamships with deeper drafts in China's rivers, all pointed to the need to accommodate foreign methodologies of studying hydraulic issues and designing solutions, and implementing foreign methods of hydraulic civil engineering. More specifically, in addition to investment in machinery for river dredging, it became necessary to use a modern scientific approach to study water flows and siltation patterns in China's rivers to identify the need for dredging and the construction of canals to bypass winding or shallow river sections. At the same time, increasing settlement in river and port cities required measures to control or prevent flooding of settled urban areas.

One solution was to send young Chinese to universities in the United States and Europe to study hydrology and hydraulic civil engineering. But it would take years for that to yield results, as candidates had to study relevant foreign languages, qualify for university education, graduate and accumulate relevant professional experience before they could assume civil engineering positions in China. Another solution was to engage expatriate hydraulic civil engineers and emulate the foreign institutions that dealt with issues of river conservancy.

The Qing government did both. For example, it dispatched Chinese students to the United States to study civil engineering.[24] But for more immediate absorption of foreign hydraulic technology, the Qing government established several conservancy boards. The main ones were the Hai-Ho Conservancy Commission, established in 1897 in Tianjin, and the Whangpoo Conservancy Board, established in 1905 in Shanghai. Other conservancy boards were established later, for example, the Huai River, which is part of the Yangtze River delta, the Liao River in Northeast China, and the Guangdong Conservancy Board in the Pearl River delta. Port authorities in other coastal cities, such as Zhifu (now Yantai), adopted similar roles.

A reason for the Qing government to attach importance to HHC and commit to improving navigation in the Hai-ho River was that both were mentioned in the 1901 international protocol (*Final Protocol for the Settlement of the Disturbances of 1900*, or *Boxer Protocol*), between the international powers and the Qing government. The protocol

---

24. Stacey Bieler, *"Patriots" or "Traitors"?: A History of American-Educated Chinese Students.*

amended the several treaties of trade and navigation China had concluded with foreign countries during the 19th century.[25] It specified the new commitments that the Qing government had agreed to as compensation for the consequences of the Boxer Rebellion.

Article 11 of this 1901 protocol specified that the Qing government agreed "to co-operate in the amelioration of the course of the rivers Peiho [Hai-ho/Hai-he] and Whangpoo [Huangpu]."[26] It noted the resumption of work in Tianjin, and for the Whangpoo River, it provided for the 'creation of a "River Board, charged with the management and control of the work of straightening the Whangpoo and improving the course of that river."[27] The agreement specified the composition of board membership as including representatives of the Chinese government and representatives of foreign traders operating in Shanghai. It set the board's annual budget at 460,000 Haikwan taels during the first 20 years, to be supplied in equal parts by the Chinese government and foreign interests. An appendix specified that the latter would take a range of forms, but in essence, taxes on the value of all goods passing through or landing along the Whangpoo River. Further negotiations led to a 1905 multilateral agreement about the WCB.[28] Article 9 stipulated that the Qing government would pay the full expense of the board's activity without levying additional taxes on merchandise or shipping but by using its revenues from the imports and sale of opium.

The 1901 protocol and the 1905 agreement established the basic foundations for the WCB: its purpose, governance structure, and finance. Some of its aspects were also applied to the HHC. In both cases, the implementation and further development of the agencies took time. In the first instance, the conservancy issues in both rivers required further research and close consideration of the most appropriate technology, but later because both agencies increasingly had to deal with a wider range of conservancy issues beyond dredging.

3   Experiences with Organizational Development and Revolution

One aspect of change over time concerned the governance structure of both agencies. The first HHC functionaries were appointed in 1897. Tianjin was the Northern base of the "Westernization Movement." Two companies associated with the movement, the China Merchants Steam Navigation Company and the Chinese Engineering and Mining

---

25. Charles I. Bevans, *Treaties and Other International Agreements of the United States of America 1776–1949: Volume 1, Multilateral 1776–1917*, 302–9.

26. Ibid., 324–28.

27. Ibid.

28. Ibid., 446–49.

Company, were located there and had a vested interest in the dredging of the Hai-ho River. The commission's supervisory board comprised the imperial circuit intendant (*daotai* 道台), the Commissioner of Customs, and two officials nominated by Wang Wenshao 王文韶 (1830–1908), the Viceroy of Zhili province (*zhili zongdu* 直隶总督), as the representatives of the two Chinese companies, as well as the Commissioner of Chinese Imperial Maritime Customs in Tianjin, and representatives of foreign merchants, foreign concessions, and the general Chamber of Commerce. Although exemplary for stakeholder engagement, the board hardly ever met, and supervision was initially in the hands of the imperial circuit intendant, the Senior Consul, and the Commissioner of Customs.[29] All activity in terms of organizing and building up the HHC and studying and resolving relevant hydraulic issues was left to an expatriate engineer-in-chief.

WCB initially had a similar structure, where the imperial circuit intendant of Shanghai shared supervision with the Commissioner of Customs in Shanghai, with one Assistant Commissioner. The supervisors left the day-to-day administration and engineering activities here to an expatriate Engineer-in-Chief. In both cases, the Engineer-in-Chief had considerable autonomy and discretion. The first activities of the engineers-in-chief focused on the resolving the Taku and Wusong sandbars in the Hai-ho and Whangpoo rivers, respectively. However, they soon identified a range of related issues that the HHC and WCB would have to study and address, such as other silt deposits, straightening of the river through canals, reinforcing embankments, and flood prevention.

Missing from the initial structure was a mechanism for stakeholder consultation. This changed in 1908 for HHC with the establishment of a Consultative Board with representatives of the foreign concessions in Tianjin. Following the establishment of the Republic of China in 1912, the structure of the WCB was changed. Both agencies were placed under the Ministry of Foreign Affairs of the central government and later under the combined responsibility of the Ministry of Foreign Affairs and the Ministry of Finance. A new 1912 international agreement reformed the financing of the WCB and established a Consultative Board, with representatives of the five nations "having the largest tonnage entering and clearing at Shanghai" and one from the Chinese Chamber of Commerce.[30]

Figure 7 shows the changes. In essence, representatives of the foreign concessions in Tianjin and Shanghai were given formal consultative roles. This served the purpose of mobilizing stakeholder interest and reaching a consensus on river regulation and navigation issues. The Chinese officials retained their supervisory roles, and the engineers-in-chief

---

29. HHC Board, *Hai-Ho Conservancy Board 1898–1919: A Resumé of Conservancy Operations on the Hai-Ho and Taku Bar*, 9.

30. Bevans, *Treaties and Other International Agreements of the United States of America 1776–1949: Volume 1*, 879–82.

performed their executive roles. As the supervisors and the members of the consultative board did not generally work in the field, the engineers-in-chief retained considerable discretion in administration and engineering.

The constitutions of both agencies provided for regular meetings of the whole board. The WCB board started meeting in 1912 and met 691 times until 1949, an average of 19 times per year, although there were no meetings during the Japanese occupation period 1937–45.[31] The HHC board met 442 times during 1902–45, an average of 10 meetings per year, including from 1937–45. Most WCB board meetings took place during 1912–32. The minutes of the WCB board meetings capture discussions about the planning, scheduling, and financing of dredging projects, as the consultative boards had to agree on all major issues relating to dredging, financial control, and engineering technology. Changes in personnel were also announced at board meetings.

As mentioned, a key change in 1912 was the financing of WCB activities. Under the 1901 protocol, the Qing government would provide 460,000 taels over 20 years. While sufficient for initial work on the Wusong sandbar, this amount was insufficient to cover the costs of additional conservancy work along the Whangpoo River. The initial two main projects were the construction of the Wusong diversion dam and what later became known as the Astraea Channel at Gaoqiao to facilitate steamship passage. In order to finance the 7.2 million tael construction cost, the WCB negotiated borrowing additional funds from the government-owned Hupu Bank, expecting to repay the loan from the annual government subvention. However, the government of the new Republic of China in 1912 reneged on the annual funding of the WCB, which was then unable to repay the loan. Following repeated negotiations with the new government and the bank, the loan was written off. Construction was still incomplete, and the WCB needed further funding. The 1912 agreement arranged for an additional conservancy charge of 3% on top of regular customs duties and of 1.5% ad valorem on duty-free goods, both to be levied by the customs service. This allowed the WCB to borrow funds from the Deutsch-Asiatische Bank to complete the Wusong project.

During the following years, China's foreign trade increased significantly, and Shanghai became a major conduit for it. Total customs tariff revenues in Shanghai increased from 22 million in 1922 to 125 million taels in 1931. That year, Shanghai accounted for 47% of China's foreign trade and 51% of its customs revenue.[32] Figure 8 shows that by the late-

---

31. Board Meeting Minutes (1912–1950), WCB vols. 25–36.

32. Yu-Kwei Cheng, *Foreign Trade and Industrial Development of China: An Historical and Integrated Analysis through 1948.*

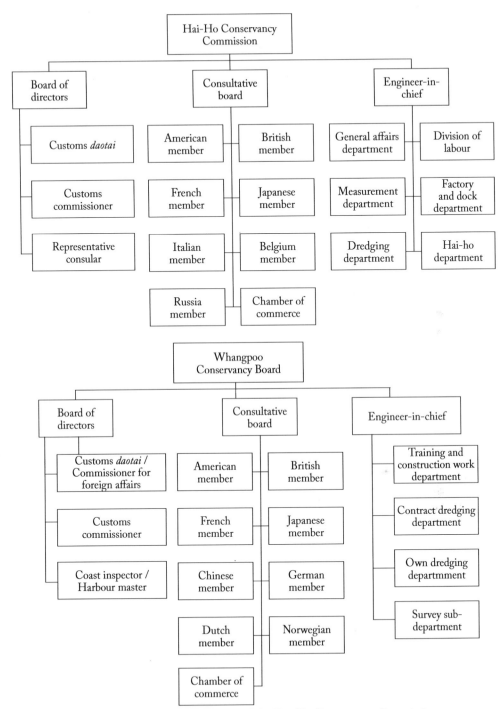

Figure 7 Governance Structures of the Hai-Ho Conservancy Commission
and the Whangpoo Conservancy Board, ca. 1920

Sources: WCB Engineer-in-Chief Quarterly Reports (1912).

1920s, the average annual WCB income was about 1.1 million taels, which allowed it to take on new conservancy initiatives along the Whangpoo River.

In the case of the HHC, Viceroy Wang Wenshao allocated 100,000 taels. In addition, the British representative in Tianjin guaranteed a public loan of 150,000 taels to finance the initial dredging work. Repayment would be with revenues of a levy of 0.5% ad valorem on all imports and exports. After the Boxer Rebellion, the local Chinese government allocated 250,000 taels to the HHC. The 1901 international protocol codified this allocation, specifying that the Qing government would allocate 60,000 taels per year to the work of the HHC for recurrent expenses.[33] These funds were insufficient to support the main project, comprising remedial measures to deal with the Taku sandbar through permanent dredging, the closing of channels and creeks so that the main river would take more of the flood tide, widening the bends in the river, and straightening the river where possible to enhance navigability. For that reason, the HHC issued its first bond in 1905. Seven other bond issues followed before 1935. Also, in 1905, the Qing government agreed to levy a surtax on the regular customs duties to guarantee the bond issues and raise additional funds.[34] This practice was continued after 1912.

Figure 8 shows that the HHC budget increased modestly from 1900 to1904. By the standards of the time, the annual incomes of both agencies indicate that they were very sizeable ventures by the late-1920s. By the early 1930s, the budgets of the HHC and the WCB diverged. One reason is that the Republic of China moved the government seat to Nanjing in 1928, and banks and businesses followed political power to Nanjing and Shanghai. Another reason is that Shanghai was the bigger of the two ports. Its trade value increased when the 1930–1934 depreciation of China's silver currency improved the international competitiveness of Chinese products, and the value of exports and surtax revenues increased.

Cooperation among dredging stakeholders involves many countries, organizations and individuals. The main action groups involved in the institution include the Chinese central government and local government, the consulates of various countries, the modern customs, the concession and its municipal affairs, the foreign merchant ships, and the citizens of the concession. Dredging requires hydrological surveys, technical schemes, and complex dredging equipment and technical ability. Because this knowledge was decentralized, even if China's governments had a monopoly on one resource, they were forced to utilize foreign

33. Bevans, *Treaties and Other International Agreements of the United States of America 1776–1949: Volume 1*, 308.

34. Long Denggao et al., "Innovative Financing Mode of Modern Public Interest Organizations: Bond Issue of the Hai-Ho Conservancy Commission," 112–23.

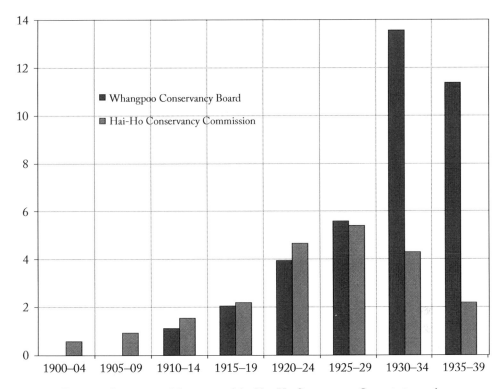

Figure 8 Quinquennial Revenues of the Hai-Ho Conservancy Commission and
the Whangpoo Conservancy Board, 1900–1939 (million Haikwang taels)

Notes: Revenues are in current prices. For the Hai-Ho Conservancy Commission, they include
revenues from the foreign trade surtax, government contributions, and income from landfill. For
the Whangpoo Conservancy Board, they only include monthly revenues from the foreign trade
surtax. The currency denominations are converted to Haikwan taels or their silver equivalent after
the currency reform of November 1935.

Sources: HHC Annual reports (1910–1940); WCB Engineer-in-Chief quarterly reports (1912–40);
exchange rates from Hsiao* and Young.†

---

* Hsiao, Liang-lin, *China's Foreign Trade Statistics, 1864–1949*, 190–196.
† Arthur N. Young, *China's Wartime Finance and Inflation, 1937–1945*, 360–361.

resource management professionals to some extent. This created space for the emergence of a collaborative mode of governance.

At an earlier stage, cooperation between "Chinese government officials and foreign involved organizations" was a remarkable institutional innovation. From the perspective of the management mode, the senior management personnel is appointed by the Chinese government. To a greater extent, the resources of various interests of China and foreign countries were integrated. It was an independent institution formed by promoting foreign merchants and the strong support and cooperation of foreign consulates, modern customs, concessions, and other foreign forces. From the perspective of the organization, it was a Chinese government organ. To maintain China's national sovereignty, the two conservancy organizations were run by officials appointed by the Chinese government. This system was like a flash in the pan, failing after just a few short years. The high costs and technical threshold of dredging utilities continue to carry on, so establishing a more effective cooperation mechanism is imperative.

Chinese and foreign stakeholders began to explore a new model of collaborative governance, and the two organizations gradually changed to the model of a "public interest organization," which is a non-governmental non-profit and independently operated professional dredging institution under the approval of the central government of China and jointly established by many governments and stakeholders. The decision-making layer *had* both the board of directors and the board of consultants. Two organizations also had "foreign" engineers-in-chief in charge of the overall operation of the organization and the full support of the Chinese and foreign governments and businesses. Moreover, the two conservancy boards had the autonomous right of income and control, establishing their financial independence and independent property rights.

4   The Engineers-in-Chief: Their Multifaceted and Pivotal Roles

Until the 1930s, the HHC and the WCB employed several expatriates, especially hydraulic and structural engineers, to design and execute technical solutions affecting the navigation of the two rivers. For example, in 1909, the WCB engineer-in-chief was assisted by a range of expatriates, including six engineers, three surveyors, and twenty work supervisors.[35] It took longer to build up the smaller HHC, where in 1912, the engineer-in-chief was

---

35. *The Directory and Chronicle for China, Japan, Corea, Indo-China, Straits Settlements, Malay States, Siam, Netherlands India, Borneo, the Philippines, Etc.*, 847.

assisted by five expatriates; two engineers, a dredging manager, a "raking manager,"[36] and a works manager.[37]

The high cost of the initial employment of expatriates was justified because there were no qualified Chinese engineers with comparable experience in managing and growing such agencies. Chinese employees were initially mainly doing manual work as fascine workers, sailors on river vessels, carpenters, coolies, launch crews, sampan men, and watchmen. From the outset, the aim of the Chinese government was for Chinese employees of the agencies to learn from expatriate staff before replacing them with trained and skilled but lower-wage Chinese engineers.

The key expatriate position was that of the engineer-in-chief. Despite the title of the position, the chief engineers took responsibility for hydro-engineering and other operations, including appointments to key supporting positions, structuring the ventures as they increased their operations, and financial management. For all intents and purposes, they were expatriate CEOs answerable to the boards of both agencies.

As is generally the case with contracted expatriate employees, there was a succession of expatriate engineers-in-chief before the appointment of the first Chinese engineer-in-chief. At the HHC:

- 1898–1904, Albert de Linde (Denmark)
- 1905–9, Abel Gaston Guïotton (France)
- 1909–13, Johannes Cornelis Vliegenthart (Netherlands)
- 1913–27, Tommaso Pincione (Italy)
- 1928–34, Jean A. Hardel (France)
- 1935–38, Poul E. Müller (Denmark)
- 1938–48, Alfred Tritthart(Austria)
- And at the WCB:
- 1906–10, Johannis de Rijke (Netherlands)
- 1912–28, August Werner Hugo von Heidenstam (Sweden)
- 1928–37, Herbert Chatley (UK)

In 1937 the WCB was the first of the two agencies to appoint a Chinese engineer-in-chief, Cho Pin Hsueh (Xue Zhuobin 薛卓斌).

---

36. The appointment of the "raking manager" was related to the solution for the Taku sandbar, which required "raking" before dredging. See De Linde, *Report on the Taku Bar Raking Scheme.*

37. *The Directory and Chronicle for China, Japan, Corea, Indo-China, Straits Settlements, Malay States, Siam, Netherlands India, Borneo, the Philippines, Etc.,* 774.

In principle, the boards of the two agencies selected the engineers-in-chief for their technical expertise, particularly in hydraulics, structural engineering, and dredging technology, but also for their experience with managing and operating comparable agencies, particularly their familiarity with ways of organizing employment practices, delegations of responsibilities and reporting, as well as supervising financial management. Their employment was therefore intended to bring broader perspectives on the functional role of the two agencies. Some were engineers at one of the agencies who were internally promoted to the position of engineer-in-chief when it became available. For example, Vliegenthart had been an engineer with the HHC since 1901 and was promoted in 1910; Guïotton had been an HHC engineer since 1902, and Pincione had been one since 1909. In Shanghai, Chatley had been Von Heidenstam's deputy until his promotion in 1928.

While the expatriate engineers-in-chief were responsible to their respective boards and were restricted in their activities by available finance and manpower, each enjoyed a high degree of autonomy in how they carried out their professional responsibilities. Of particular significance was their ability to combine theory and practice to offer advanced and scientific approaches to the governance of the Hai-ho and Whangpoo rivers.

Most had extensive experience in hydraulic engineering. For example, De Rijke worked as an expatriate hydraulic engineer with the Department of Public Works in Japan from 1873 to1903.[38] By contrast, De Linde was a general engineer who had worked in Tianjin since 1888 and had been involved in railway construction.[39] However, De Linde traveled to China and studied the 1887–88 Yellow River flood disaster from 1889 to 1890, particularly how the flood affected the Tianjin port and Hai-ho River navigation.[40] Hence, although not a specialist, he was familiar with scientific hydraulics when appointed in 1898. He also understood the shortcomings of traditional Chinese hydraulic solutions. For example, he reflected on a mistake in China's traditional solution to managing the Yongding River 永定河 Southwest of Beijing, a major tributary of the Hai-ho River:

> The best way to govern the rushing rivers is to build a wide and large embankment. It is believed that this can accommodate a sufficient amount of water. The Yongding River began to expand from the Lugou Bridge and even from the riverbed three miles downstream,

---

38. During the years from 1872 to 1903, eleven Dutch civil engineers came to Japan, and attained great achievement in the fields of investigation, planning and execution of public works. Johannis De Rijke, who stayed in Japan for almost 30 years, from September 1873 to June 1903, played a very large part in the development of Hydraulic Engineeringin Japan. Yoshiyuki Kamibayashi, "The Background of GA. Escher, Hollander Engineer Who Supported J. de Rijke for 40 Years," in *Doboku-shikenkyūdai*, 399–406.

39. Povl Vinding, "Albert de Linde," in *Dansk Biografisk Leksikon*, 3rd ed.

40. Albert De Linde, *Report of the Hai-Ho River Improvement and the Rivers of Chihli*.

causing a rapid drop in flow rate, which inevitably forms sediments and shoals. Originally, it was hoped to reduce the resistance of the water flow, but the direct consequence of the river's excessive width is the elevation of the riverbed.[41]

5   Comprehensive River Conservancy Solutions and Modern Dredging

For both the Hai-ho and the Whangpoo rivers, the first task of the engineers-in-chief was to focus on resolving the sandbar problem: the Taku sandbar in the Hai-ho River and the Wusong sandbar in the Whangpoo River. De Linde and De Rijke did not start from zero, as both had previously studied the issues before the establishment of the conservancy agencies. Their reports on how to tackle sandbars are the earliest examples of the application of foreign hydraulic technology. Linde (for the Taku bar) and De Rijke (for the Wusong bar) had to expand on their initial reports and recommendations and turn them into much more comprehensive plans. In the process, they added new structural features to the initial dredging plans to influence or divert the river flows and improve navigability. Consequently, the plans were based on comprehensive surveys of water flows and siltation patterns and close consideration of solutions, yielding integrated solutions.

In Tianjin, there had been growing awareness in the late-19th century of the increasing problems that the Taku sandbank caused for navigation on the Hai-ho River and their relation to the earlier Yellow River floods. Already in 1890, De Linde had submitted the first report.[42] In 1895, the Tianjin Chamber of Commerce, together with the Commissioner of Customs in Tianjin, Gustav von Detring, commissioned De Linde to provide further advice on possible ways to improve the navigability of the Hai-ho River.[43] His 1896 report was based on a study of the sediment samples, water flows, and sedimentation patterns in the Hai-ho, particularly near the Taku sandbar, taking into account hydrology, geology, waves, tides, and coastal flows.[44] Apart from implementing engineering works to straighten some of the bends in the river and dam some tributaries, he proposed raking the sandbar to allow the water flow to carry most of the sediment out to sea. De Linde's report was comprehensive because it also proposed the construction of a shipyard for assembly and maintenance and staff training. Following the establishment of the HHC in 1897,

41. HHC Board. *Hai-Ho Conservancy Board 1898–1919: A Resumé of Conservancy Operations on the Hai-Ho and Taku*, 13.

42. De Linde, *Report of the Hai-Ho River Improvement and the Rivers of Chihli.*

43. Shi Jianyun, "A Brief Account of the Relationship between the Chamber of Commerce and the Rural Economy: Reading Notes on the Archives of the Tianjin Chamber of Commerce," 24–41.

44. Albert De Linde, *Report Peiho, Tientsin and Taku: Proposed Improvement If Navigable Channel.*

De Linde was hired to implement his plan. Progress was delayed by the Boxer Rebellion and the siege of Tianjin in 1900.

In the case of the Whangpoo River, in 1876, Escher and De Rijke had been the first to submit a report that recommended dredging.[45] By contrast, an 1882 report by a German-American team recommended very expensive engineering solutions.[46] After dredging during 1882–83 proved ineffective, Shanghai Harbour Master A. M. Bisbee shone his light on the issue. In his 1894 report, he too recommended expensive engineering works, particularly a comprehensive rectification of the Whangpoo River from Wusong kou (where the Whangpoo enters the Yangtze River) to the Jiangnan shipyard at the Wusong sandbar.[47]

In 1897 the Shanghai Chamber of Commerce commissioned De Rijke to have another look at the issue. This time De Rijke carried out a systematic hydraulic survey and mapping of the Whangpoo River basin. A year later, he again recommended dredging the Wusong sandbar, but this time with two alternative engineering solutions.[48] Option A proposed the construction of a 10-kilometer canal to the Yangtze River from Gaoqiao. Option B proposed to block the old river channel and excavate a new 33-kilometer river channel from Wusong kou to the Jiangnan shipyard.[49] After the establishment of the WCB in 1905, the Qing government made funds available, and the WCB board employed De Rijke to implement Option B.[50] As mentioned, the WCB raised additional funding through a loan from the Hupu Bank because option B required a range of construction works in addition to excavating a new channel. Work commenced, and—although still incomplete by 1910—steamships that previously had to anchor at Woosung could now precede upriver and dock there.

In both cases, the engineers-in-chief were responsible for the technical activities and for the organizational management of the day-to-day operations of their agencies. In addition, they were responsible for the hydraulic research on both rivers, including analysis of the research results in the context of relevant foreign professional literature. This research informed the technical activities of both agencies.

---

45. Escher, George Arnold, and Johannis De Rijke. *Report upon the Woosung Bar.*

46. Ludwig Franzius and Lindon Wallace Bates, *Project for the Improvement of the Hwang Pu River to the Port of Shanghai.*

47. Escher, George Arnold, and Johannis De Rijke, *Woosung Inner Bar: With an Appendix Consisting of the Report on the Bar (1876).*

48. Johannis De Rijke, *Report to the Shanghai General Chamber of Commerce on the Water Approaches to Shanghai, Dated Tokio, January 10, 1898.*

49. Von Heidenstam, Project for the Continued Whangpoo Regulation (1912), WCB vol. 74.

50. Frans-Paul van der Putten, *Corporate Behaviour and Political Risk: Dutch Companies in China 1903–1904,* 152–57.

For example, during his 19-year tenure at the WCB, Von Heidenstam proved to be a prolific publicist of the outcomes of his team's research. Certainly, after the 1912 reorganization of the funding arrangements, the number of publications supported by the WCB increased significantly. The agency issued more than 30 publications during this period. Consequently, Von Heidenstam left a considerable legacy of technical documents and publications, covering the results of hydraulic surveying and hydrographical mapping, port planning, engineering design, and other technical elements, as well as comparative analyses of the Whangpoo and Shanghai data relative to key ports in Britain and the United States. Von Heidenstam also published on the prospects for further port development in Shanghai to support China's foreign trade and the hydraulics of the much bigger Yangtze River. Such published reports not only informed the WCB board but also informed engineering colleagues in other countries, and of course, the mid-level managers and engineers employed by the WCB.

Both De Rijke and Von Heidenstam were convinced that increasing the tidal water volume of the Whangpoo River would increase the scouring force of the freshwater runoff, helping to remove sediment. Consequently, one element of option B was to concentrate and guide the river's water flow to strengthen the flow's force and thus maximize the scouring effect and minimize sedimentation. Although this principle was simple enough, the specific details of the size and location of structures and the location and depth of required dredging work were more difficult to establish. Von Heidenstam, therefore, ordered meticulous ongoing observations and analyses of water flows, sedimentation, and the impact of the ebb tide, to inform the ongoing construction and dredging work.[51] Two additional reasons for the simultaneous surveying and construction and dredging were that the water flows and sedimentation patterns of the Whangpoo River changed over time, so that planning work was an ongoing process, and the increasing size of steamships with deeper drafts required deeper channels to reach Shanghai.

It is difficult to provide a concise overview of the published and archival documentation regarding the foreign engineers-in-chief and their assistants, the multitude of hydraulic issues they resolved along the Hai-ho and Whangpoo rivers and their tributaries, and the way in which they built the increasingly diversified operations of these two organizations. In all, these instances demonstrate that the engineers-in-chief brought significant changes to the two agencies that constituted the introduction of foreign technology. This involved systematic surveying, scientific observations of water flows and siltation patterns, the use, engineering, and maintenance of new machinery and equipment for dredging and excavation, the development of new construction techniques, as well as the establishment

---

51. Von Heidenstam, *Project for the Continued Whangpoo Regulation (1912)*, WCB vol. 74.

of new organizational procedures to manage increasingly diversified operations. This chapter discusses some instances that demonstrate how new hydraulic technology and management were introduced and adapted to suit local circumstances in China.

Furthermore, as dredging was a key part of the activities of both agencies, they were in a position to switch from manual dredging to purchasing the latest steam-powered mechanical dredging technology. In 1902, the HHC purchased its first mechanical dredger, the Beihe 北河, from the A. F. Smulders shipyard in Rotterdam (Netherlands). This was followed by a grab dredge, which the HHC's engineering works assembled from a self-built hull and grabs supplied by Priestman Bros in Hull (UK). The engineering works also assembled the two mud traps. Subsequently, the HHC purchased the Xihe 西河, Yanyun 燕云, Xinhe 新河, Zhonghua 中华, and Gaolin 高林 dredgers from engineering firms in Japan, Britain, and the Netherlands, and an icebreaker made by the Jiangnan Shipyards in Shanghai. In 1921, the HHC purchased the Kuaili 快利 self-propelled suction dredger from the UK.

Initially, the WCB relied on outsourcing to complete planned work. After the 1912 reorganization, it expanded by purchasing large and medium-sized dredgers and auxiliary ships. During 1916–1930, it had a fleet of four "King Kong" dredgers: "Sea Whale" (Hai-jing 海鲸), "Sea Tiger" (Hai-hu 海虎), "Sea Dragon" (Hai-long 海龙) and "Sea Elephant" (Hai-xiang 海象), as well as a number of smaller dredging facilities and other supporting vessels.

Both initiated their own shipyards for the assembly and repair of dredging equipment as well as other engineering facilities. In 1908, HHC built the Xiao-Liu Zhuang 小刘庄 Shipyard, and in 1924, it purchased the Xinhe Shipyard, where it assembled and repaired other vessels, including dredgers. The WCB used a series of automatic tide gauges and other specialized equipment for research purposes. In 1912 it established the Wusong and Zhongsha self-recording water level stations, followed in later years by a series of stations in different locations along the Whangpoo River. These stations accumulated hydraulic data that informed the analysis of water flows and siltation.[52]

6   Enterprise Operation and Management

The two conservancy organizations' development involved various aspects of enterprise management, of which the archival records contain many examples. This included production decisions, personnel management, financial management and reporting, taxation

---

52. "Meeting Minutes of the Advisory Panel of Experts on the Shanghai Port Investigation," WCB vol. 4, 42.

and investment, purchase and subcontracting contract drafting and signing procedures, announcements to stakeholders and the public, publicity and communications, etc. Consequently, they grew with the size of their operations and the diversification of their responsibilities, and it was up to the engineers-in-chief to instigate this change. For example, in 1901, the HHC consisted of the General Affairs Department, Division of Labour, Measurement Department, Factory and Dock Department, Dredging Department, and the Hai-ho Department.[53] In 1912, the WCB consisted of four departments: training and construction works, contract dredging work, dredging under its own administration, and surveying water flows and silt.[54]

In a Western context, such changes in the structure of both organizations are not unusual for large ventures. However, for China, it was, both because of the unusually large size of these organizations by Chinese standards and the traditional reliance of the Chinese on organizational structures enmeshed with local bureaucracy. The expansion of both agencies was accompanied by new appointments of engineers and managers. For example, the senior management of the WCB after the 1912 reorganization comprised assistant to the engineer-in-chief, assistant chief engineer, general supervisor, chief surveyor, associate surveyor, chief supervisor, engineering secretary, and the like. Almost all technical key positions were non-Chinese employees.[55] Gradually both agencies made more Chinese appointments to mid-level and senior management positions as Chinese graduates returned from studies overseas and/or accumulated relevant experience in China.

The activities of the HHC and the WCB expanded in both size and diversity. However, from the outset, they also purchased supplies from other companies and subcontracted work to such companies. As both agencies were accountable to multiple interests, some of which were represented on their boards, it was paramount that the engineers-in-chief reported comprehensively and that the boards reported to stakeholders transparently. For the HHC, the 1905 revised provisions and the 1912 regulation mentioned the processes for the procurement of machinery and equipment, including the tendering, bidding, selection and subcontracting processes, discussions among the board of directors, and the publication of relevant details.[56]

The WCB used a similar model. Regardless of the type of equipment and materials purchased and the financial amounts involved, the bidding process was conducted openly

---

53. Zhou Xingjia, ed., *History of Tianjin Dredging Co. Ltd*, 8.

54. Engineer-in-Chief, WCB Engineer-in-Chief Quarterly Report, 1912 Q3.

55. Shanghai hangdaoju jushi bianxiezu, ed., *History of Shanghai Dredging Co. Ltd*, 15.

56. Long Denggao et al, *Tianjin Dredging Co. Ltd.: 120 Years of History*, 20. Details the tendering process for the construction of the Wanguo bridge万国桥 (now Jiefang bridge 解放桥) across the Hai-ho River in 1923. 17 firms submitted 31 designs, before a French engineering company was announced as the successful contractor.

and transparently. The archival records contain evidence from many cases, large and big. For example, three companies participated in a total of seven types of materials in a 1929 bidding process for a contract to supply wrought iron materials to WCB. The WCB board of directors negotiated with firms, including the dimensions, price, quality, and delivery period. The engineer-in-chief decided to purchase 200 materials at a total price of 4,000 taels. The WCB not only invited tenders for the procurement of equipment and materials, but it also invited bids for the sale of used equipment and materials and documented this. For example, in 1929, it recorded the details of the sale of scrap iron and old chains, for which eight companies submitted bids. The WCB board was strict in refusing bids of associated companies and personalized transactions. For example, in 1923, it invited tenders to procure new barges. Kiangnan Dock & Engineering Works, a "Westernisation enterprise" in Shanghai owned by the Chinese government (which was represented on the board), was one of the eleven bidding companies. Nevertheless, the board awarded the contract to the lowest price tender.[57]

Another organizational and management technology that the boards implemented was the open recruitment and promotion of personnel based on qualifications, experience, and performance. This was despite the fact that all employees were formally employed by the Qing government or later the government of the Republic of China, and these states did not necessarily use such principles. The degree of openness was such that by 1927, the HHC board agreed that for each new hiring of specialized technicians, it would publicize their qualifications, knowledge, and experience, as well as their responsibilities and salaries.[58] The WCB records also contain ample evidence of its open recruitment and retention methods. The resumes and qualifications of candidates for employment were closely reviewed, and appointments were confirmed by the WCB board of directors. All employment contracts were signed by the WCB engineer-in-chief.[59] The strict regulation of merit-based selection, recruitment, and retention policies seem to have been modeled on the British civil service system.[60]

The responsibilities of employees were specified as clearly as possible in the employment contracts and strictly enforced by the boards. The contracts of the engineers-in-chief contained such details. For example, the contracts on which the HHC hired De Linde in

---

57. WCB Board Meeting Minutes.

58. The methods for employing engineer-in-chief and technicians are outlined in the reorganization of the Hai-ho Conservancy Commission and the relief measures for Hai-ho River, HHC vol. 4, 676.

59. WCB Board Meeting Minutes.

60. The procedures and standards of employee recruitment were similar to those of foreign employees in The Customs Service, where the "recommendation–examination" system intended to offer equal opportunity and a mechanism to select the best talent. See Li Hu, "The Foreigner Recruitment System in China's Modern Customs Service, 1854–1911," 23–27.

1898 and the WCB hired De Rijke in 1905 specified not only their generous entitlements and their responsibilities but also the penalties they faced in case of underperformance. For example, De Linde's contract stated: "If De Linde has misunderstood and has done something wrong, he can be immediately expelled by the general assembly."[61] And De Rijke's contract: "If J.de Rijke has failed to comply with the obligations set out in the contract, the Chinese government will be able to dismiss him and cancel the contract." Other employment contracts, whether with Chinese or foreign nationals, contained similar clauses. In addition, both agencies were strict in pursuing cases of fraud and misuse of agency resources.

On the other hand, both organizations offered relatively generous benefits designed to maximize employee retention regardless of nationality. Retention was a significant issue with both expatriate and Chinese employees, as qualified, skilled, and experienced employees were in short supply throughout China at the time. General skill shortages meant that experienced Chinese employees at both agencies could easily find higher-paid employment elsewhere. Most expatriates retained family commitments in their home countries, often limiting their stay in China. Consequently, at the WCB, five years or more employment would qualify employees for one year's salary at separation. In addition, 6% of an employee's monthly salary was withheld and contributed to a pension fund, to which the WCB contributed an additional equivalent of 10% of the salary. Employment contracts also included provisions for sick leave and medical care.[62]

Last but not least, both organizations were formally subject to Chinese laws governing public sector accountability. However, as agencies with a range of stakeholders—Chinese and international—both went well beyond these legal requirements regarding the frequency of reporting and transparency in financial reporting. In essence, the reason for this was to sustain the trust of stakeholders through openness about the collection, processing and transmission of information. As a consequence, both agencies issued quarterly and annual reports and engaged qualified third parties for the independent auditing of financial accounts. In addition, the annual audit reports provided independent information to the boards.[63] In fact, both agencies used an open bidding system to engage independent third parties for the annual audits.

Apart from transparency to stakeholders, regular reporting also served the purpose of maximizing internal lines of communication, responsibility, and purpose. This benefited overall efficiency and was particularly important as both organizations grew and diversified

---

61. HHC Board, *Hai-Ho Conservancy Board 1898–1919: A Resumé of Conservancy Operations on the HaiHo and Taku Bar*, 16.

62. See staff assignment and welfare. WCB vols. 50–60, 184, 310.

63. WCB Board Meeting Minutes.

their activities with a transient mid- and senior-level workforce. Documentation, therefore, served as an explicit corporate memory that was not lost when employees resigned and left China.

As a consequence, both agencies left vast archival records. The HHC archives comprise more than 2,000 volumes. The main parts are 376 volumes of documents until 1949, in addition to thousands of volumes of technical archives and many publications. More than 90% of the records are in English. The yearly activities related to the Hai-ho River and changes to the composition and activities of the HHC. Financial and audit statements are reported in the annual reports of the HHC board. They were originally written and printed in English and after 1928 also in Chinese. The WCB annual reports contain similar data but more financial details, given the larger size of the organization.

7   The Engineers-in-Chief's Leadership and Rewards

The engineers-in-chief of both agencies communicated project planning and implementation to their boards of directors, consultative boards, and other parties through their regular reports. The total number of reports from the HHC engineer-in-chief is 1,683, including 29 in 1927 alone. The WCB board released the quarterly reports of the WCB engineer-in-chief after 1917. They detail the current production equipment, technology development and changes, human resources, construction schedule, number of dredging vessels and equipment, as well as surveying and mapping of hydraulic data.

These reports confirm the crucial role of the engineers-in-chief. As mentioned, China was entirely unfamiliar with the modern technology of river conveyance and managing organizations for that purpose. Both organizations relied extensively on the leadership of the engineers-in-chief for this. For example, in 1897, Wang Wenshao, the Viceroy of Zhili, announced: "Linde is appointed as Engineer-in-Chief, and in charge of all projects regarding Hai-ho River," and "All employees must obey the Engineer or he will dismiss them at once," adding that anyone obstructing the engineer's work would suffer consequences at the local court.[64] From the outset, De Linde was given considerable authority and, therefore, the freedom and responsibility to organize the HHC and its activities as he saw fit, only limited by the annual budget and the board's approval. His successors and his WCB counterparts carried similar responsibilities and freedoms.

The responsibility, authority, and independence of the engineers-in-chief were crucial for the technology-intensive organizations that they led and shaped. In exercising their

---

64. HHC Board, *Hai-ho Conservancy Board 1898–1919*, 16.

responsibilities, they translated foreign experiences with hydraulics and the management of public organizations and applied them to Chinese circumstances. They mobilized foreign equipment and trained Chinese mid-level colleagues in technology and management. Their work results are illustrated by their agencies' size, diversification, and budgets.

Their efforts did not go unnoticed. When De Linde's contract ended in 1904, the Chinese HHC board members, the imperial circuit intendant in Tianjin Tang Shaoyi 唐绍仪 (1862–1938) and Minister of Beiyang Yuan Shikai 袁世凯 (1859–1916), recommended De Linde to the emperor for a third-class "Second Treasure" award.[65] Likewise, when De Rijke's contract ended in 1910, the Viceroy of the Two Rivers, Zhang Renjun 张人骏 (1846–1927), recommended him to the emperor for an award.[66]

In addition, the engineers-in-chief indirectly facilitated the introduction of hydraulic technology and related organizational capabilities into the provincial and regional conservancy agencies that later emerged. None less than Zhang Jian 张謇 (1853–1926), a well-known entrepreneur and later Minister of Agriculture and Commerce of the Republic of China, publicly called for the study and application of modern hydraulic technology and for investment in river conservancy, stating "for the immediate future the work should be supervised by Dutch or foreign experts."[67] He headed the Huai Ho Conservancy Bureau (1913) and the National Conservancy Bureau (1914). He was instrumental in the establishment of the Directorate General of Flood Relief and Conservancy (1915), which supervised the establishment of other conservancy agencies. Employees at such agencies were introduced to foreign hydraulic technology through studying the publications of the well-documented and much better-endowed experiences of the HHC and WCB. Foreign hydraulic technology was also introduced into the teaching program of the Conservancy Engineering College (1915) in Nanjing, which supplied graduates for employment as hydraulic civil engineers in China. In these ways, foreign hydraulic technology and management started to spread to other parts of China after their introduction in the 1890s.

8   Conclusion

This chapter has shown that by the late 19th century, there was a need in China to mobilize foreign hydraulic technology to help resolve major problems with floods and river

---

65. Long Denggao et al., *Tianjin Dredging Co. Ltd: 120 Years of History*, 26.

66. Play for Whangpoo Conservancy Board engineer-in-chief De Rijke was hired and achieve the completion of the project route access, now the expiration of the contract, please drink reward. For the report, please refer to the collection of China first archives, no. 03-7561-034.

67. Jian Zhang, *Conservancy Work in China: Being a Series of Documents and Reports*, 22.

navigation, both in terms of understanding the fundamental essence of these problems and in institutionalizing the solutions. As China did not have a ready supply of suitably qualified and experienced engineers, the immediate solution was to recruit expatriates. And because China did not have sufficient resources, these expatriate engineers were, in the first instance, mobilized to study and resolve issues at the interface of imperial China and the foreign presence—in the treaty ports of Tianjin and Shanghai.

The solutions took the form of conservancy agencies for the Hai-ho River and Whangpoo River, led by highly autonomous expatriate engineers-in-chief. Employed by the Chinese government, these professionals were given the responsibility and authority to design and implement solutions that improved the navigability of both rivers and resolved other issues. At the same time, they established the organization of both agencies until they could be led by suitably qualified and experienced Chinese colleagues in the 1930s.

The two agencies were initially closely supervised by the Chinese state and focused on resolving navigation issues. However, in their existence, they morphed into stakeholder-oriented agencies that served a public interest and took on a diverse range of activities beyond navigability. The relevance of the diversified activities of both agencies and their engagement of professional engineers and administrators was an important reason for their longevity.

The engineer-in-chief responsibility system was a unique system in the dredging industry in modern China. It gave China advanced technology and an international perspective. Indirectly, the initiatives of the engineers-in-chief improved the performance and efficiency of both conservancy agencies, possibly even to the extent of encouraging the development of organizations that later became the Chinese state-owned enterprises CCCC Tianjin Dredging Company Ltd. and CCCC Shanghai Dredging Company Ltd., which now offer their dredging and engineering services around the world.

References

Asen, Daniel. *Death in Beijing: Murder and Forensic Science in Republican China*. Cambridge: Cambridge University Press, 2016.

Baark, Erik. *Lightning Wires: The Telegraph and China's Technological Modernization, 1860–1890*. Westport, CO: Greenwood Press, 1997.

Bessant, John, and Rush Howard. "Building Bridges for Innovation: The Role of Consultants in Technology Transfer." *Research Policy* 1 (1995): 97–114.

Bevans, Charles I. *Treaties and Other International Agreements of the United States of America 1776–1949: Volume 1, Multilateral 1776–1917*. Washington, DC: Department of State, 1968.

Bickers, Robert, and Jackson Isabella, eds. *Treaty Ports in Modern China: Law, Land and Power*. London: Palgrave, 2016.

Bieler, Stacey. *"Patriots" or "Traitors"?: A History of American-Educated Chinese Students.* Armonk, NY: M. E. Sharpe, 2004.

Blom, F. J. "Hydraulic Engineering in China." *De Ingenieur* 49 (1915): 1000–1010.

Blue, Gregory. "Joseph Needham: A Publication History." *Chinese Science* 1 (1997): 90–132.

Cheng, Yu-Kwei. *Foreign Trade and Industrial Development of China: An Historical and Integrated Analysis through 1948.* Washington, DC: The University Press of Washington D.C., 1956.

Chiang, Yung-Chen. *Social Engineering and the Social Sciences in China, 1919–1949.* Cambridge: Cambridge University Press, 2001.

Lin, Chih-Lung. "Reinhardt, Anne, *Navigating Semi-Colonialism: Shipping, Sovereignty, and Nation-Building in China, 1860–1937.*" *Frontiers of History in China* 2 (2019): 286–89.

De Linde, Albert. *Report Peiho, Tientsin and Taku: Proposed Improvement If Navigable Channel.* Tianjin: The Tientsin Press, 1897.

———. *Report of the Hai-Ho River Improvement and the Rivers of Chihli* (Reprinted from Report of 1890). Tianjin: The Tientsin Press, 1900.

———. *Report on the Taku Bar Raking Scheme.* Tianjin: The Tientsin Press, 1906.

De Rijke, Johannis. *Report to the Shanghai General Chamber of Commerce on the Water Approaches to Shanghai, Dated Tokio, January 10, 1898.*

Escher, George Arnold, and Johannis De Rijke. *Report upon the Woosung Bar.* Shanghai: The North-China Herald Office, 1876.

———. *Woosung Inner Bar: With an Appendix Consisting of the Report on the Bar (1876).* Shanghai: Kelly and Walsh, 1894.

Franzius, Ludwig, and Lindon Wallace Bates. *Project for the Improvement of the Hwang Pu River to the Port of Shanghai.* London V. Brooks, Day & Son, 1902.

Glass, Amy Jocelyn, and Kamal Saggi. "Multinational Firms and Technology Transfer." *Social Science Electronic Publishing* 4 (2010): 495–513.

Hai-Ho Conservancy Commission Archive (HHC).

Harris, Lane Jeremy. *The Post Office and State Formation in Modern China, 1896–1949.* PhD diss., University of Illinois at Urbana-Champaign, 2012.

HHC Board. *Hai-Ho Conservancy Board 1898–1919: A Resumé of Conservancy Operations on the Hai-Ho and Taku Bar Compiled by Order of the Board.* Tianjin: The Tientsin Press, 1919.

Hsiao, Liang-lin. *China's Foreign Trade Statistics, 1864–1949.* Cambridge, MA: Harvard University Press, 1974.

Kamibayashi, Yoshiyuki. "The Background of GA. Escher, Hollander Engineer Who Supported J. De Rijke for 40 Years." *Doboku-shikenkyūdai* 19 (1999): 399–406.

Keightley, David N. "'Benefit of Water': The Approach of Joseph Needham." *The Journal of Asian Studies* 2 (1972): 367–71.

Kenneth Pomeranz, *The Making of a Hinterland.* University of California Press, 1993.

Köll, Elisabeth. *Railroads and the Transformation of China.* Cambridge, MA: Harvard University Press, 2019.

Li, Hu. "The Foreigner Recruitment System in China's Modern Customs Service (1854–1911)." *History Teaching* 1 (2006): 23–27.

Lin, Justin. "The Needham Puzzle: Why the Industrial Revolution Did Not Originate in China." *Economic Development and Cultural Change* 2 (1995): 269–92.

Lockwood, Edward T. "Floods and Flood Prevention in China." *Far Eastern Survey* 21 (1935): 164–68.

Long, Denggao, et al. *Tianjin Dredging Co. Ltd.: 120 Years of History*. Beijing: Tsinghua University Press, 2017.

Long, Denggao, Gong Ning, and Yi Wei. "Innovative Financing Mode of Modern Public Interest Organizations: Bond Issue of the Hai-Ho Conservancy Commission." *Modern History Studies* 1 (2018): 112–23.

Meng, Yue. "Hybrid Science versus Modernity: The Practice of the Jiangnan Arsenal, 1864–1897." *East Asian Science Technology & Medicine* 16 (1999): 13–52.

Nield, Robert. *China's Foreign Places: The Foreign Presence in China in the Treaty Port Era, 1840–1943*. Hong Kong: Hong Kong University Press, 2015.

Thammarutwasik, Paiboon. "The Food Research Centre—Assisting Small and Medium Sized Industry." In *Case Studies in Food Product Development*, edited by Mary Earle and Richard Earle, 53–66. Cambridge: Woodhead Publishing, 2008.

The Directory and Chronicle for China, Japan, Corea, Indo-China, Straits Settlements, Malay States, Siam, Netherlands India, Borneo, the Philippines, & Etc. Hong Kong: Daily Press Office, 1909, 1912.

Tianjin Municipal Archives (Tianjin, China).

Pietz, David A. *Engineering the State: The Huai River and Reconstruction in Nationalist China, 1927–1937*. New York: Routledge, 2002.

———. "Controlling the Waters in Twentieth-Century China: The Nationalist State and the Huai River." In *A History of Water: Series I, Volume 1: Water Control and River Biographies*, edited by Terjeand Tvedt and Eva Jakobsson, 92–119. London: I. B. Tauris, 2006.

Prescott, E. C. "The Transformation of Macroeconomic Policy and Research." *American Economist* 1 (2006): 3–20.

Shi, Jianyun. "A Brief Account of the Relationship between the Chamber of Commerce and the Rural Economy: Reading Notes on the Archives of the Tianjin Chamber of Commerce." *China Economic History Research* 4 (2001): 24–41.

Shanghai hangdaoju jushi bianxiezu, ed. *History of Shanghai Dredging Co. Ltd.* Shanghai: Wenhui Press, 2010.

Zhou, Xingjia, ed. *History of Tianjin Dredging Co. Ltd.* Beijing: China Communications Press, 2000.

The First Historical Archives of China (Beijing, China), the collection of historical archives. File No: 03-7561-034.

Tsu, Jing, and Benjamin A. Elman, eds. *Science and Technology in Modern China, 1880s–1940s*. Leiden: Brill, 2014.

Van de Ven, Hans. *Breaking with the Past: The Maritime Customs Service and the Global Origins of Modernity in China*. New York: Columbia University Press, 2014.

Van der Putten, Frans-Paul. *Corporate Behaviour and Political Risk: Dutch Companies in China 1903–1941*. PhD diss., University of Leiden, The Netherlands, 2001.

Vinding, Povl. "Albert de Linde," in *Dansk BiografiskLeksikon, 1979–84*. 3rd ed. Copenhagen: Gyldendal. Accessed on April 18, 2019. http://denstoredanske.dk/index.php?sideId=293607

Wang, Ai. *City of the River: The Hai River and the Construction of Tianjin, 1897–1948*. PhD diss., Washington State University, 2014.

Wei, Chunjuan Nancy, and Darryl E. Brock, eds. *Mr. Science and Chairman Mao's Cultural Revolution: Science and Technology in Modern China.* Lanham, MD: Lexington Books, 2013.

Whangpoo Conservancy Board Archive (WCB).

Ye, Shirley. "Corrupted Infrastructure: Imperialism and Environmental Sovereignty in Shanghai, 1873–1911." *Frontiers of History in China* 3 (2015): 428–56.

———. "River Conservancy and State-building in Treaty Port China." In *Treaty Ports in Modern China: Law, Land and Power*, edited by Robert Bickers and Isabella Jackson, 121–38. London: Palgrave, 2016:

Young, Arthur Nichols. *China's Wartime Finance and Inflation, 1937–1945.* Cambridge, MA: Harvard University Press, 1965.

Yoon, Wook. "Dashed Expectations: Limitations of the Telegraphic Service in the late Qing." *Modern Asian Studies* 2 (2015): 832–57.

ABOUT THE AUTHORS

Denggao LONG, Professor of Economics, School of Social Sciences, Tsinghua University; Chair, Center for Chinese Entrepreneur Studies, Tsinghua University; Chair, Center for Economic History, Tsinghua University. He is a member of the Expert Advisory Committee of the Overseas Chinese Affairs Office of the State Council, Peoples Republic of China; member of the China Economic and Social Council; Vice President of the Overseas Chinese History Society of China; member of Academic Degree Committee, Institute of Economics, Chinese Academy of Social Science; Chief Expert of National Social Science Fund of China. He also obtained the Laureate of the Sun Yefang Economic Science Award in 2018; *Excellent of Research, First-class, 2007– 2010*, The State Council of Overseas Chinese Affair, China; *Prize of Humanities and Social Sciences in Higher Education in China, Second Place, 2003*, Ministry of Education, China; *Prize of Humanities and Social Sciences in Beijing, First-class, 2020*.

Wei YI, Research fellow, School of Social Sciences, Tsinghua University, and Center for Chinese Entrepreneur Studies, Tsinghua University. She has a diversified Academic Educational Background. Ph.D. in Economics, Tsinghua University; Mater of Business Administration (MBA), and Bachelor in Engineering. She also has the certificate of Project Management Professional (PMP), and "Green Belt" in 6 Sigma Program. She undertook industrial history and economic history-related academic research, Identifying, developing, and executing strategies for research. Take part in the research projects and published multiple papers in top journals, such as *Economic Research Journal, Research in Chinese Economic History, Frontier of History in China, China Economist*, etc.